DRAMAS, FIELDS, AND METAPHORS

Symbolic Action in Human Society

SYMBOL, MYTH, AND RITUAL SERIES

General Editor: Victor Turner

DRAMAS, FIELDS, AND METAPHORS

Symbolic Action
in Human Society

VICTOR TURNER

Cornell University Press

ITHACA AND LONDON

Copyright © 1974 by Cornell University

All rights reserved. Except for brief quotations in a review, this book, or parts thereof, must not be reproduced in any form without permission in writing from the publisher. For information address Cornell University Press, 124 Roberts Place, Ithaca, New York 14850.

First published 1974 by Cornell University Press.
First printing, Cornell Paperbacks, 1975.
Sixth printing 1990.

International Standard Book Number 0-8014-9151-7
Library of Congress Catalog Card Number 73-16968
Printed in the United States of America

⊗ The paper in this book meets the minimum requirements of the American National Standard for Information Sciences—Permanence of Paper for Printed Library Materials, ANSI Z39.48–1984.

TO ALEX AND RORY

Foreword

Recently both the research and theoretical concerns of many anthropologists have once again been directed toward the role of symbols—religious, mythic, esthetic, political, and even economic—in social and cultural processes. Whether this revival is a belated response to developments in other disciplines (psychology, ethology, philosophy, linguistics, to name only a few), or whether it reflects a return to a central concern after a period of neglect, is difficult to say. In recent field studies, anthropologists have been collecting myths and rituals in the context of social action, and improvements in anthropological field technique have produced data that are richer and more refined than heretofore; these new data have probably challenged theoreticians to provide more adequate explanatory frames. Whatever may have been the causes, there is no denying a renewed curiosity about the nature of the connections between culture, cognition, and perception, as these connections are revealed in symbolic forms.

Although excellent individual monographs and articles in symbolic anthropology or comparative symbology have recently appeared, a common focus or forum that can be provided by a topically organized series of books has not been available. The present series is intended to fill this lacuna. It is designed to include not only field monographs and theoretical and comparative studies by anthropologists, but also work by scholars in other disciplines, both scientific and humanistic. The appearance of studies in such a forum encourages emulation, and emulation can produce fruitful new theories. It is therefore our hope that the series will serve as a house of many mansions, providing hospitality for the practitioners of any discipline that has a serious and creative concern with comparative symbology. Too often, disciplines are sealed off, in sterile pedantry, from significant intellectual influences. Nevertheless, our primary aim is to bring to public attention works on ritual and myth written by anthropologists, and our readers will find a variety of strictly anthropological approaches ranging from formal analyses of systems of symbols to empathetic accounts of divinatory and initiatory rituals.

VICTOR TURNER

University of Chicago

Contents

Illustrations

Preface

"Dramas," "passages," "action," "processes"—these are the key words in the titles of the essays in this book. Alongside them are such terms as "metaphors" and "paradigms." The book attempts in fact to probe and describe the ways in which social actions of various kinds acquire form through the metaphors and paradigms in their actors' heads (put there by explicit teaching and implicit generalization from social experience), and, in certain intensive circumstances, generate unprecedented forms that bequeath history new metaphors and paradigms. In other words, I do not see social dynamics as a set of "performances" produced by a "program," as certain of my colleagues, notably the New Anthropologists, believe to be the case. Living action, for the human species, can never be the logical consequence of any grand design. This is not because of the inveterate tendency of man's "free will" to resist manifest good and manifest reasonableness, as Dostoevsky, Berdyaev, Shestov, and other "alienated" Russians would have it, but because of the processual structure of social action itself. Van Gennep made a striking discovery when he demonstrated, in his comparative work on rites of passage, that human culture had become cognizant of a tripartite movement in space-time. His focus was restricted to ritual, but his paradigm covers many extra-ritual processes. He insisted that in all ritualized movement there was at least a moment when those being moved in accordance with a cultural script were liberated from normative demands, when they were, indeed, betwixt and between successive lodgments in jural political systems. In this gap between ordered worlds almost anything may happen.

In this interim of "liminality," the possibility exists of standing aside not only from one's own social position but from all social positions and of formulating a potentially unlimited series of alternative social arrangements. That this danger is recognized in all tolerably orderly societies is made evident by the proliferation of taboos that hedge in and constrain those on whom the normative structure loses its grip during such potent transitions as extended initiation rites in "tribal" societies and by legislation against those who in industrial societies utilize such "liminoid" genres as literature, the film, and the higher journalism to subvert the axioms and standards of the *ancien régime*—both in general and in particular cases.

Without liminality, program might indeed determine performance. But, given liminality, prestigious programs can be undermined and multiple alternative programs may be generated. The result of confrontations between monolithic, power-supported programs and their many subversive alternatives is a sociocultural "field" in which many options are provided, not only between programmatic *gestalten* but also between the parts of different programs. As my colleague Harold Rosenberg, the art critic, has often argued, the culture of any society at any moment is more like the debris, or "fall-out," of past ideological systems, than it is itself a system, a coherent whole. Coherent wholes may exist (but these tend to be lodged in individual heads, sometimes in those of obsessionals or paranoiacs), but human social groups tend to find their openness to the future in the variety of their metaphors for what may be the good life and in the contest of their paradigms. If there is order, it is seldom preordained (though transiently bayonets may underpin some political schema); it is achieved—the result of conflicting or concurring wills and intelligences, each relying on some convincing paradigm.

When one surveys large spans of social processes, one sees an almost endless variety of limited and provisional outcomes. Some seem to fall on the programmatic side of the scale, others eschew precise structural articulation. But the besetting quality of human society, seen processually, is the capacity of individuals to stand at times aside from the models, patterns, and paradigms for behavior and thinking, which as children they are conditioned into accepting, and, in rare cases, to innovate new patterns themselves or to assent to innovation. There is nothing mysterious about these capacities if we are to accept the testimony of evolutionary biology. Evolving species are adaptive and labile; they escape the constraints of that form of genetic programming which dooms a species to extinction under conditions of radical environmental change. In the evolution of man's symbolic "cultural" action, we must seek those processes which correspond to open-endedness in biological evolution. I think we have found them in those liminal, or "liminoid" (postindustrial-revolution), forms of symbolic action, those genres of free-time activity, in which all previous standards and models are subjected to criticism, and fresh new ways of describing and interpreting sociocultural experience are formulated. The first of these forms are expressed in philosophy and science, the second in art and religion.

This book is concerned both with the strength and vitality of certain "root paradigms," such as the acceptance of martyrdom for the sake of an altruistic cause—as in the somewhat contrasting cases of Becket and Hidalgo—and with the social dramas where conflicting groups and personages attempt to assert their own and deplete their opponents' paradigms—as in the confrontations between Henry II and Becket and between Hidalgo and his former friends, who for various reasons supported Spanish hegemony over Mexico. I have also considered the processes through which religious paradigms are continually reinvested with vitality, such as pilgrimages, which commit individuals unreservedly to the values of a particular faith in order to make not merely acceptable but glowing the hardships and unforeseen disasters of long journeys across several national frontiers. Religious paradigms are also maintained by the periodic emergence of counterparadigms which under certain conditions become reabsorbed in the initial and central paradigm. The essay "Metaphors of Antistructure in Religious Culture" exemplifies this process in the

context of Indian culture. I believe that it has a still wider application and has something to say about developmental cycles in European and Chinese religion. Yesterday's liminal becomes today's
stabilized, today's peripheral becomes tomorrow's centered. I am
not here advocating a cyclical repetitive view of the human historical process. Rather I am suggesting that the cyclical repetitive view is itself only one among a number of possible processual
alternatives. At the other extreme we may find history regarded
as a succession of unique, unrepeated phases in which all forward
movement is the result of inspirations owing nothing to the past.
Between these poles many degrees of mutual accommodation are
possible. I would suggest that what have been regarded as the
"serious" genres of symbolic action—ritual, myth, tragedy, and
comedy (at their "birth")—are deeply implicated in the cyclical
repetitive views of social process, while those genres which have
flourished since the Industrial Revolution (the modern arts and
sciences), though less serious in the eyes of the commonality (pure
research, entertainment, interests of the elite), have had greater
potential for changing the ways men relate to one another and the
content of their relationships. Their influence has been more in-
sidious. Because they are outside the arenas of direct industrial
production, because they constitute the "liminoid" analogues of
liminal processes and phenomena in tribal and early agrarian societies, their very outsiderhood disengages them from direct functional action on the minds and behavior of a society's members.
To be either their agents or their audience is an *optional* activity—
the absence of obligation or constraint from external norms imparts to them a pleasurable quality which enables them all the
more readily to be absorbed by individual consciousnesses. Plea-
sure thus becomes a serious matter in the context of innovative
change. In this book I have not taken up this point, but my concern with complex societies in change (twelfth-century England,
nineteenth-century Mexico, medieval India, medieval and modern
Europe and Asia as settings for pilgrimage processes) points toward this formulation.

In the present context, "fields" are the abstract cultural domains where paradigms are formulated, established, and come into conflict. Such paradigms consist of sets of "rules" from which many kinds of sequences of social action may be generated but which further specify what sequences must be excluded. Paradigm conflict arises over exclusion rules. "Arenas" are the concrete settings in which paradigms become transformed into metaphors and symbols with reference to which political power is mobilized and in which there is a trial of strength between influential paradigm-bearers. "Social dramas" represent the phased process of their contestation. These abstract formulations underlie the essays that make up the book. I have ranged widely through geography and history, over India, Africa, Europe, China, and Meso-America, from ancient society through the medieval period to modern revolutionary times. I know that I have trespassed beyond the limits of my disciplinary competence on several occasions. My excuse is that I regard mankind as one in essence though manifold in expression, creative and not merely adaptive in his manifoldness. Any serious study of man must follow him wherever he goes and take into serious account what Florian Znaniecki called the "humanistic coefficient," whereby sociocultural systems depend not only for their meaning but also for their existence upon the participation of *conscious* human agents and upon men's relations with one another. It is this factor of "consciousness" which should lead anthropologists into extended study of complex literate cultures where the most articulate conscious voices of values are the "liminoid" poets, philosophers, dramatists, novelists, painters, and the like.

This book is programmatic perforce because it strays beyond disciplinary frontiers. Its main imperfections derive from such incursive nomadism. But I would plead with my colleagues to acquire the humanistic skills that would enable them to live more comfortably in those territories where the masters of human thought and art have long been dwelling. This must be done if a unified science of man, an authentic anthropology, is ever to become possible. I am an advocate not of abandoning the methods of behavioral science but of applying them to the behavior of an innovative, liminal creature, to a species whose individual members have included Homer, Dante, and Shakespeare, as well as Galileo, Newton, and Einstein.

Acknowledgments

Four of these essays have been published previously. The author is grateful to John Wiley & Son ("Metaphors of Anti-structure in Religious Culture"), first written for Allan Eister, ed., *Changing Perspectives in the Scientific Study of Religion*, 1974; to *Worship* 46 (August–September 1972):390–412; 46 (October 1972):482–494 ("Passages, Margins, and Poverty: Religious Symbols of Communitas"); to *History of Religions* 12, no. 3 (1973):191–230 ("The Study of Pilgrimages as Social Processes") by permission of the University of Chicago Press, Copyright © 1973 by the University of Chicago; and to *Social Science Information* 7, no. 6 (1968):55–61 ("The Word of the Dogon").

The opportunity to write "The Study of Pilgrimages as Social Processes" was afforded me by the Lichstern Fund of the Department of Anthropology and by a grant from the Division of the Social Sciences at the University of Chicago. I am most grateful to both these sources of assistance.

My thanks are due to Father Jorge Serrano-Moreno, S.J., who patiently acted as my research assistant in the collection of Mexican data. His research was financed by the Wenner-Gren Foundation for Anthropological Research, to whose generous support we are both indebted.

I am particularly thankful to have had the constant advice and stimulus of my colleagues and students of the Committee on Social Thought and of the Department of Anthropology of the University of Chicago. I would also like to thank Jerald Brown, who, when he was a graduate student at Cornell University, gave me much valuable information about the then incipient counterculture. The staff of Cornell University Press have contributed their skills to the making of this book, and, indeed, of this whole series. My thanks are due to them. Finally, I would like once more to acknowledge my debt to my wife, Edie, for her incomparable help with this book as with all my other publications.

V. T.

DRAMAS, FIELDS, AND METAPHORS

Symbolic Action in Human Society

CHAPTER 1

Social Dramas and
Ritual Metaphors[1]

In this chapter I shall trace some of the influences that led to the formulation of concepts I developed in the course of my anthropological field work and to consider how they may be used in the analysis of ritual symbols. In moving from experience of social life to conceptualization and intellectual history, I follow the path of anthropologists almost everywhere. Although we take theories into the field with us, these become relevant only if and when they illuminate social reality. Moreover, we tend to find very frequently that it is not a theorist's whole system which so illuminates, but his scattered ideas, his flashes of insight taken out of systemic context and applied to scattered data. Such ideas have a virtue of their own and may generate new hypotheses. They even show how scattered facts may be systematically connected! Randomly distributed through some monstrous logical system, they resemble nourishing raisins in a cellular mass of inedible dough. The intuitions, not the tissue of logic connecting them, are what tend to survive in the field experience. I will try later to locate the sources of some insights that helped me to make sense of my own field data.

The concepts I would like to mention are: "social drama," "the processual view of society," "social anti-structure," "multivocality," and "polarization of ritual symbols." I mention these in the order of their formulation. All are pervaded by the idea that human social life is the producer and product of time, which be-

[1] First presented at the Department of Anthropology, University of California at San Diego, in October 1971.

comes its measure—an ancient idea that has had resonances in the very different work of Karl Marx, Emile Durkheim, and Henri Bergson. Following Znaniecki, the renowned Polish sociologist, I had already come, before doing field work, to insist on the dynamic quality of social relations and to regard Comte's distinction between "social statics" and "social dynamics"—later to be elaborated by A. R. Radcliffe-Brown and other positivists—as essentially misleading. The social world is a world in becoming, not a world in being (except insofar as "being" is a description of the static, atemporal models men have in their heads), and for this reason studies of social structure *as such* are irrelevant. They are erroneous in basic premise because there is no such thing as "static action." That is why I am a little chary of the terms "community" or "society," too, though I do use them, for they are often thought of as static concepts. Such a view violates the actual flux and changefulness of the human social scene. Here I would look, for example, to Bergson rather than, say, to Descartes, for philosophical guidance.

However, I am alive to the virtues of Robert A. Nisbet's warning in *Social Change and History* (1969:3–4) about the use of "becoming" and similar notions, such as "growth" and "development," which rest fundamentally on organic metaphors. Nisbet has drawn our attention to a whole metaphorical family of sociological and sociophilosophical terms such as "genesis," "growth," "unfolding," "development," on the one hand, and "death," "decadence," "degeneration," "pathology," "sickness," and so on, which take off originally from the Greek idea of "*physis*." This term literally means "growth," from φύ-ειτ, to produce, Indo-European root BHU. It is the "key concept of Greek science," φυσική meant "natural science," as in physiology, physiognomy, and so on. This family also derives from the Roman and Latinized European basic concept of nature, the Latin translation or rather mistranslation of *physis*. "Nature" is from "natus" meaning "born," with overtones of "innate," "inherent," "immanent," from the Indo-European root GAN. The "nature" family is cognate with the "gen" family, generate, genital, general, gender, genus, generic, and with the Germanic kind, kin, kindred. All these terms "have immediate and unchallengeable reference to the organic world, to the life-cycles of plants and organisms" (pp. 3–4), where they are literal and empirical in meaning. But "applied to *social* and *cultural* phenomena these words are not literal. They are *metaphoric*" (p. 4, my italics). Hence they may be misleading; even though they draw our attention to some important properties of social existence, they may and do block our perception of others. The metaphor of social and cultural systems as machines, popular since Descartes, is just as misleading.

I am not opposed to metaphor here. Rather, I am saying that one must pick one's root metaphors carefully, for appropriateness and potential fruitfulness. Not only Nisbet but Max Black, the Cornell philosopher, and others have pointed out how "perhaps every science must start with metaphor and end with algebra; and perhaps without the metaphor there would never have been any algebra" (Black, 1962:242). And, as Nisbet says:

Metaphor is, at its simplest, a way of proceeding from the known to the unknown. [This corresponds, curiously, with the Ndembu definition of a symbol in ritual.] It is a way of cognition in which the identifying qualities of one thing are transferred in an instantaneous, almost unconscious, flash of insight to some other thing that is, by remoteness or complexity, unknown to us. The test of essential metaphor, Philip Wheelwright has written, is not any rule of grammatical form, but rather the quality of semantic transformation that is brought about [1969:4].

Metaphor is, in fact, metamorphic, transformative. "Metaphor is our means of effecting instantaneous fusion of two separated realms of experience into one illuminating, iconic, encapsulating image" (p. 4). It is likely that scientists and artists both think primordially in such images; metaphor may be the form of what M. Polanyi calls "tacit knowledge."

The idea of society as being like a "big animal" or a "big machine," as James Peacock has pithily put the matter (1969:173), would be what Stephen C. Pepper has called a "root metaphor" (1942:38-39). This is how he explains the term:

The method in principle seems to be this: A man desiring to understand the world looks about for a clue to its comprehension. He pitches upon some area of common-sense fact and tries to see if he cannot understand other areas in terms of this one. The original area then becomes his *basic analogy* or *root metaphor*. He describes as best he can the characteristics of this area, or if you will, "discriminates its structure." A list of its structural characteristics becomes his basic concepts of explanation and description. [E.g., the gen-words, the kin words, the nature words.] We call them a set of categories [a possibly exhaustive set of classes among which all things might be distributed]. . . . In terms of these categories he proceeds to study all other areas of fact whether uncriticized or previously criticized. He undertakes to interpret all facts in terms of these categories. As a result of the impact of these other facts upon his categories, he may qualify and readjust the categories so that a set of categories commonly changes and develops. Since the basic analogy or root metaphor normally (and probably at least in part necessarily) arises out of common sense [which is the normal understanding or general feeling of mankind, but for anthropologists this operates in a specific culture], a great deal of development and refinement of a set of categories is required if they are to prove adequate for a hypothesis of unlimited scope. Some root metaphors prove more fertile than others, have greater power of expansion and adjustment. These survive in comparison with the others and generate the relatively adequate world theories [1942:91-92].

Black prefers the term "conceptual archetype" to "root metaphor," and defines it as a "systematic repertoire of ideas by means of which a given thinker describes, by *analogical extension*, some domain to which those ideas do not immediately and literally apply" (1962:241). He suggests that if we want a detailed account of a particular archetype, we require a list of key words and expressions, with statements of their interconnections and their paradigmatic meanings in the field from which they were originally drawn. This should then be supplemented by analysis of the ways in which the original meanings become extended in their analogical use.

The illustration Black offers of the influence of an archetype on a theorist's work is of exceptional interest to me, for this very case had a profound effect on my own early attempts to characterize a "social field." Black examines the writings of the psychologist Kurt Lewin whose "field theory" has been fruitful in generating hypotheses and stimulating empirical research. Black finds it "ironical" that Lewin

formally disclaims any intention of using models. "We have tried," he says, "to avoid developing elaborate models; instead we have tried to represent the dynamic relations between the psychological facts by mathematical constructs at a sufficient level of generality." Well [Black goes on], there may be no specific models envisaged; yet any reader of Lewin's papers must be impressed by the degree to which he employs a vocabulary indigenous to *physical* theory. We repeatedly encounter such words as "field," "vector," "phase-space," "tension," "force," "valence," "boundary," "fluidity"—visible symptoms of a massive archetype awaiting to be reconstructed by a sufficiently patient critic" [p. 241].

Black is not upset about all this on the ground of general principles of sound method. He feels that if an archetype, confused though it may be in details, is sufficiently rich in implicative power it may become a useful speculative instrument. If the archetype is sufficiently fruitful, logicians and mathematicians will eventually reduce the harvest to order. "There will always be competent technicians who, in Lewin's words, can be trusted to build the highways 'over which the streamlined vehicles of a highly mechanized logic, fast and efficient, can reach every important point on fixed tracks'" (p. 242). There, of course, we have another uninhibited flood of metaphors.

Nisbet, too, as well as Black and Pepper, holds that "complex philosophical systems can proceed from metaphorical premises." For example, Freudianism, he says, "would have little substance left once stripped of its metaphors" (p. 5)—Oedipus complex, topographical and economic models, defense mechanisms, Eros and Thanatos, and so on. Marxism, too, sees social orders as "forming embryonically" in the "wombs" of preceding orders, with each transition akin to "birth," and requiring the assistance of the "midwife," force.

Both Black and Nisbet admit the tenacity as well as the potency of metaphors. Nisbet argues that what we usually call revolutions in thought are

quite often no more than the mutational replacement, at certain critical points in history, of one foundation-metaphor by another in man's contemplation of universe, society, and self. Metaphoric likening of the universe to an *organism* in its structure will yield one set of derivations; derivations which become propositions in complex systems of philosophy. But when, as happened in the 17th Century, the universe is likened instead to a *machine*, not merely physical science but whole areas of moral philosophy and human psychology are affected [p. 6].

I believe it would be an interesting exercise to study the key words and expressions of major conceptual archetypes or foundation metaphors, both in the periods during which they first appeared in their full social and cultural settings and in their subsequent expansion and modification in changing fields of social relations. I would expect these to appear in the work of exceptionally liminal thinkers—poets, writers, religious prophets, "the unacknowledged legislators of mankind"—just before outstanding limina of history, major crises of societal change, since such shamanistic figures are possessed by spirits of change before changes become visible in public arenas. The first formulations will be in multivocal symbols and metaphors—each susceptible of many meanings, but with the core meanings linked analogically to the basic human problems of the epoch which may be pictured in biological, or mechanistic, or some other terms—these multivocals will yield to the action of the thought technicians who clear intellectual jungles, and organized systems of univocal concepts and signs will replace them. The change will begin, prophetically, "with metaphor, and end, instrumentally, with algebra." The danger is, of course, that the more persuasive the root metaphor or archetype, the more chance it has of becoming a self-certifying myth, sealed off from empirical disproof. It remains as a fascinating metaphysics. Here, root metaphor is opposed to what Thomas Kuhn has called "scientific paradigm," which stimulates and legitimates empirical research, of which it is indeed the product as well as the producer. For Kuhn, paradigms are "accepted examples of actual scientific practice—which includes law, theory, application and instrumentation together— which provide models from which spring coherent traditions of scientific research" (1962:10)—Copernican astronomy, Aristotelian or Newtonian "dynamics," wave optics, and others. My own view of the structure of metaphor is similar to I. A. Richards' "interaction view"; that is, in metaphor "we have two thoughts of different things *active* together and supported by a single word, or phrase, whose meaning is a resultant of their *interaction*" (1936:93). This view emphasizes the dynamics inherent in the metaphor, rather than limply comparing the two thoughts in it, or regarding one as "substituting" for the other. The two thoughts are active together, they "engender" thought in their coactivity.

Black develops the interaction view into a set of claims:

1. A metaphorical statement has two distinct subjects—a principal subject and a "subsidiary" one. Thus if one says—as Chamfort does in an example cited by Max Black—that "the poor are the negroes of Europe," "the poor" is the principal subject and the "negroes" the subsidiary one.

2. These subjects are best regarded as "systems of things," rather than things as elements. Thus, both "poor" and "negroes" in this metaphorical relation are themselves multivocal symbols, whole semantic systems, which bring into relation a number of ideas, images, sentiments, values, and stereotypes. Components of one system enter into dynamic relations with components of the other.

3. The metaphor works by applying to the principal subject a system of "associated implications" characteristic of the subsidiary subject. In the metaphor cited, for instance, the "poor" of Europe could be regarded not only as an oppressed class, but also as sharing in the inherited and indelible qualities of "natural" poverty attributed to black Americans by white racists. The whole metaphor is thereby charged with irony and provokes a rethinking of the roles both of the (European) poor and the (American) blacks.

4. These "implications" usually consist of commonplaces about the subsidiary subject, but may, in suitable cases, consist of deviant implications established ad hoc by the author. You need have only proverbial knowledge, as it were, to have your metaphor understood, not technical or special knowledge. A "scientific model" is rather a different kind of metaphor. Here "the maker must have prior control of a well-knit theory," says Black, "if he is to do more than hang an attractive picture on an algebraic formula. Systematic complexity of the source of the model and capacity for analogical development are of the essence" (1962:239).

5. The metaphor selects, emphasizes, suppresses, and organizes features of the principal subject by implying statements about it that normally apply to the subsidiary subject.

I have mentioned all this merely to point out that there are certain dangers inherent in regarding the social world as "a world in becoming," if by invoking the idea "becoming" one is unconsciously influenced by the ancient metaphor of organic growth and decay. Becoming suggests genetic continuity, telic growth, cumulative development, progress, etc. But many social events do not have this "directional" character. Here the metaphor may well select, emphasize, suppress, or organize features of social relations in accordance with *plant* or *animal* growth processes, and in so doing, mislead us about the nature of the *human* social world, *sui generis*. There is nothing wrong with metaphors or, *mutatis mutandis*, with models, provided that one is aware of the perils lurking behind their misuse. If one regards them, however, as a species of liminal monster, such as I described in *The Forest of Symbols* (1967), whose combination of familiar and unfamiliar features or unfamiliar combination of familiar features provokes us into thought, provides us with new perspectives, one can be excited by them; the implications, suggestions, and supporting values entwined with their literal use enable us to see a new subject matter in a new way.

The "becoming" metaphor fits fairly well, despite the apparent quarrel between functionalists and cultural evolutionists, with the structural-functionalist orthodoxy or paradigm, that gave rise to what Kuhn would have called the "normal science" of British social anthropology when I went into the field. For functionalism, as Nisbet has argued, following Wilbert Moore, from Durkheim through Radcliffe-Brown to Talcott Parsons, tried to present a unified theory of order *and* change based on a biological metaphor—it tries to draw the *motivational* mechanisms of change from the same conditions from which are drawn the concepts of *social order.* In other words, we have here the biological notion of immanent causation, an inner growth principle, as well as a homeostatic control mechanism. The simple, like the grain of mustard seed, *grows* into the complex, through various preordained stages. There are various micromechanisms of change in each specific sociocultural system, just as in modern evolutionary theory there are in biological entities and colonies, such as tensions, strains, discrepancies, and disharmonies, which are internal, endogenous, to them and provide the motor causes for change. In the social process—meaning by "process" here merely the general course of social action—in which I found myself among the Ndembu of Zambia, it was quite useful to think "biologically" about "village life-cycles" and "domestic cycles," the "origin," "growth," and "decay" of villages, families and lineages, but not too helpful to think about change as *immanent* in the structure of Ndembu society, when there was clearly "a wind of change," economic, political, social, religious, legal, and so on, sweeping through the whole of central Africa and originating *outside* all village societies. The functionalists of my period in Africa tended to think of change as "cyclical" and "repetitive" and of time as structural time, not free time. With my conviction as to the dynamic character of social relations I saw movement as much as structure, persistence as much as change, indeed, persistence as a striking aspect of change. I saw people interacting, and, as day succeeded day, the consequences of their interactions. I then began to perceive a form in the process of social time. This form was essentially *dramatic*. My metaphor and model here was a human esthetic form, a product of *culture* not of nature. A cultural form was the model for a social scientific concept. Once more I have to admit a debt to Znaniecki (I am also indebted to Robert Bierstedt's seminal article, 1968, pp. 599–601, for the following summary of his views), who, like some other social thinkers, was disposed to maintain the neo-Kantian distinction between two kinds of system—natural and cultural—which exhibit differences not only in composition and structure, but also—and most importantly—in the character of the elements that account for their coherence. Natural systems, Znaniecki always argued, are objectively given and exist independently of the experience and activity of men. Cultural systems, on the contrary, depend not only for their meaning but also for their existence upon the participation of conscious, volitional human agents and upon men's continuing and potentially changing relations with one another. Znaniecki had his own label for this difference. He called it the "humanistic coefficient," and it is this concept that sharply separated his approach from that of most of his contemporaries on the American scene. Everywhere in his work he emphasized the role of conscious agents or actors—an emphasis which his opponents were inclined to criticize as the "subjective" point of view. It is persons as the objects of the actions of others, however, not as subjects, that meet his criteria for sociological data. Among the sources of these data Znaniecki listed the personal experiences of the sociologist, both original and vicarious;

observation by the sociologist, both direct and indirect; the personal experience of other people; and the observations of other people. This emphasis supported his use of personal documents in sociological research. This whole approach I continue to find most congenial.

I felt that I had to bring the "humanistic coefficient" into my model if I was to make sense of human social processes. One of the most arresting properties of Ndembu social life in villages was its propensity toward conflict. Conflict was rife in the groups of two dozen or so kinsfolk who made up a village community. It manifested itself in public episodes of tensional irruption which I called "social dramas." Social dramas took place in what Kurt Lewin might have called "aharmonic" phases of the ongoing social process. When the interests and attitudes of groups and individuals stood in obvious opposition, social dramas did seem to me to constitute isolable and minutely describable units of social process. Not every social drama reached a clear resolution, but enough did so to make it possible to state what I then called the "processional form" of the drama. I had no thought, at that time, of using such a "processual unit," as I came to call the genus of which "social drama" is a species, in cross-societal comparison. I did not think it to be a universal type, but subsequent research —including work for a paper on "An Anthropological Approach to the Icelandic Saga" (1971)—has convinced me that social dramas, with much the same temporal or processual structure as I detected in the Ndembu case, can be isolated for study in societies at all levels of scale and complexity. This is particularly the case in political situations, and belongs to what I now call the dimension of "structure" as opposed to that of "communitas" as a generic mode of human interrelatedness. Yet there is communitas, too, in one stage of the social drama, as I hope to show, and perhaps the capacity of its successive phases to have continuity is a function of communitas.

Not all processual units are "dramatic" in structure and atmosphere. Many belong under the rubric of what Raymond Firth has called "social organization" and defines as "the working arrangements of society . . . the process of ordering of action and of relations in reference to given social ends, in terms of adjustments resulting from the exercise of choices by members of the society" (*Essays on Social Organization and Values*, 1964:45). Among these "harmonic" processual units would be what I call "social enterprises," primarily economic in character, as when a modern African group decides to build a bridge, school, or road, or when a traditional Polynesian group, like Firth's Tikopia, decides to prepare turmeric, a plant of the ginger family, for ritual dye or other purposes (Firth 1967:416–464); either group is concerned with the outcomes of these decisions on social relations within the group over time. Here individual choice and considerations of utility are discriminating features.

A recent book by Philip Gulliver (1971), which is a microanalysis of social networks (another interesting metaphor to be probed with reference to how it is used by anthropologists) in two small local communities among the Ndendeuli people of southern Tanzania, also represents a conscious attempt to describe dynamic processes over a period in nondramatic terms. Gulliver wished to direct especial attention and give added emphasis to the cumulative effect of an endless series of incidents, cases, and events that might be quite as significant in affecting and changing social relationships as the more dramatic encounters. Lesser events, he argues, serve gradually to set the stage for the bigger encounters. Gulliver urges that careful attention should be paid to "the continuum of interaction amongst a given collection of people" (p. 354). He warns that we should not "concentrate so greatly on conflict situations that we neglect the equally important situations of cooperation—though the latter are likely to be less dramatic" (p. 354). I agree with Gulliver, though I share Freud's view that disturbances of the normal and regular often give us greater insight into the normal than does direct study. Deep structure may be revealed through surface anti-structure or counter-structure—terms I discuss in Chapter 7, "Metaphors of

Anti-structure." I will not here follow up Gulliver's interesting views on such formulations as "action-set," "network," "decision making," "role playing," and others. He has a lot of sturdy wisdom on those—but they would take us from the main themes. Gulliver cautions against the view, familiar since Weber, that

assumes a rationality in men that we know by experience is often absent. Men can misconceive a situation and its possibilities, they can be stimulated by high emotion or by depression to make moves and decisions that otherwise they might not, they can be stupid, obstinate, short-sighted, or they may be calculating, alert, intelligent, or something in between. Yet social scientists often ignore these critical factors which affect decision-makers [pp. 356–357].

In the social drama, however, though choices of means and ends and social affiliation are made, stress is dominantly laid upon loyalty and obligation, as much as interest, and the course of events may then have a tragic quality. As I wrote in my book *Schism and Continuity* (1957), in which I began to examine the social drama, "the situation in an Ndembu village closely parallels that found in Greek drama where one witnesses the helplessness of the human individual before the Fates; but in this case [and also in the Icelandic one, as I have found] the Fates are the necessities of the social process" (p. 94). Conflict seems to bring fundamental aspects of society, normally overlaid by the customs and habits of daily intercourse, into frightening prominence. People have to take sides in terms of deeply entrenched moral imperatives and constraints, often against their own personal preferences. Choice is overborne by duty.

Social dramas and social enterprises—as well as other kinds of processual units—represent sequences of social events, which, seen retrospectively by an observer, can be shown to have structure. Such "temporal" structure, unlike atemporal structure (including "conceptual," "cognitive," and "syntactical" structures), is organized primarily through relations in time rather than in space, though, of course, cognitive schemes are themselves the result of a mental process and have processual qualities. If one were able to arrest the social process as though it were a motion film and were then to examine the "still," the coexisting social relations within a community, one would probably find that the temporary structures were incomplete, open-ended, unconsummated. They would be, at most, on their way to an ending. But if one had the science-fiction means of penetrating into the minds of the arrested actors, one would undoubtedly find in them, at almost any endopsychical level existing between the full brightness of conscious attention and the darker strata of the unconscious, a set of ideas, images, concepts, and so on, to which one could attach the label "atemporal structures." These are models of what people "believe they do, ought to do, or would like to do" (Audrey Richards, 1939:160). Perhaps in individual cases these are more fragmentary than structural, but if one were to look at the whole group one would find that what ideas or norms an individual lacks or fails to put into systematic relation with other ideas, other individuals do possess or have systematized. In the intersubjective collective representations of the group one would discover "structure" and "system," "purposive action patterns" and, at deeper levels, "categorical frames." These individual and group structures, carried in people's heads and nervous systems, have a steering function, a "cybernetic" function, in the endless succession of social events, imposing on them the degree of order they possess, and, indeed, dividing processual units into phases. "Structure is the order in a system," as Marvin Harris has said. The phase structure of social dramas is not the product of instinct but of models and metaphors carried in the actors' heads. It is not here a case of "fire finding its own form," but of form providing a hearth, a flue, and a damper for fire. Structures are the more stable aspects of action and interrelationship. What the philosopher John Dewey has called the "more rapid and irregular events" of the social process are converted into "slower and regular rhythmic events" through the cybernetic effects of cognitive and normative/structural models.

Some of the "regular rhythmic events" can be measured and expressed in statistical form. But here we shall be first of all concerned with the shape, the diachronic profile of the social drama. I would like to stress as strongly as I can that I consider this processual approach decisive as a guide to the understanding of human social behavior. Religious and legal institutions, among others, only cease to be bundles of dead or cold rules when they are seen as phases in social processes, as dynamic patterns right from the start. We have to learn to think of societies as continuously "flowing," as a "dangerous tide . . . that never stops or dies. . . . And held one moment burns the hand," as W. H. Auden once put it. The formal, supposedly static, structures only become visible through this flow which energizes them, heats them to the point of visibility—to use yet another metaphor. Their very stasis is the effect of social dynamics. The organizational foci of temporal structures are "goals," the objects of action or effort, not "nodes," mere points of diagrammatic intersection or lines of rest. Temporal structure, until at rest and therefore atemporal, is always tentative; there are always alternative goals and alternative means of attaining them. Since its foci are goals, psychological factors, such as volition, motivation, span of attention, level of aspiration, and so on, are important in its analysis; contrastingly, in atemporal structures these are unimportant, for such structures reveal themselves as already exhausted, achieved, or, alternatively as axioms, self-evident cognitive or normative frames to which action is subsequent and subordinate. Again, since the goals significantly include social goals, the study of temporal structures involves the study of the communication process, including the sources of pressures to communicate within and among groups; this leads inevitably to the study of the symbols, signs, signals, and tokens, verbal and nonverbal, that people employ in order to attain personal and group goals.

Social dramas, then, are units of aharmonic or disharmonic process, arising in conflict situations. Typically, they have four main phases of public action, accessible to observation. These are:

1. *Breach* of regular, norm-governed social relations occurs between persons or groups within the same system of social relations, be it a village, chiefdom, office, factory, political party or ward, church, university department, or any other perduring system or set or field of social interaction. Such a breach is signalized by the public, overt breach or deliberate nonfulfillment of some crucial norm regulating the intercourse of the parties. To flout such a norm is one obvious symbol of dissidence. In a social drama it is not a crime, though it may formally resemble one; it is, in reality, a "symbolic trigger of confrontation or encounter," to use Frederick Bailey's terms. There is always something altruistic about such a symbolic breach; always something egoistic about a crime. A dramatic breach may be made by an individual, certainly, but he always acts, or believes he acts, on behalf of other parties, whether they are aware of it or not. He sees himself as a representative, not as a lone hand.

2. Following breach of regular, norm-governed social relations, a phase of mounting *crisis* supervenes, during which, unless the breach can be sealed off quickly within a limited area of social interaction, there is a tendency for the breach to widen and extend until it becomes coextensive with some dominant cleavage in the widest set of relevant social relations to which the conflicting or antagonistic parties belong. It is now fashionable to speak of this sort of thing as the "escalation" of crisis. If it is a social drama involving two nations in one geographical region, escalation could imply a stepwise movement toward antagonism across the dominant global cleavage between communist and capitalist camps. Among the Ndembu, the phase of crisis exposes the pattern of current factional intrigue, hitherto covert and privately conducted, within the relevant social group, village, neighborhood, or chiefdom; and beneath it there becomes visible the less plastic, more durable, but nevertheless gradually changing basic Ndembu social structure, made up of relations that have a high degree of constancy and consistency—that are

supported by normative patterns laid down in the course of deep regularities of conditioning, training, and social experience. Even beneath these cyclical structural changes, other changes in the ordering of social relations emerge in social dramas—those, for example, resulting from the incorporation of the Ndembu into the Zambian nation, the modern African world, the Third World, and the whole world. I discuss this aspect briefly in the Kamahasanyi case in *The Drums of Affliction* (1968a). This second stage, *crisis*, is always one of those turning points or moments of danger and suspense, when a true state of affairs is revealed, when it is least easy to don masks or pretend that there is nothing rotten in the village. Each public crisis has what I now call liminal characteristics, since it is a threshold between more or less stable phases of the social process, but it is not a sacred limen, hedged around by taboos and thrust away from the centers of public life. On the contrary, it takes up its menacing stance in the forum itself and, as it were, dares the representatives of order to grapple with it. It cannot be ignored or wished away.

3. This brings us to the third phase, *redressive action*. In order to limit the spread of crisis, certain adjustive and redressive "mechanisms," (and here I joyfully borrow a metaphor from physics) informal or formal, institutionalized or ad hoc, are swiftly brought into operation by leading or structurally representative members of the disturbed social system. These mechanisms vary in type and complexity with such factors as the depth and shared social significance of the breach, the social inclusiveness of the crisis, the nature of the social group within which the breach took place, and the degree of its autonomy with reference to wider or external systems of social relations. They may range from personal advice and informal mediation or arbitration to formal juridical and legal machinery, and, to resolve certain kinds of crisis or legitimate other modes of resolution, to the performance of public ritual. The notion of "escalation" can apply to this phase also: in a complex, industrial society, for example, antagonists might move a dispute up from a court

of lower jurisdiction to the supreme court through intervening judicial stages. In the Icelandic *Njál's Saga*, escalation characterizes the set of dramas that make up the saga. It begins with simple breaches of local order, minor crisis, and informal redress, mainly at the level of household communities in a small region of the South Quarter of tenth-century Iceland, which cumulate, despite temporary settlement and adjustment of claims, until, finally, a public breach that triggers the tragic main drama takes place: a *goði*, or priest chieftain, who is also a good man, is killed wantonly by his foster brother, the most intransigent of Njál's sons. The resulting crisis phase involves a major cleavage between factions consisting of the major lineages and *sibs* (here meaning bilateral vengeance and blood-compensation groups) in southern and southeastern Iceland, and the parties seek redress at the Althing and Fifth Court, the general assembly of Icelanders. *Njál's Saga* pitilessly reveals how Iceland just could not produce the adequately sanctioned judicial machinery to handle large-scale crisis, for inevitably, the Althing negotiations break down, and there is regression to crisis again, sharpened crisis, moreover, that can only be resolved by the total defeat and attempted annihilation of one party. The fact that though there was a general assembly of Icelanders there was no Icelandic nation was represented by the absence of national laws with teeth in them, the teeth of punitive sanctions jointly applied by the leading men of all four Quarters. I have discussed elsewhere (1971) some of the various historical, environmental, and cultural reasons why the Icelandic commonwealth failed to become a state, lost its independence (in 1262), and accepted Norwegian overlordship. I was set on the track of these reasons by treating the saga literature as a series of social dramas. The sagas reveal that local feuds which could only be transiently contained by enlightened individuals generated forces over time which sundered Iceland and revealed the weakness of its uncentralized, acephalous polity. When one is studying social change, at whatever social level, I would give one piece of advice: study carefully what happens in phase three, the would-be redressive phase of social dramas, and ask whether the redressive machinery is capable of handling crises so as to restore, more or less, the status quo ante, or at least to restore peace among the contending groups. Then ask, if so, how precisely? And if not, why not? It is in the redressive phase that both pragmatic techniques and symbolic action reach their fullest expression. For the society, group, community, association, or whatever may be the social unit, is here at its most "self-conscious" and may attain the clarity of someone fighting in a corner for his life. Redress, too, has its liminal features, its being "betwixt and between," and, as such, furnishes a distanced replication and critique of the events leading up to and composing the "crisis." This replication may be in the rational idiom of a judicial process, or in the metaphorical and symbolic idiom of a ritual process, depending on the nature and severity of the crisis. When redress fails there is usually regression to crisis. At this point direct force may be used, in the varied forms of war, revolution, intermittent acts of violence, repression, or rebellion. Where the disturbed community is small and relatively weak vis-à-vis the central authority, however, regression to crisis tends to become a matter of endemic, pervasive, smoldering factionalism, without sharp, overt confrontations between consistently distinct parties.

4. The final phase I distinguished consists either of the *reintegration* of the disturbed social group or of the social recognition and legitimization of irreparable schism between the contesting parties—in the case of the Ndembu this often meant the secession of one section of a village from the rest. It frequently happened then that after an interval of several years, one of the villages so formed would sponsor a major ritual to which members of the other would be expressly invited, thus registering reconciliation at a different level of political integration. I describe one such ritual, Chihamba, in *Schism and Continuity* (1957:288–317) and how it functioned to reconcile the sponsoring village, Mukanza, with several other villages, including one

formed by the fission of one of its previous component sections. From the point of view of the scientific observer the fourth phase—that of temporary climax, solution, or outcome—is an opportunity for taking stock. He can now analyze the continuum synchronically, so to speak, at this point of arrest, having already fully taken into account and represented by appropriate constructs the temporal character of the drama. In the particular case of a "political field," for example, one can compare the ordering of political relations which preceded the power struggle erupting into an observable social drama with that following the redressive phase. As likely as not, as Marc Swartz and I pointed out in the Introduction to *Political Anthropology* (1966), the scope and range of the field will have altered; the number of its parts will be different; and their magnitude will be different. More importantly, the nature and intensity of the relations between parts, and the structure of the total field, will have changed. Oppositions may be found to have become alliances, and vice versa. Asymmetric relations may have become egalitarian ones. High status will have become low status and vice versa. New power will have been channeled into old and new authority and former authority defenestrated. Closeness will have become distance, and vice versa. Formerly integrated parts will have segmented; previously independent parts will have fused. Some parts will no longer belong to the field, others will have entered it. Institutionalized relationships will have become informal; social regularities will have become irregularities. New norms and rules may have been generated during attempts to redress conflict; old rules will have fallen into disrepute and have been abrogated. The bases of political support will have altered. Some components of the field will have less support, others more, still others will have fresh support, and some will have none. The distribution of the factors of legitimacy will have changed, as also the techniques used by leaders to gain compliance. These changes can be observed, ascertained, recorded, and in some cases their indices can even be measured and expressed in quantitative terms.

Yet through all these changes, certain crucial norms and relationships—and other seemingly less crucial, even quite trivial and arbitrary—will persist. The explanations for both constancy and change can, in my opinion, only be found by systematic analysis of *processual* units and temporal structures, by looking at phases as well as atemporal systems. For each phase has its specific properties, and each leaves its special stamp on the metaphors and models in the heads of men involved with one another in the unending flow of social existence. In keeping with my explicit comparison of the temporal structure of certain types of social processes with that of dramas on the stage, with their acts and scenes, I saw the phases of social dramas as cumulating to a climax. I would point out too that at the linguistic level of "parole," each phase has its own speech forms and styles, its own rhetoric, its own kinds of nonverbal languages and symbolisms. These vary greatly, of course, cross-culturally and cross-temporally, but I postulate that there will be certain important generic affinities between the speeches and languages of the crisis phase everywhere, of the redressive phase everywhere, of the restoration of peace phase everywhere. Cross-cultural comparison has never applied itself to such a task because it has limited itself to atemporal forms and structures, to the products of man's social activity abstracted from the processes in which they arise, and, having arisen, which they channel to a varying extent. It is much easier to prop oneself on the "paradigmatic" crutch, coolly remote from the vexatious competitiveness of social life. Such cross-cultural comparison, moreover, cannot be made until we have many more extended-case studies. An extended-case history is the history of a single group or community over a considerable length of time, collected as a sequence of processual units of different types, including the social dramas and social enterprises mentioned already. This is more than plain historiography, for it involves the utilization of whatever conceptual tools social anthropology and cultural anthropology have bequeathed to us. "Processualism" is a term that includes "dramatistic analysis."

Processual analysis assumes cultural analysis, just as it assumes structural-functional analysis, including more static comparative morphological analysis. It negates none of these, but puts dynamics first. Yet in the order of presentation of facts it is a useful strategy to present a systematic outline of the principles on which the institutionalized social structure is constructed and to measure their relative importance, intensity, and variation under different circumstances with numerical or statistical data if possible. In a sense the social activities from which one elicits a "statistical structure" can be characterized as "slow process," in that they tend to involve the regular repetition of certain acts, as distinct from the rapid process seen, for example, in social dramas, where there is a good deal of uniqueness and arbitrariness. All is in motion but some social flows move so slowly relatively to others that they seem almost as fixed and stationary as the landscape and the geographical levels under it, though these too, are, of course, forever in slow flux. If one has the data to analyze a sequence of crucial processual units over, say, twenty or thirty years, one can see changes even in the slow processes, even in societies thought of as "cyclical" or "stagnant," to use the favorite terms of some investigators. But I do not want to present here methods of studying social processes—I have given examples of this in *Schism and Continuity* (1957), *The Drums of Affliction* (1968a), the analysis of the *Mukanda* rites in *Local-Level Politics* (1968b), and in various papers. This approach is an abiding concern of mine, and within it I made my first attempt to produce a paradigm for the analysis of ritual symbols. Nor do I wish just now to discuss the theory of conflict which obviously influences my "dramatistic" formulation.

I want rather to do something quite different, as far different as "anti-structure" is from "structure," though processualism would see both terms as intrinsically related, perhaps even as not contradictory in the ultimate, nondualistic sense. A mathematical equation needs its minus signs as well as its pluses, negatives as well as positives, zeros as well as numbers: the equivalence of two expressions is affirmed by a formula containing negations. It may be said that positive structuralism can only become processualism by accepting the concept of social anti-structure as a theoretical operator. There is nothing really mystical about this. For example, Znaniecki argued with reference to what he called "cultural systems":

The people who share a certain set of interconnected systems (and among these systems there are usually also certain social groups— territorial, genetic or telic) may be more or less conscious of this fact, and more or less willing to influence one another for the benefit of their common civilization and to influence this civilization for their mutual benefit. This consciousness and willingness, in so far as they exist, constitute a social bond uniting these people over and above any formal social bonds which are due to the existence of regulated social relations and organized social groups. . . . If the term "community" is limited to the humanistic reality embracing such phenomena . . . as the development of new cultural ideals and attempts at their realization apart from organized group action, . . . there is no doubt but that a "community" in this sense can be scientifically studied, and that sociology is the science to study it as one of the specifically social data [1936, chapter 3].

Here we have what I would call "communitas" or social anti-structure (since it is "a bond uniting . . . people over and above any formal social bonds," that is, "positive" structure) being re-garded as a reputable object of scientific study. In my recent work I have been struck by the way in which pilgrimages ex-emplify such anti-structural communities—perhaps Znaniecki had observed communitas in its Polish setting most vividly made vis-ible at the hilly shrine of Our Lady of Czenstochowa, as I have seen it in its Mexican setting at the basilica of Our Lady of Guadalupe, and more recently at the remote shrine of Our Lady of Knock in County Mayo, Ireland.

In a sense, the "social drama" concept is within the brackets of positive structural assertions; it is concerned mainly with rela-tions between persons in their status-role capacity and between groups and subgroups as structural segments. "Conflict" is the other side of the coin of "cohesion" here, with "interest" the motive binding or separating these persons, these men in servitude to structural rights and obligations, imperatives, and loyalties. But, as Znaniecki pointed out, there is a bond uniting people over and above their formal bonds. Therefore one should not limit one's inquiry to a particular social structure but look for the grounds of action in generic communitas. This was the reason that prompted me to begin the research that has so far resulted in only a few publications, one of which was *The Ritual Process* (1969). The reader should not think that I have forgotten the importance of the sociology of symbols. There are symbols of structure and symbols of anti-structure, and I wish to consider first the social bases of both. Like Znaniecki, I looked for evidences of the development of new cultural ideals and attempts at their realization and at various modes of social behavior that did not proceed from the structural properties of organized social groups. I found in the data of art, literature, philosophy, political and juridical thought, history, comparative religion, and similar documents far more suggestive ideas about the nature of the social than in the work of colleagues doing their "normal social science" under the then prevailing paradigm of structural functionalism. These notions are not always put forward with direct or obvious reference to social relations—often they are metaphorical or allegorical—sometimes they appear in the guise of philosophical concepts or principles, but I see them as arising in the experience of human coactivity, including the deepest of such experiences. For example, I have recently been paying attention to the notion that the familiar distinction made in Zen Buddhism between the concepts *prajñā* (which very approximately means "intuition") and *vijñāna* (very roughly, "reason" or "discursive understanding") are rooted in the contrasting social experiences I have described, respectively, as "communitas" and "structure." Briefly to recapitulate the argument in *The Ritual Process*, the bonds of communitas are anti-structural in that they are undifferentiated, equalitarian, direct, nonrational (though not *irrational*), I-Thou or Essential We relationships, in Martin Buber's sense. Structure is all that holds people apart, defines their differences, and constrains their actions, including social structure in the British anthropological sense. Communitas is most evident in "liminality," a concept I extend from its use in Van Gennep's *Les Rites de passage* to refer to any condition outside or on the peripheries of everyday life. It is often a sacred condition or can readily become one. For example, the world over, millenarian movements originate in periods when societies are in liminal transition between different social structures.

With these distinctions in mind let us now look at what Suzuki Daisetz Teitaro, probably the greatest scholar in Zen studies writing English, has to say about the *prajñā/vijnañā* contrast. Suzuki (1967) writes:

To divide is characteristic of *vijñāna* (discursive understanding,) while with *prajñā* (intuition) it is just the opposite. *Prajñā* is the self-knowledge of the whole, in contrast to *vijñāna*, which busies itself with parts. *Prajñā* is an integrating principle, while *vijñāna* always analyzes. *Vijñāna* cannot work without having *prajñā* behind it; parts are parts of the whole; parts never exist by themselves, for, if they did, they would not be parts—they would even cease to exist [pp. 66–67].

This "wholeness" of *prajñā* resembles Znaniecki's idea of "community" as the real source of the interconnection of cultural and social systems and subsystems. These cannot be interconnected on their own level, so to speak; it would be misleading to find their integration there—what unites them is their common ground in living community or communitas. Other explanations are specious and artificial, however ingenious, for partness can never by itself be made into wholeness—something additional is required. Suzuki expresses this with exceptional clarity (p. 67) as follows:

Prajñā is ever seeking unity on the grandest possible scale, so that there could be no further unity in any sense; whatever expressions or statements it makes are thus naturally beyond the order of *vijñāna*. *Vijñāna* subjects them to intellectual analysis, trying to find something comprehensible according to its own measure. But *vijñāna* cando this for the obvious reason that *prajñā* starts from where *vijñāna* cannot penetrate. *Vijñāna*, being the principle of differentiation, can never see *prajñā* in its oneness, and it is because of the very nature of *vijñāna* that *prajñā* proves utterly baffling to it.

Prajñā, as Suzuki understands it, would be the source of "foundation"—or root metaphors, since these are eminently synthetic: on them *vijñāna* then does its work of discriminating the structure of the root metaphor. A metaphor is a *"prajñā*-artifact," if you like, a system of categories derived from it would be a *"vijñāna*-artifact." Blaise Pascal's distinction between *l'esprit de finesse* and *l'esprit de géometrie* may represent something similar.

I would probably differ from Suzuki in some ways and find common ground with Durkheim and Znaniecki in seeking the source of both these concepts in human social experience, whereas Suzuki would probably locate them in the nature of things. For him communitas and structure would be particular manifestations of principles that can be found everywhere, like *Yin* and *Yang* for the Chinese. Indeed, *prajñā*,—intuition—is its becoming conscious of itself. Yet we find him identifying *prajñā* with the Primary Man (*gennin*) in "his spontaneous, free-creating, non-teleological activities" (p. 80); he also declares that *prajñā* is "concrete in every sense of the term. . . . [and therefore] the most dynamic thing we can have in the world" (p. 80). These (and other) characteristics seem to me to be ways of talking about human experiences of that mode of coactivity I have called communitas.

I had not read Suzuki, though I had seen quotations from his writings, before I wrote *The Ritual Process*, but in that book, on the basis of experiences and observations in the field, social experience as a person, readings in the experiences of others, and the fruits of discussion with others I came up with several statements about communitas that resemble Suzuki's on *prajñā*. For example: communitas is society experienced or seen as "an unstructured or rudimentarily structured and relatively undifferentiated *comitatus,* community, or even communion of equal individuals" (p. 96). Also: "communitas is a relationship between concrete, historical, idiosyncratic individuals," "a direct, immediate and total confrontation of human identities" (pp. 131–132). In other passages I link communitas with spontaneity and freedom, and structure with obligation, jurality, law, constraint, and so on.

But though one would have to bring within the scope of the paradigm "structure" many features of the social drama, and the other Kurt Lewin–based concepts I used, to describe the Kenneth Burkean "scene" on which the "actors" played out their "acts" with regard to certain "purposes"—such as "field," "locomotion," "positive and negative valence," and the like, still some of its aspects escape into the domain of anti-structure, and even of communitas. For instance, after showing the various structural strategies employed by the main political faction of Mukanza Village to prevent the ambitious Sandombu from making good his claim to the headmanship, notably their accusation that he had slain his classificatory mother by sorcery, I show how when his rivals had forced him into exile they began to repine, for reasons of communitas. Their consciences began to trouble them over him, as often happens when people deny their past experiences of communitas. They began to think: was he not blood of their blood, born from the same womb (the very term used for a matrilineal group) as they? Had he not been part of their corporate life? Had he not contributed to their welfare, paying for the education of their children, finding jobs for their young men when he was a foreman on a government road gang for the PWD? His plea to return was allowed. A new misfortune led to a new divination, which found, *inter alia,* that Sandombu had not been guilty of the sorcery of which he had been accused, that an outsider had caused the woman's death. A ritual was performed, for which Sandombu paid a goat. He planted a tree symbolic of matrilineage unity to his dead mother's sister, and he and his main antagonists prayed there to the shades and were reconciled. Powdered white clay, symbolizing the basic values of Ndembu society—good health, fertility, respect for elders, observance of kinship dues, honesty, and the like, briefly a master symbol of structure imbued with communitas—was sprinkled on the ground round the tree and the several kinds of kin present were anointed with it. Here clearly it was not mere self-interest or the letter of the law that prevailed but its spirit, the spirit of communitas. Structure is certainly present but its divisiveness is muted into a set of interdependencies: it is seen here as a social instrument or means, neither as an end in itself nor as providing goals for competition and dissidence. One might also postulate that the coherence of a completed social drama is itself a function of communitas. An incomplete or irresoluble drama would then manifest the absence of communitas. Consensus on values, too, is not the basic level here. Consensus, being spontaneous, rests on communitas, not on structure.

The term "anti-structure" is only negative in its connotations when seen from the vantage point or perspective of "structure." It is no more "anti" in its essence than the American "counter-culture" is merely "counter." "Structure" may just as legitimately be viewed as "anti" or at least as a set of limitations, like William Blake's "limit of opacity." If one is interested in asking some of the questions formulated in the earliest days of sociology, and now relegated to the philosophy of history, such as, "Where are we going?" or "Where is society going?" or "Whither goes the world?" it might be well to see structure as limit rather than as theoretical point of departure. The components of what I have called anti-structure, such as communitas and liminality, are the conditions for the production of root metaphors, conceptual archetypes, paradigms, models for, and the rest. Root metaphors have a "thusness" or "thereness" from which many subsequent structures may be "unpacked" by *vijñāna* consciousness or *l'esprit de géometrie*. What could be more positive than this? For metaphors share one of the properties I have attributed to symbols. I don't mean multivocality, their capacity to resonate among many meanings at once like a chord in music, though root metaphors are multivocal. I mean a certain kind of polarization of meaning in which the subsidiary subject is really a depth world of prophetic, half-glimpsed images, and the principal subject, the visible, fully known (or thought to be fully known component), at the opposite pole to it, acquires new and surprising contours and valences from its dark companion. On the other hand, because the poles are "active together" the unknown is brought just a little more into the light by the known. To be brought fully into the light is the work of another phase of liminality: that of imageless thought, conceptualization at various degrees of abstractness, deduction both informal and formal, and inductive generalization. Genuine creative imagination, inventiveness, or inspiration goes beyond spatial imagination or any skill in forming metaphors. It does not necessarily associate visual images with given concepts and proportions. Creative imagination is far richer than imagery; it does not consist in the ability to evoke sense impressions and it is not restricted to filling gaps in the map supplied by perception. It is called "creative" because it is the ability to create concepts and conceptual systems that may correspond to nothing in the senses (even though they may correspond to something in reality), and also because it gives rise to unconventional ideas. It is something like Suzuki's view of *prajñā* in its purity. This is the very creative darkness of liminality that lays hold of the basic forms of life. These are more than logical structures. Every mathematician and every natural scientist would, I think, agree with Mario Bunge that

without imagination, without inventiveness, without the ability to conceive hypotheses and proposals, nothing but the "mechanical" operations can be performed, i.e., the manipulations of apparatus and the application of computation algorithms, the art of calculating with any species of notation. The invention of hypotheses, the devising of techniques, and the designing of experiments, are clear cases of imaginative, [purely "liminal"] operations, as opposed to "mechanical" operations. They are not purely logical operations. Logic *alone* is as incapable of leading a person to new ideas as grammar *alone* is incapable of inspiring poems and as theory of harmony *alone* is incapable of inspiring sonatas. Logic, grammar, and musical theory enable us to detect formal mistakes and good ideas, as well as to develop good ideas, but they do not, as it were, supply the "substance," the happy idea, the new point of view [1962:80].

This is the "flash of the fire that can." To revert to Suzuki's interpretation of the Zen vocabulary,[2] *vijñāna* alone is incapable of leading a person to new ideas. Yet in the social and natural worlds as we know them both *vijñāna* and *prajñā* are necessary for scientific theories, poems, symphonies, for intuition and reasoning or logic. In the area of social creativity—where new social and cultural forms are engendered—both structure and communitas are necessary, or both the "bound" and the "unbound." To view "societas" as human process, rather than as an atemporal timeless or eternal system modeled either on an organism or a machine, is to enable us to concentrate on the relationships, existing at every point and on every level in complex and subtle ways, between communitas and structure. We must devise approaches that safeguard both archmodalities, for in destroying one we destroy both and must then present a distorted account of man with man. What I call liminality, the state of being in between successive participations in social milieux dominated by social structural considerations, whether formal or unformalized, is not precisely the same as communitas, for it is a sphere or domain of action or thought rather than a social modality. Indeed, liminality may imply solitude rather than society, the voluntary or involuntary withdrawal of an individual from a social-structural matrix. It may imply alienation from rather than more authentic participation in social existence. In *The Ritual Process* I was mostly concerned with the social aspects of liminality, for my

----

[2] But not Nagarjuna's; he sees logic and intuition as essentially equal expressions of the only adequate stance toward *prajñā*, silence.

emphasis was still on Ndembu society. There liminality occurs in the middle phase of the rites of passage which mark changes in a group's or individual's social status. Such rites characteristically begin with the subject's being symbolically killed or separated from ordinary secular or profane relationships, and conclude with a symbolic birth or reincorporation into society. The intervening liminal period or phase is thus betwixt and between the categories of ordinary social life. I then tried to extend the concept of liminality to refer to any condition outside, or on the peripheries of, everyday life, arguing that there was an affinity between the middle in sacred time and the outside in sacred space. For liminality among the Ndembu is a sacred condition. Among them, too, it is one in which communitas is most evident. The bonds of communitas, as I said, are anti-structural in the sense that they are undifferentiated, equalitarian, direct, nonrational (though not irrational), I-Thou relationships. In the liminal phase of Ndembu rites of passage, and in similar rites the world over, communitas is engendered by ritual humiliation, stripping of signs and insignia of preliminal status, ritual leveling, and ordeals and tests of various kinds, intended to show that "man thou art dust!" In hierarchical social structures communitas is symbolically affirmed by periodic rituals, not infrequently calendrical or tied in with the agricultural or hydraulic cycle, in which the lowly and the mighty reverse social roles. In such societies, too, and here I begin to draw my examples from European and Indian history, the religious ideology of the powerful idealizes humility, orders of religious specialists undertake ascetic lives, and *per contra*, cult groups among those of low status play with symbols of power and authority. The world over, millenarian and revivalistic movements, as I mentioned earlier, originate in periods when societies are in liminal transition between major orderings of social structural relations. In the second half of *The Ritual Process* I gloss my illustrations from the traditional cultures of Africa, Europe, and Asia with comments on modern culture, referring briefly to Leo Tolstoy, Mahatma Gandhi, Bob Dylan, and such current phenomena as the Chicago Vice Lords and the California Hell's

Angels. In 1970–1971 in Chicago a number of our seminar papers explored further aspects of communitas and liminality in connection with such topics as bureaucratic corruption in India and the Hindu tradition of gift-giving (Arjun Appadurai), trickster myths in Africa (Robert Pelton), Russian populism in the nineteenth century (Daniel Kakulski), countercultural communes (David Buchdahl), and symbol and festival in the "Évènements de Mai-Juin 1968," the Paris student uprising (Sherry Turkle). All these stimulating contributions contained a number of symbols of anti-structure, both as liminality and communitas. One student of Russian literature, Alan Shusterman, presented a paper on another type of liminality. His paper, called "Epileptics, Dying Men and Suicides: Liminality and Communitas in Dostoevsky," showed how in the Christian tradition as represented in Dostoevsky's Russia, "the lack of communitas . . . creates both an unviable liminality and the feeling of despair." His argument extended the application of the concept of liminality to ranges of data I have not myself taken into account. But with regard to this question of the contrast between the liminalities of solitude and communitas much remains to be said. Many existentialist philosophers, for example, view what they term "society" as something inimical, hostile to the authentic nature of the individual. Society is what some of them term the "seat of objectivity" and therefore antagonistic to the subjective existence of the individual. To find and become himself, the individual must struggle to liberate himself from the yoke of society. Society is seen by existentialism as the captor of the individual, very much in the same way as Greek religious thought, particularly in the mystery cults, viewed the body as the captor of the soul. To my mind these thinkers have failed to make the analytical distinction between communitas and structure; it is structure they seem to be talking about when they speak as Martin Heidegger does of the social self as the "unauthentic part of human-being." But they are really addressing themselves to a communitas of "authentic individuals" or trying to liberate such individuals from social structure. One might ask who is the audience of these prolific if alienated prophets of uncommunication? But this is diverging from my main topic, which is to consider the relations between social drama, processual analysis, anti-structure, and semantic study of ritual symbols.

Since I regard cultural symbols including ritual symbols as originating in and sustaining processes involving temporal changes in social relations, and not as timeless entities, I have tried to treat the crucial properties of ritual symbols as being involved in these dynamic developments. Symbols instigate social action. The question I am always asking the data is: "How do ritual symbols work?"

In my view they condense many references, uniting them in a single cognitive and affective field. Here I will refer the reader to my Introduction to *Forms of Symbolic Action* (1970b). In this sense ritual symbols are "multivocal," susceptible of many meanings, but their referents tend to polarize between physiological phenomena (blood, sexual organs, coitus, birth, death, catabolism, and so on) and normative values of moral facts (kindness to children, reciprocity, generosity to kinsmen, respect for elders, obedience to political authorities, and the like). At this "normative" or "ideological" pole of meaning, one also finds reference to principles of organization: matriliny, patriliny, kingship, gerontocracy, age-grade organization, sex-affiliation, and others. The drama of ritual action—the singing, dancing, feasting, wearing of bizarre dress, body painting, use of alcohol or hallucinogens, and so on, causes an exchange between these poles in which the biological referents are ennobled and the normative referents are charged with emotional significance. I call the biological referents, insofar as they constitute an organized system set off from the normative referents, the "orectic pole," "relating to desire or appetite, willing and feeling," for symbols, under optimal conditions, may reinforce the will of those exposed to them to obey moral commandments, maintain covenants, repay debts, keep up obligations, avoid illicit behavior. In these ways *anomie* is prevented or avoided and a milieu is created in which a society's members cannot see any fundamental conflict between themselves as individuals and society. There is set up, in their minds, a symbiotic interpenetration of individual and society. All this would fit in admirably with Durkheim's notion of morality as essentially a social phenomenon. But I am suggesting that this process only works where there is already a high level of communitas in the society that performs the ritual, the sense that a basic generic bond is recognized beneath all its hierarchical and segmentary differences and oppositions. Communitas in ritual can only be evoked easily when there are many occasions outside the ritual on which communitas has been achieved. It is also true that if communitas can be developed within a ritual pattern it can be carried over into secular life for a while and help to mitigate or assuage some of the abrasiveness of social conflicts rooted in conflicts of material interest or discrepancies in the ordering of social relations.

However, when a ritual does work, for whatever reason, the exchange of qualities between the semantic poles seems, to my observation, to achieve genuinely cathartic effects, causing in some cases real transformations of character and of social relationships. I refer, for example, to the extended case history of an Ndembu patient in a series of curative rituals, Kamahasanyi by name, in *The Drums of Affliction* (1968a, chapters 4–6), for an illustration of this. The exchange of qualities makes desirable what is socially necessary by establishing a right relationship between involuntary sentiments and the requirements of social structure. People are induced to want to do what they must do. In this sense ritual action is akin to a sublimation process, and one would not be stretching language unduly to say that its symbolic behavior actually "creates" society for pragmatic purposes—including in society both structure and communitas. More than the manifestation of cognitive paradigms is meant here. Paradigms in ritual have the orectic function of impelling to action as well as to thought. What I have been doing in all this, perhaps, is trying to provide an alternative notion to that of those anthropologists who still work, despite explicit denials, with the paradigm of Radcliffe-Brown and regard religious symbols as reflecting or expressing social structure and promoting social integration. My view would also differ from that of certain anthropologists who would regard religion as akin to a neurotic symptom or a cultural defense mechanism. Both these approaches treat symbolic behavior, symbolic actions, as an "epiphenomenon," while I try to give it "ontological" status. Hence my interest in ritualization in animals. Of course, there remains the problem, to which I cannot claim to have given any satisfactory answer, and which several of my critics have mentioned (for example, Charles Leslie in a perceptive review of *The Ritual Process*), not of "why people continue to create symbolic ritual systems in a world full of secularization processes, but of why these systems ever go stale or become perverted, and of why people lose belief, often with anxiety, fear and trembling, but also with a sense of liberation and relief" (1970:702–704). Here I would point to the long endeavor of Emile Durkheim to establish the reality of the object of faith which in his view has always been society itself under innumerable symbolic guises, without accepting the intellectual content of traditional religions. Traditional religions were doomed in his eyes by the development of scientific rationalism, but he believed that his theory would save what it seems to be destroying by showing that in the last analysis men have never worshiped anything other than their own society. Yet it is clear that Durkheim's "religion of society" like Auguste Comte's "religion of humanity" has never had much appeal to the mass of ordinary mankind. I cite these authors because both clearly felt the need of quickly converting their "sense of liberation" into a moral, even pseudoreligious system, a curious egolatry. Here I think the whole matter of symbolism is very relevant, as is the matter of what is symbolized. And here, too, I think the distinction between communitas and social structure has a contribution to make.

References

Bierstedt, Robert. 1968. "Florian Znaniecki." In *International Encyclopedia of the Social Sciences*. Ed. David L. Sills. New York: Macmillan and Free Press.

Black, Max. 1962. *Models and Metaphors: Studies in Language and Philosophy*. Ithaca: Cornell University Press.

Bunge, Mario. 1962. *Intuition and Science*. Englewood Cliffs, N.J.,: Prentice-Hall.

Firth, Raymond. 1964. *Essays on Social Organization and Values*. London: Athlone.

——. 1967. *The Work of the Gods in Tikopia*. London: Athlone.

Gulliver, Philip. 1971. *Neighbours and Networks*. Berkeley: University of California Press.

Kuhn, Thomas S. 1962. *The Structure of Scientific Revolutions*. Chicago: University of Chicago Press.

Leslie, Charles. 1970. Review of *The Ritual Process*. *Science* 168 (May 8): 702–704.

Nisbet, Robert A. 1969. *Social Change and History: Aspects of the Western Theory of Development*. London: Oxford University Press.

Peacock, James L. 1969. "Society as Narrative." In *Forms of Symbolic Action*. Ed. Robert F. Spencer. Seattle: University of Washington Press.

Pepper, Stephen C. 1942. *World Hypotheses*. Berkeley: University of California Press.

Richards, Audrey. 1939. *Land, Labour and Diet in Northern Rhodesia*. Oxford: Oxford University Press.

Suzuki, D. T. 1967. "An Interpretation of Zen Experience." In *The Japanese Mind: Essentials of Japanese Philosophy and Culture*. Ed. Charles A. Moore. Honolulu: East–West Center Press.

Turner, Victor. 1957. *Schism and Continuity in an African Society*. Manchester: Manchester University Press.

——, ed. 1966. With M. Swartz and A. Tuden. Introduction to *Political Anthropology*. Chicago: Aldine.

——. 1967. *The Forest of Symbols: Aspects of Ndembu Ritual*. Ithaca: Cornell University Press.

——. 1968a. *The Drums of Affliction*. Oxford: The Clarendon Press.

——. 1968b. "Mukanda: The Politics of a Non-Political Ritual." In *Local-Level Politics*. Ed. M. Swartz. Chicago: Aldine.

———. 1969. *The Ritual Process: Structure and Anti-structure*. Chicago: Aldine.

———. 1970. Introduction to *Forms of Symbolic Action*. Ed. R. Spencer. Seattle: University of Washington Press.

———. 1971. "An Anthropological Approach to the Icelandic Saga." In *The Translation of Culture: Essays to E. E. Evans-Pritchard*. Ed. T. Beidelman. London: Tavistock.

Toulmin, Stephen. 1953. *The Philosophy of Science*. New York: Harper.

Znaniecki, F. 1936. *The Method of Sociology*. New York: Farrar and Rinehart.

CHAPTER 2

Religious Paradigms and Political Action: Thomas Becket at the Council of Northampton

It has been said that almost every schoolchild in England knows the main outlines of the story of Thomas Becket, archbishop of Canterbury, who was murdered in his cathedral on December 29, 1170, by four knights of King Henry II, the first royal Plantagenet. I beg leave to doubt the literality of this statement after having recently heard in the Canterbury cloisters a mother tell her ten-year-old daughter that Becket was a "bishop whose 'ead was cut off by old 'Enery the Heighth." Nevertheless, the tale and the myth of Becket have survived eight centuries and can still arouse fierce partisanship, for there was a clash of wills between monarch and prelate which both masked and milked a fatal affinity of temperament; this was caught up into an accelerating cleavage between church and state and was compounded by the first serious stirrings of nationalist sentiment in England and France. In the complex social field within which both archantagonists operated there were many other opposed and developing social trends which reinforced their personal quarrel: the rift between urban and rural subsystems, between country aristocracy and town burghers, between feudal relations and market relations; the still unresolved ethnic tension between Norman conquerors and Anglo-Saxon indigenes; the incipient struggle for secular power between the throne and the barony; the opposition between secular and regular clergy—and other conflicts and struggles which we will encounter in the course of this analysis. These and other social conflicts drew cultural support from divergent theories: one school of thought held that a papal monarchy should direct all the spiritual and temporal affairs of Christendom, another that society ought to be dualistically organized into separate but equal spheres of state and church; then there was the polarization, memorably discussed by Fritz Kern (*Kingship and Law in the Middle Ages*, 1970), between the complex of rights summarized under "the divine right of kings" and the right of resistance to the arbitrary use of royal power, a right which conflated ancient Germanic tribal custom and the Christian tenet that it is one's bounden duty to resist tyrants as expressed in Acts 5:29: "We ought to obey God rather than men." Quite early, too, under the influence of the German monk Manegold of Lautenbach, who wrote in the late eleventh century, the doctrine of popular sovereignty and the vassal's right of resistance in face of the lord's breach of fidelity began to gain ground. In the legal sphere, the burgeoning of studies in canon law, especially at the University of Bologna where the great Gratian and Pope Alexander III (before his elevation to the papacy) taught and Becket for a while studied, exacerbated the struggle between ecclesiastical and royal courts for jurisdiction over several important categories of offences and for the right to indict and punish clerics who had committed serious crimes. Within the Catholic church the formal structuring implied by the ferment in canon law was countered to some extent by a renewed stress on the contemplative life by some Cluniac and most Cistercian religious houses. Yet the very success of reformed monasticism increased the operative scope of canon law.

All these conflicts and more besides were caught up in the Becket affair. It is here, I think, that the social drama approach I have advocated in other connections can be shown to be a useful tool for distinguishing between the roles and estimating the significance of general propensities in specific situations. Indeed, the Becket case lends itself almost too readily to treatment by the

social dramatistic technique. Becket's public life was nothing if
not dramatic, full of strong situations. This has been gratefully
recognized by generations of playwrights, from Will Mountfort
and John Bancroft who, in the late seventeenth century wrote a
tedious anticlerical play *Henry the Second* (to which John
Dryden contributed a hackneyed prologue) through Lord Tennyson (who in his play *Becket* tut-tutted over Henry's sex life) to
such modern celebrities as T. S. Eliot (*Murder in the Cathedral,*
1935), Christopher Fry (*Curtmantle,* 1961), and Jean Anouilh
(*Becket of the Honor of God,* 1960; film version, *Becket*). Novelists have borrowed their plot lines from Becket's story: for instance, Shelley Mydans' *Thomas* (1965) and Alfred Duggan's *My
Life for My Sheep* (1955). Historians, too, have seized upon the
dramatic aspect of the confrontation between archbishop and
king in order to take vehement sides. In the eighteenth century
George Lord Lyttleton made a lengthy case for Henry—in three
massive volumes—which elicited a slimmer but vigorous riposte in
one volume from the Reverend Joseph Berington, who implied that
the noble lord falsified his case "from the prejudications of low
bigotry, from dislike of characters, or from a paltry policy"
(1790:62–63). In the nineteenth century, though respect for the
scientific method had grown, nationalist fervor tinctured interpretation, and the age of Darwin revived ancient conflicts between
church and state exacerbated by evolutionary theory and in the
heat of evolutionist controversy. Thus the Reverend Henry Hart
Milman writes of the horror of Becket's murder running throughout Christendom and of the Passion of the Martyr St. Thomas,
while the Reverend James C. Robertson, the equally clerical but
"anti-Romanist" editor of the major work of historical scholar-
ship, the *Materials for the History of Thomas Becket* (1875–
1883), which comprise seven volumes of the Pipe Rolls series,
concludes that Becket's program might have made England "the
most priest-ridden and debased of modern countries" rather than
"the freest," manifesting "a spirit which would aim at the establishment of priestly tyranny and intolerance" (1859:320). The

famous legal historians Frederick Pollock and Frederic William
Maitland (1895:124-131) seem to favor Henry who, they say,
handed down to his successors a larger body of purely temporal
justice than was to be found elsewhere. In fact, Winston Churchill
wrote of him (*The History of the English-Speaking Peoples*, vol.
1, p. 175) that he "laid the foundations of the English Common
Law, upon which succeeding generations would build. Changes in
the design would arise, but its main outlines would not be altered."
In the twentieth century controversy has been less acrid and attempts have been made to strike a balance between the conflicting
claims of Thomas and Henry, especially in the work of Mme
Raymonde Foreville, author of *L'Eglise et la royauté en Angleterre
sous Henri II Plantagenet* (1943), and the Benedictine monk Dom
David Knowles, eminent Cambridge University historian of the
High Middle Ages, who wrote *The Episcopal Colleagues of Archbishop Thomas Becket* (1951) and *Thomas Becket* (1970). Both
these modern scholars, however, fully admit the dramatic quality
of the main events.

Paul Alonzo Brown (1930:9) has asserted that there are "three
Beckets: the Becket of History, the Becket of Legend, and the
Becket of Literature," which can be readily isolated though they
overlap. I will argue that these three are interrelated in a symbolic
field which contains a set of paradigms or models for behavior
drawn from the Christian religious tradition. My theoretical concern is not quite that of the historians, though I rely upon their
findings, nor is it that of the constitutional historians, though I am
indebted to their conclusions. Nor am I operating as a structural
anthropologist who might fruitfully analyze the variations of the
original Becket legend—as distinct from the abundantly docu-
mented Becket history—in terms of "mythemic" analysis. Since
I am a social anthropologist with a long-term bias toward the
analysis of microevents I shall use the social dramatistic framework
that I developed first in the study of small-scale central African
village societies and have later begun to apply to the local feuds of
medieval Iceland. But I shall use this framework primarily as a

device for isolating from the sequence of events dominated by the Becket-Henry confrontation those which unambiguously evince the presence and activity of certain consciously recognized (though not consciously grasped) cultural models in the heads of the main actors which I shall call root paradigms. These have reference not only to the current state of social relationships existing or developing between actors, but also to the cultural goals, means, ideas, outlooks, currents of thought, patterns of belief, and so on, which enter into those relationships, interpret them, and incline them to alliance or divisiveness. These root paradigms are not systems of univocal concepts, logically arrayed; they are not, so to speak, precision tools of thought. Nor are they stereotyped guidelines for ethical, esthetic, or conventional action. Indeed, they go beyond the cognitive and even the moral to the existential domain, and in so doing become clothed with allusiveness, implicitness, and metaphor—for in the stress of vital action, firm definitional outlines become blurred by the encounter of emotionally charged wills. Paradigms of this fundamental sort reach down to irreducible life stances of individuals, passing beneath conscious prehension to a fiduciary hold on what they sense to be axiomatic values, matters literally of life or death. Root paradigms emerge in life crises, whether of groups or individuals, whether institutionalized or compelled by unforeseen events. One cannot then escape their presence or their consequences. I believe that Thomas Becket came more and more fully under the sway of a linked set of such root paradigms as his relationship with Henry moved from the private to the public sphere, from amity to conflict, and as his attitude shifted from self-interest to self-sacrifice on behalf of a system of religious beliefs and practices, which itself concealed, even from Becket, intuition of the central good of human communitas.

Part of any investigation is the investigator—his motives and circumstances. How and why did I come to select the Becket-Henry drama for detailed attention? I will spare the reader a recital of my personal beliefs and prejudices—these in any case emerge clearly enough in my work as in everyone else's and are as contradictory as anyone else's who eschews the systematic creation of a *Weltanschauung* as self-defense or apologia. The immediate cause of my interest in Becket was an interest in the comparative study of pilgrimage systems. This itself was an outgrowth of my investigation of the relations between liminality, communitas, and social structure in *The Ritual Process* (1969). Pilgrimages, so it seemed to me, were, to put it crudely in social science jargon, "functional equivalents," in complex cultures dominated by the major historical religions, partly of *rites de passage* and partly of "rituals of affliction" (rites to cure illness or dispel misfortune) in preliterate, small-scale societies. Since historical religions are ideally "optative" or "voluntaristic" in character, as opposed to the "ascribed" character of tribal religions, and since their ultimate goal is salvation, or liberation from the ills of the sensorily perceived social and natural worlds, people choose to go on pilgrimages rather than have to undergo initiation, and, furthermore, go for the good of their souls rather than for the health of their bodies. Nevertheless, there remains a strong component of obligatoriness, of the duty to go on pilgrimage, in cultures where pilgrimage systems are strongly developed—particularly, of course, in Islam and in Judaism before the destruction of the temple. Many of the faithful of most major religions hope like tribesmen to be cured of the ills or difficulties of body, mind, or soul whether by miraculous power or better morale, by making the penitential journey to some pilgrim shrine. Usually such shrines are marginal or liminal to the major centers both of political or ecclesiastical organization, and usually, too, those who have recorded their experiences as pilgrims speak glowingly of what I would describe as the "communitas" relationship which develops between travelers to and worshipers at the shrines.

My wife and I decided to visit some shrines where pilgrimages were still actively occurring to see what their symbolism was and what went on at them. We traveled to Mexico, Ireland, and England, and collected a fair quantity of observational and documentary data at each site studied. Since most pilgrimages are long established and we wished to study their vicissitudes over time, we were compelled to look at written historical records where these were available and to record oral traditions wherever we could obtain them. Among other fascinating places we came across Canterbury, once one of the four great pilgrim centers of Christendom—along with the Holy Sepulcher at Jerusalem, the apostolic churches in Rome, and the great shrine of St. James at Compostella in northwestern Spain. Even today the absence of a shrine to St. Thomas seems to be more potent than the presence of shrines in many other places in drawing hundreds of thousands of visitors—and many of them are de facto pilgrims—from all over Europe and, indeed, from America, Asia, and Australia as the Canterbury Cathedral Visitors' Book attests. Henry VIII had the medieval shrine destroyed and Thomas' bones scattered—not burnt as one legend has it. Now only a plaque and a circle on the paving stones commemorate the site and fact of the murder, but incessantly throughout the summer months parties of visitors speaking all the tongues of Europe come with their guides to this spot and listen to the grim, heroic story of Thomas' end—with its final question unanswered: did he stage-manage his death through pride or accept it with Christian resignation and humility? Did he seek glory or die for a principle? Did Thomas succumb, as T. S. Eliot makes him fear he might succumb, to the "last temptation"? "The last temptation is the greatest treason: To do the right deed for the wrong reason."

It was not merely the superabundance of available data in the immediate aftermath of the 1970 commemoration of the eighth centenary of the death of St. Thomas Becket which made me focus especially closely on the career of the archbishop who had once been chancellor of the king's domains. By a strange, felicitous fluke the English Thomas story converged with my other main theoretical preoccupation at the time—the study of Icelandic sagas (and Icelandic history generally)—as source materials for a comparative study of processual structures. I am interested in the formal aspects of temporality in human social life—how certain events seem to develop along patterned lines so that it is possible to elicit a consecutive series of recognizable phases from the welter of data. It is not only institutionalized processes, such as judicial and ritual processes, that have diachronic form or structure, but also ungoverned events, such as political or religious movements. But where processes are unconditioned, undetermined, or unchanneled by explicit customs and rules, my hypothesis would be that the main actors are nevertheless guided by subjective paradigms—which may derive from beyond the mainstream of sociocultural process with its ensocializing devices such as education and limitation of action models in stereotyped situations. Such paradigms affect the form, timing, and style of the behavior of those who bear them. Actors who are thus guided produce in their interaction behavior and generate social events which are nonrandom, but, on the contrary, structured to a degree that may in some cultures provoke the notion of fate or destiny to account for the experienced regulation of human social affairs. Greek tragedy and Icelandic saga are genres that recognize this implicit paradigmatic control of human affairs in public areas, where behavior which appears to be freely chosen resolves at length into a total pattern. One has, of course, to account for the almost instinctual manner in which root paradigms are accepted by the individual and their social consequences are fatalistically regarded—both in the mirror of literature and art and on the stage of history—by the masses. Here I would propose an as yet untested hypothesis: that in man, as in other living species, genotypical goals prevail over phenotypical interests, the general good over the individual welfare—that is, in the relatively rare instances in which there is direct confrontation between the two drives. Almost always there is room for compromise and maneuver. Root paradigms are the cultural transliterations of genetic codes—they represent that in the human individual as a cultural entity which the DNA and RNA codes represent in him as a biological entity, the species life raised to the more complex and symbolic organizational level of culture. Furthermore, insofar as root paradigms are religious in type they entail some aspect of self-sacrifice as an evident sign of the ultimate predominance of group survival over individual survival. Here, too, I would suspect a connection between root paradigms and the experience of communitas, an "essential we" relationship (to quote Buber) which is at the same time a generic human bond underlying or transcending all particular cultural definitions and normative orderings of social ties. The root paradigm—as distinct from what is probably in each culture a wide range of quotidian or situational models for behavior under the sign of self or factual interest—is probably concerned with fundamental assumptions underlying the human societal bond with preconditions of communitas. Perhaps the best expression of the central Christian root paradigm is not in the mythic or parabolic forms invoked, as we shall see, explicitly by Becket, but William Blake's passage on the offering up of self as a precondition of conversing "as Man with Man in Ages of Eternity" (Plate 96, line 6, of his *Jerusalem*). In it this heretical antichurchman compresses the *Via crucis* theme into six lines:

> Jesus said: "Wouldest thou love one who never died
> For thee, or ever die for one who had not died for thee?
> And if God dieth not for Man & giveth not himself
> Eternally for Man, Man could not exist; for Man is Love
> As God is Love; every kindness to another is a little Death
> In the Divine Image, nor can Man exist but by Brotherhood
> [*Jerusalem*, Plate 96: lines 23–28]

Here the notion of love as the basal societal bond is related to the notion of both real and symbolic death—to be in a true social relation to another human being one must die to one's "selfhood," a term which for Blake is *inter alia* a shorthand for the ambitious, competitive world of social status and role-playing.

I mention all this because I came across an Icelandic saga in the traditional fatalistic vein on the life and death of Thomas Becket which underlined the issues I have just been raising. This was *Thómas Saga Erkibyskups,* meticulously edited by Eiríkr Magnús-son and published in two volumes of the great "Rolls Series" in 1875 and 1883 as part of the *Materials for the History of Thomas Becket,* edited by the Reverend James C. Robertson. Thus pilgrimage, history, myth, and saga met at last and compelled me to examine the Becket affair. In it one could see a pilgrimage system in its very genesis. The saga style made evident to me the fatalistic quality of Becket's relationship to Henry, its social historical dimension, so to speak, while the other histories dwelt in the main on Becket's freely making the choices which placed him in his final predicament. I will draw on the saga and on the contemporary historical sources, such as William of Canterbury, Edward Grim, Guernes de Pont-Sainte-Maxence, William Fitzstephen, John of Salisbury, and others, to present in social drama form certain crucial episodes in Becket's career. I want particularly to trace in these the development of Becket's commitment to the Christian root paradigm of martyrdom, of underlining the ultimate value of a cause by laying down one's life for it.

It should be stressed, however, that every sacrifice requires not only a victim—in this case a self-chosen victim—but also a sacrificer. That is, we are always dealing not with solitary individuals but with systems of social relations—we have drama, not merely soliloquy. In the case considered the sacrificer was Henry, who, whether he was directly responsible for the murder or not (and I am inclined to think that his grief on first hearing of it was true grief, not just for public effect), at any rate in certain crucial moments almost egged Thomas on to commit himself to the martyr's path. There is constantly a curious complicity between the two, with Henry daring Thomas to make good his asseverations about the honor of the church. Thomas was at the beginning only reluctantly holy. This comes through clearly in a tale cited by William Fitzstephen, Thomas' friend and one of his best biographers, which, whether myth or truth, rings precisely true to the characters of the great antagonists. It relates of the grand time of their friendship when Thomas was the king's chancellor, and when, as Fitzstephen writes:

the king and he would play together like boys of the same age: in hall, in church they sat together, or rode out. One day they were riding together in the streets of London; the winter was severe: the king saw an old man coming, poor, in thin and ragged garb, and he said to the chancellor: "Do you see him?" "I see," said the chancellor. The king: "How poor he is, how feeble, how scantily clad. Would it not be great charity to give him a thick, warm cloak?" The chancellor: "Great indeed; and, my king, you ought to have a mind and an eye to it." Meanwhile the poor man came up; the king stopped and the chancellor with him. The king pleasantly accosted him and asked if he would have a good cloak. The poor man, who knew them not, thought that this was a jest, not in earnest. The king to the chancellor: "*You* shall do this great charity," and laying hands on his hood he tried to pull off the cape—a new and very good one of scarlet and grey—which the chancellor wore, and which he strove to retain. Then was there great commotion and noise, and the knights and nobles in their train hurried up wondering what might be the cause of so sudden a strife; no one could tell; both were engaged with their hands and more than once seemed likely to fall off their horses. At last the chancellor, long reluctant, allowed the king to win, to pull off his cape and give it to the poor man. Then first the king told the story to his attendants; great was the laughter of all; some offered their capes and cloaks to the chancellor. And the poor old man went off with the chancellor's cape, unexpectedly happy, and rich beyond expectation, and giving thanks to God" [in Robertson, *Materials*, 1833, vol. 3:22].

In this remarkable scene Henry bullies Becket into being good. The style is friendly horseplay, but in it we detect, having historical hindsight, the overbearing, overweening, Angevin temperament that would soon be so menacing for Becket. We can also see in this episode the beginnings of Becket's obstinate resistance and can deduce from the quick generosity of the knights and nobles with their offer of cloaks to replace the grudging alms, the strange charm which Becket could exert on members of his own circle. Perhaps, too, we have here a dim foreshadowing, in the poor man's response, of Becket's posthumous miraculous powers. From this scene of sunlight with a faint shadow I wish to pass to the dark scenario of the Council of Northampton where the wills of Thomas and Henry revealed themselves as implacably opposed, and the causes they stood for seemed just as irreconcilable. I shall discuss this meeting much as I would describe and analyze a major political or jural event in a preliterate society, since the main actors are hardly more in number than those of an African village council, their confrontations are likewise face to face, and their rhetoric and gestures have much in common with those of tribal lawmen. In brief, I shall study Northampton as a social drama and submit it to situational analysis. But there is one major difference between the two cases. The meeting at Northampton was not concerned with resolving the problems of a handful of villages or even of a whole chiefdom. Within it coiled the tensions of the changing structure of Europe, and the form and content of its discourse were drawn from many centuries of literate debate. Although the actors were few, their interactions lend themselves only superficially to small group analysis, for each man there was the representative of many persons, relationships, corporate interests, and institutional aims. Each was the incumbent of an office, some of several offices. Such representative figures have carefully to weigh their words, to ponder courses of action, and sometimes to prefer judicious silence to the best-chosen words. It is all the more remarkable, therefore, to observe at Northampton how flushed and intemperate great prelates and magnates became, and how overtly dramatic, even melodramatic, grew their deeds. All this clearly betrays the presence of naked confrontation and the absence of adequate means of mediation. It is in this desperate impasse that the root paradigm we shall discuss came to claim Becket's full attention and to dominate his development from that time forth. When a great man's back is against the wall, he seizes roots not straws. Yet if we are to sense and weigh what Becket thought and did we must place his actions in their full dynamic context (see Chart 1, Chronology, p. 73).

The Council of Northampton was at once the climax of a long bout or battle of principles between Becket and Henry and the beginning of a new struggle. Most of us know how Henry, to gain control of church as well as state, had tempted Becket with the double mandate of chancellorship and the see of Canterbury, supreme office of the Catholic church in England. The king wanted his friend to become the instrument of his will, and through him to make the realm of England obedient to "government of idea," Henry's idea—one which could not tolerate an ungoverned space, such as was represented by the independent sphere of the church. Becket's insistence on resigning from the post of chancellor, allegedly on the scruple of potential conflict of interests, can now be seen as his first blow for the independence of most ecclesiastical matters from royal control. His resignation flouted the king's wishes and demonstrated his commitment to his new ecclesiastical status which was at the opposite pole from the monarchy. Becket then threw himself into the practice of religious austerity, further signalizing his separation from the past, where he had been known throughout Europe for the sumptuousness and magnificence of his style of living. To an anthropologist the whole extraordinary business of Becket's life and death after his installation takes on the stylized character of an initiation ceremony— an initiation into the status of martyr. It will become clear that he was propelled along this path or passage by certain images and ideas (which in their patterning made up a paradigm). This pattern, stamped on the real events of history by a primary process at first unpent by royal edict but afterward governed by its own inner law, took the cultural shape of the martyr's way and brought ever more clearly before Becket's consciousness the glorious goal of the martyr's crown, to be won by a painful death rather by a meritorious life. It must have been clear to Thomas from the first that he could not make Henry come to Canterbury as Pope Gregory VII, the redoubtable former monk Hildebrand,

Chart 1. Chronology of Becket's Martyrdom

B.C. 516? Zachary, prophet, slain
A.D. 33 Crucifixion
A.D. 35 Stephen martyred

EUROPE	ENGLAND	THOMAS
	597 St. Augustine in England	
910 Start of Cluniac reform		
962 Otto I, Holy Roman Emperor		
	1012 Archbp. Alphege martyred by Danes	
	1066 Archbp. Lanfranc pushed Cluniac reforms	
1073–1085 Pope Gregory VII		
1077 Emp. Henry IV "went to Canossa," penitent to Gregory		
1095 Reforms of Council of Clermont		
	1097 Archbp. Anselm exiled by Henry I	
		1118 Birth of Thomas
		1143 Entered Archbp. Theobald's household
	1154–1189 Reign of Henry II	1154 Became archdeacon
	1155–1172 Struggle between church and royal court system	1155 Became chancellor
1162 Pope Alexander III exiled by Barbarossa to Sens		1162 Became Archbp. of Canterbury
	1163 Council of Westminster	
1164 Antipope Paschal III appointed by Barbarossa	1164, Jan. 14 Constitutions of Clarendon Oct. 6 Council of Northampton	1164, Jan. 14 Constitutions of Clarendon Oct. 6 Council of Northampton Oct. 12 Thomas sick Oct. 13 Tues. Mass of St. Stephen. Thomas fled Nov. 2 Escaped to France
1166 Vézelay excommunications		1166 Vézelay excommunications
1170 July 22 Fréteval reconciliation		1170 July 22 Thomas reconciled with Henry Dec. 1 Returned to England
Dec. 24 Henry: "Who will rid me of this low born priest?" Conspiracy of knights		
		Dec. 25 Preached sermon prophesying his death Dec. 29, Tues. Murder of Thomas in cathedral 1173 Canonized
	1174 Henry's penitence at Canterbury	
1177 Defeat of Barbarossa by Pope's forces		
		1220 Translation of body to new shrine. 200,000 present

had compelled Emperor Henry IV to "come to Canossa" (see Chart 2 for interrelations between monarchs opposing or supporting the autonomy of canon law). William the Conqueror had given the English monarchy too strong a position vis-à-vis the English church for that. Force could not conquer the Angevin. Besides, Becket somehow wished to win Henry's soul rather than to destroy him. It is significant that despite his occasional threats to do so Thomas never actually used the ultimate thunders of the church—excommunication and interdiction—against Henry and England. If he would win he must win by antiforce or by demonstrating to the world that if Henry used force against him, such force would be unjust. The paradigm of martyrdom nerved him to dare Henry and the secular power *à l'outrance*.

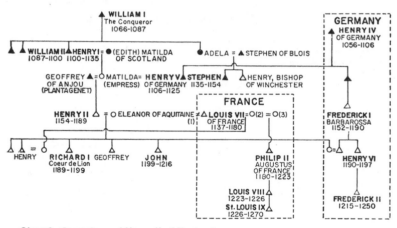

Chart 2. Genealogy of Henry II of England

But some time was left to Thomas yet. Shortly after he became archbishop, Becket identified himself with the church and demanded that certain lands within his diocese be taken from their lay incumbents and restored to their former control by the church. Then he claimed all clerical patronage within his diocese, thus directly challenging a royal prerogative. But what angered Henry most was Becket's insistence that "criminous clerks" should be tried and punished by ecclesiastical courts under canon law, not civil law. This ran counter to the course being following by Henry and his competent advisers—including Thomas himself before his installation—of bringing the entire legal system under centralized royal control and devising a system of justice that would be both profitable for Henry and equitable for all. If "clerks," that is, persons in holy orders of however low a degree, were to be immune from the king's writ, then clearly an absolute limit symbolized by "the benefit of clergy" had been set to the state's authority. It has, of course, been cogently argued by Lord Acton that one important source of English liberties lay precisely in this legal duality. People could play one set of lawmen against the other. But Henry, though quite disorganized in his personal habits, was always seeking to impose the maximum of discipline and order on others. He could not do this readily if an important area of social control fell outside the scope of his authority. What enraged him was that his friend Thomas, to whom he had entrusted the task of subduing the church to the monarchy, should betray him by declaring that there were many things that might not be rendered unto Caesar. I propose to pass over the complicated tale of the councils of Westminster (October 2, 1163) and Clarendon (January 14, 1164), in which the openly hostile Henry tried to impose his will on Thomas. Generally, he had his way and it was the archbishop who made the concessions. However, it was Henry's determination to secure the royal prerogative once and for all and with it, it would seem, Becket's ruin and humiliation as churchman and as man, that drove him on to summon a royal council at Northampton on October 6, 1164.

Something should first be said, however, about the Constitutions of Clarendon (Robertson, *Materials*, 1883, vol. 5:71), which Henry had forced the bench of English bishops to accept at the celebrated meeting there, for these set the terms of the Northampton confrontation. Becket himself had then quailed and faltered and sought to appease the king. He had not reckoned on Henry's insistence on demanding solemn assent to a written list

of propositions; he had thought that a verbal assurance, a gentle-
mans' agreement, would have sufficed and that subsequent difficulties could have been smoothed away by tact and turning a
blind eye, the ancient English genius for compromise. What, then,
were these propositions? The Constitutions were given under
sixteen headings. David Knowles holds that six of them, at least,
"traversed the rights of the church" (1970:89–92). Henry justi-
fied the Constitutions by claiming that they were based on the
customs of fifty years earlier, in the reign of his maternal grand-
father Henry I. Regal custom thus clashed with canon law. The
controversial clauses included the right of the king's justice to
summon criminous clerks to come before the king's court "to
answer there concerning matters which shall seem to the king's
court to be answerable there" (Clause III). They also declared
that "it is not lawful for archbishops, bishops and beneficed
clergy to depart from the kingdom without the lord king's leave"
(IV). Again, immunity was conferred against excommunication
or interdiction laid by a senior cleric on all who held land primarily from the king and on all officers of his demesne (VII).
The king's court was also declared the final court of appeal;
indeed "if the archbishop should fail to do justice, the case must
be finally brought to the lord king" (VIII). This article was
aimed at preventing appeals to Rome, just as churchmen had
been forbidden by Clause IV to visit the Pope without royal
permission. Finally, by Clause XII, the king claimed the right to
summon the clergy to his own chapel to elect an archbishop or
bishop, who would then have to "do homage and fealty to the
lord king as his liege lord for his life and limbs and earthly
honour, saving his order, before he is consecrated." This clause,
of course, referred directly to the investiture controversy which
divided church and state throughout Europe at the time. Under
canon law the church claimed that election should be freely made
by "canonical electors, viz, the clergy of the church with local
notabilities, monastic and lay" (Knowles, 1970:92). Emperors
and kings had claimed that the choice be made by the suzerain

himself—as indeed, William the Conqueror had insisted on doing a century earlier—unopposed then by Lanfranc, his archbishop. Clause XVI hit the common people hard—it declared that sons of villeins ought not to be ordained without the consent of the lord on whose lands they were known to have been born. This aimed to strangle one of the few possibilities of upward mobility accessible to the commonality at the time—ascent through ordination and education up the ecclesiastical ladder. Henry aimed to generalize the principles of feudal monarchy throughout all social domains and to decree one law for the lion and the ox.

I have barely touched on the Constitutions and the problems they raise, but the drift is clear. They represent Henry's most determined attempt to mobilize the sanctions of organized and legitimate force behind the protonationalist monarchy and behind the politicoeconomic structures of feudalism, which with all their internal contradictions represent a principle opposed to the internationalism, learning, and potential social mobility then represented by the Catholic church, in the *fine fleur* of the Cluniac reform and before the emergent arrogance of Caesaropapalism. Becket dismayed the other bishops by giving way, without consulting them, to Henry's demands. As Knowles points out, they had "stood firm even in the face of the fury of the king—'as is the roaring of a lion, so is the fury of a king'—and the threats of the barons, who at one point broke in upon the bishops threatening violence" (Knowles, 1970: 87–88). Thus, as Becket's implacable rival, Gilbert Foliot, bishop of London, was later to point out, Becket's "sudden tack off course" (Knowles, 1970:88) seemed like defection from the church's cause—an outcome the bishops had always feared from the former king's chancellor and henchman. To most of the bishops Becket was always an outsider—baseborn, never a monk, a worldly, sophisticated administrator. It is clear that Becket bitterly repented of his wavering. When he realized that the Constitutions were to be written down, he refused to sign the roll. Shortly afterward, in dejection he wrote to Pope Alexander III, begging absolution for his sin of disloyalty. He suspended himself from the service of the altar for the symbolic forty days, until the rescript came to him from the pope at Sens in France where the pope himself was then dwelling in exile, a refugee under the protection of the pious French monarch Louis VII from the fury of Emperor Frederick Barbarossa, who spoke of Rome as his fief and the pope as his vassal and who recognized a schismatic antipope. Alexander in his usual agony of diplomatic tact reproved Becket for his ostentatious austerities and counseled him not to provoke Henry further. Much of the papacy's financial support came from Henry's treasury, and Alexander could not afford to affront the English monarch too blatantly. But Becket was by now becoming increasingly committed to a policy of steady opposition to Henry's purposes, and this commitment was strengthened by the pope's condemnation of ten of the Clarendon clauses. Alexander could hardly avoid doing this in view of their assault on ecclesiastical rights. Becket then made two attempts to cross the channel—both foiled—to confess his fault in person to the pope. In these he was, of course, contravening the fourth Clarendon clause forbidding clerics to depart from the kingdom without the royal permission. Thomas made one last effort at reconciliation when he waited on Henry at Woodstock. But his former friend merely asked with reference to his abortive flights: "Do you find my kingdom not big enough for both of us?" (Robertson, *Materials*, 1883, vol. 3:294). The stage was now set for the decisive meeting at Northampton.

In previous studies I have used the notion of social drama as a device for describing and analyzing episodes that manifest social conflict. At its simplest, the drama consists of a four-stage model, proceeding from breach of some relationship regarded as crucial in the relevant social group, which provides not only its setting but many of its goals, through a phase of rapidly mounting crisis in the direction of the group's major dichotomous cleavage, to the application of legal or ritual means of redress or reconciliation between the conflicting parties which compose the action set.

The final stage is either the public and symbolic expression of reconciliation or else of irremediable schism. The first stage is often signalized by the overt, public breach of some norm or rule governing the key relationship which has been transformed from amity to opposition. Now there are a number of variations possible with regard to the sequence of the phases and to the weight accorded to them. Again, when there is a rapid sequence of social dramas it is hard to tell whether what one is observing at a given moment in the series is breach, crisis (when sides are being taken, coalitions formed and fissures spread and deepen through a number of coordinated and contiguous relationships between persons and groups), or the application of redressive machinery. In the case of the royal council at Northampton, for example, the action begins when Henry alleges that Thomas has broken the law—a breach, incidentally of a constitution issued by the king since Clarendon and bearing the Clarendon stamp. Henry wishes to begin the drama at the redressive stage, and with himself as judge. One cannnot decide whether it is Henry who has broken the tacit norm or at least gentleman's agreement between king and archbishop not to meddle in one another's affairs, or whether Thomas' alleged breach of the letter of the new law was the instigating factor. At any rate, the real issue was not the breach of this or that rule, but of who was master. It is obvious that Thomas saw the matter as a test of wills and that Henry was indeed trying to provoke a showdown, converting a power field into a force field, potency into act, with the terms materially in his favor. Each contestant was cashing in his resources of power, influence, prestige, wealth, numerical following, organization, internal and external support of every type in a trial of strength. At any rate breach soon became crisis and crisis grew so severe that available, formal means of redress proved inadequate, throwing back the situation into deeper crisis and preparing the way for the ultimate drama, six years later, of the murder in the cathedral with its symbolic deposits of martyrdom and pilgrimage.

Henry's pretext for Northampton was the affair of John the

Marshal. "This baron, a member of the exchequer staff, claimed land at Mundham that was part of the archiepiscopal manor of Pagham" (Knowles, 1970:94). The king, as mentioned earlier, had issued a constitution giving a vassal the right of appeal to his over-lord

if the latter failed after two days to do him justice in a plea in his court. All that he then needed to do was to swear with two oath-helpers that his case had been unjustly delayed. John the Marshal, wishing to ingratiate himself with Henry, followed the procedure just mentioned, swearing, so his opponents said, upon a troper (a liturgical book) which he had brought with him to elude the charge of perjury, that is, of foreswearing upon the Gospel. [Note here how Becket's mainly clerical biographers impute some sort of blasphemy to many of the actions that support the king's cause.] The king seized his opportunity and summoned the archbishop to answer in the royal court [again in keeping with the Clarendon clause which declared the king's court to be the final court of appeal]. The biographers dis-agree over what followed. Some say that the archbishop fell sick and sent his excuses, which were not accepted as genuine. Others say that he produced evidence in his favour and refused to answer an unjust summons. In any case, Henry cited him once more to appear in his presence at a royal council at Northampton on 6 October" [Knowles, 1970:94].

There is no lack of documentation on the council; there are seven lengthy narratives and several briefer accounts; two of the narratives are from eyewitnesses, William Fitzstephen and Herbert of Bosham. It is clear from these that Henry's intention was to run Thomas into the ground, to destroy him. Characteristically Henry was late for the meeting, for on his way he "went hawking along every river and stream." At the start Thomas still had some faint hopes of a reconciliation, but the tone was set by Henry's refusal to "admit Thomas to the favor of a kiss, according to the English custom" after the king had attended his first mass in the palace chapel. After much wrangling Henry forced his cousin, the elderly Bishop of Winchester, to pronounce the sentence on

Thomas in the case of John the Marshal—who never turned up for the proceedings. Thomas had been found guilty of contempt of court for having failed to appear three weeks earlier to answer the suit of John the Marshal, and for having offered no "essoin," that is, excuse for nonappearance. The main actors at Northampton were the king and Thomas, the king's barons, and the bench of bishops. The barons and bishops were by no means solidary groups, and Knowles has written a fascinating book on *The Episcopal Colleagues of Archbishop Thomas Becket* (1951), detailing the alliances and dissensions within the episcopal ranks as the Becket/Henry drama played itself out. But it is a feature of the present case that the bishops, one by one, some through cowardice, some through knavery, and others out of blank misunderstanding, drew away from Becket as he grew more obdurate. Even the pope had continually tried to reach compromises with Henry; Becket's opposition to royal demands seemed stupid, arrogant, even uncharitable since it exposed his friends and relatives to royal vengeance. At any rate, in the first round at Northampton, Henry, the bishop of Winchester, in an undertone urged Thomas to accept sentence quietly. Thomas retorted ironically: "This is a new kind of judgment, perhaps according to the new canons promulgated at Clarendon" (Robertson, *Materials*, 1883, vol. 4:312). The fine proposed was £500, and all the bishops, except his ancient enemy Gilbert Foliot of London, acted as Thomas' guarantors.

But Henry was by this time really bloody-minded, and on the following day the monarch demanded that Thomas pay him £300 which he had received while the castles of Eye and Berkhamsted were in his charge as chancellor. Thomas protested that this was a new suit, for which he had not been cited and therefore had had no time to prepare a defense. Besides, he remarked informally, the king knew quite well that he had used the money to repair the Tower of London and the castles themselves.

"Not on my authorization," Henry retorted, "I demand judgment" (Robertson, *Materials*, 1883, vol. 3:53).

For the sake of peace Thomas agreed to pay this; remarkably, a nobleman, William of Eynsford—whom Becket had recently excommunicated and absolved—came forward to offer security for the debt (the sum Thomas owed the king has been computed at about $32,000 in modern American cash terms). He was joined in this by the earl of Gloucester—which indicated that Thomas had some support at this time from the baronry. But next day the financial demands went on. Henry probed Thomas to the root. What had happened, he asked, to the thousand marks (two-thirds of a pound) that Thomas had borrowed during the Toulouse war? Notice how Henry seems to be reminding Thomas of his moral debt—rather than his financial one—to the king when Thomas had as client been the king's chancellor. Thomas replied that the money had been a gift expended, in fact, in the king's service. Henry demanded more security. Five laymen came forward and offered to go bail for Thomas. But the king was implacable. He asked Thomas to account for all the proceeds of the archbishopric during its vacancy and for the revenues of all the other bishoprics and abbacies he had held during his chancellorship. The sum demanded was at least 30,000 marks (about $800,000 today). Thomas said that he needed time to do the proper accountancy work; he would do it if time were granted. Henry said, "You must then give security." Herbert of Bosham writes that at this "all [Thomas's] wisdom was devoured." He could hardly speak but he yet asked to consult his clergy. This was quite a tactical move for it made clear to Henry that the bishops were not to be classified as barons—though in terms of the royal writ inviting them to the council they had been summoned in their role as English feudal magnates—but as representatives of the universal church. Thomas thus hoped to divide the bishops from the barons and precipitate a manifest state-church confrontation. But all Thomas succeeded in doing was in estranging his friends in the baronry and dividing the churchmen. Thomas spent the whole of Saturday in consultation with his bishops and abbots. Gilbert Foliot reminded Thomas of his commoner origin—he was a burgher of London, of the Norman merchant class, not of the landed gentry to which Foliot and several other bishops belonged—and urged him to resign "to avoid ruining the Church and all of us." Henry of Winchester, the royal bishop, once a playboy but now an elder statesman, defended Thomas' position, arguing that if the primate of all England resigned how could any future prelate oppose the king's will? Others urged various forms of compromise. Several said that it would be better for Thomas to suffer than the whole English church. But the true tenor of Henry's desires became clear when Winchester went to the king with an offer of two thousand marks to get Thomas off the hook. Henry turned it down flat. Now the good men of God really had the fear of God in them, for they saw that Henry wanted to doom Thomas, no less. No compromise seemed possible. All the king's demands had been trumped up; what he lusted for was the downfall of Thomas, possibly his imprisonment and the lingering death this often entailed. The king demanded that the bishops themselves should pass sentence on Thomas, since the barons had declared themselves, as laymen, incompetent to do this. The next day Thomas found that only Winchester and Worcester of the bishops seemed to realize that the principle of ecclesiastical freedom—and perhaps beyond that, freedom in the realm of England—was at stake; it was not just a matter of the king's protecting himself from the past financial dealings of a supposedly dishonest official, auditing his tax return, as it were.

On Monday, Thomas fell ill; the tension of the debates, his long ride from Canterbury to Northampton, the king's delay in coming, all these stirred up his old complaint, kidney stone, and he writhed with renal colic. Henry believed that as before he was merely feigning illness and sent the Earl of Leicester and the Earl of Cornwall—the highest ranking officials of the kingdom—to find out the true facts. They realized he was really sick but asked him whether he was prepared to submit his accounts. Thomas replied that he would appear in court next day, if he had to be carried there, and would then "answer as God wills." They then "encouraged" him by telling him that some nobles were conspiring to kill him, and that the king, following certain Angevin and Norman precedents, was planning to have him imprisoned for life or mutilated—his eyes put out and his tongue cut off.

This was Thomas' low point, the rock bottom of his life, Black Monday. Picture the gloom and desperation of the scene. There was Thomas, sick on his pallet in St. Andrew's monastery outside Northampton town, having been debarred by royal pressure from taking up the more comfortable quarters to which his rank entitled him—but in a strange way foreshadowing his exile among Cistercian monks in Pontigny and his attempt to emulate the humility of the ideal monk. The king was all cold cruelty, masked in moral law and accusation. The weather was dank and dull, as I have often known it myself in the Northampton area in autumn. The savage, illiterate barons had uttered their appalling menaces. Becket was a ruined man, foredoomed. How could this tall man, always intent on glory, snatch victory from this disaster, this unnerving mood? Almost all the bishops, his recent Job's comforters, had abandoned him, quailing from the physical threat in the castle where the king and his barons reveled and raved. The great lords had rejected him. It was in these circumstances that courage came back to Becket from the paradigm glowing redly in his mind, the *via crucis* pattern of martyrdom. Years ago, Becket had gone to school at Merton in Surrey. His teacher had been a Prior Robert. This Robert's successor at Merton was another Prior Robert, and out of some quirk of nostalgia Thomas had appointed the second Robert his confessor. In his darkest hour Thomas confessed his despair, and Prior Robert in the Abbey confessional encouraged him to say a votive mass next morning, Tuesday, October 13—not the regular mass of the day according to the ceremonial of the Roman church—but the mass of the protomartyr of the Christian church, St. Stephen, whose day follows Christmas, the celebration of the birth of Jesus Christ.

All the historical evidence points to Thomas' decision to say this challenging mass as the turning point toward his martyrdom. Henry had browbeaten him once more, as in the friendly affair of the cloak, just a further step toward the martyr's crown. Tuesday was thick with symbols. It has not passed unnoticed by the makers of the Thomas legend that Tuesdays were crucial days for the archbishop. As Tennyson puts it in his *Becket,* following Robert of Gloucester's late thirteenth-century metrical history of the *Life and Martyrdom of Thomas Becket:*

> On a Tuesday was I born and on a Tuesday
> Baptised; and on a Tuesday did I fly
> Forth from Northampton; on a Tuesday passed
> From England into bitter banishment;
> On a Tuesday at Pontigny came to me
> The ghostly warning of my martyrdom;
> On a Tuesday from mine exile I returned,
> And on a Tuesday—— [he was murdered].

Not only did Becket say St. Stephen's mass out of season, but he said it in St. Stephen's Chapel at the Cluniac monastery of St. Andrew's. Before he set forth, on this day scheduled to be the last of the great council, most of the bishops, led by Foliot of London, called on Thomas. They tried to persuade him to resign and throw himself on Henry's mercy. But he was already resolved to fight matters out with the spiritual sword for he replied vigorously: "The sons of my own mother [that is, the church] have fought against me" (Robertson, *Materials,* 1875, vol. 1:205)—a citation from the Canticle of Canticles 1:5 (Vulgate): "Filii matris meae pugnaverunt contra me." He then ordered the bishops to excommunicate any of the laity who might raise their hands against him. Foliot, leader of the king's party among the bishops, refused to accept this injunction. Thomas then dismissed them and they hurried off to court. Nevertheless, the bishops of Winchester and Salisbury lingered after the rest to give him a few words of encouragement before he went to celebrate mass.

St. Stephen's mass has for its opening words or introit: "Princes sat and spoke against me: and the wicked persecuted me . . . but thy servant is occupied in thy statutes" (Psalms 118). I have given the impression that apart from his immediate entourage and a few sympathetic bishops Thomas was without support. This was decidedly not the case, for the common people of Northampton thronged around him whenever he moved from St. Andrew's Abbey to the castle and back again. Anouilh was literally incorrect—he followed Augustin Thierry, the nine-teenth-century French historian translated by William Hazlitt in this—when he declared Becket to have been an Anglo-Saxon, for Becket's parents both came from near Caen in Normandy to settle in London, but he was right in stressing the support given him by the masses, most of whom were of indigenous origin, Anglo-Saxons or Celts. The London burghers, merchants, and guild craftsmen also gave him considerable support, and for years St. Thomas Becket was the patron saint of the Brewers' Company, of which he was allegedly the founder. On the morning of October 13, despite the persecution of princes, the commonality gathered round Thomas like a shield as with his procession of priests and choristers, wearing his most sacred garments, includ-ing the pallium, a circular band of white wool symbolizing the fullness of the episcopal power enjoyed by the pope and shared in by archbishops, Thomas entered the Chapel of St. Stephen to say mass. Even the pallium has martyrological associations, for the pallia are made of the wool of two lambs blessed in the church of St. Agnes in Rome on her feast day. St. Agnes was a fourth-century virgin-martyr, beheaded, at the age of thirteen, at the order of the prefect of Rome under the Emperor Maximian Herculeus. Becket, always a highly conscious man with a flair for the symbolism of public life, was probably not unaware of the multivocal meaning of the pallium—which symbolized not only his archiepiscopal authority devolving from the papacy but also the image of martyrdom in the case of church against empire.

In the presence of his own "sheep and lambs," as Becket often called the people of England committed to his pastoral care, Becket celebrated the mass of the protomartyr, with its gospel reference (Matt. 23:34–39) to Zachary slain between the altar and the temple—a curious prophecy of his own fate in his own cathedral of Canterbury just over six years later, Thomas is recorded as having become so caught up in the emotions stirred by the words of the epistle recording Stephen's stoning for defending the early Christian church and of the gospel with its reference to the persecution of "prophets and wise men and scribes" that "he wept and sighed frequently" (Winston, 1967: 183).

To my mind the confession on October 12 and the martyr's mass on October 13, in the desperate circumstances of Northampton, represented Thomas' decisive conversion to the role of champion of the church, who would prevail as "a lamb led to the slaughter" over the "lion king," Henry the raging Angevin. Becket knew that if he was to be a winner he would have to be a loser, since he had no force at his command other than the spiritual weapons of the church, excommunication and the interdict. Such weapons clearly did not terrify all, since the De Broc family who gave Becket's four slayers hospitality and guidance before the martyrdom lay under excommunication by Becket at the time. It was the root paradigm of martyrdom—with its rich symbolism of blood and paradise—which gave him a frame and fortification for the final trial of will with Henry whom he had loved and whom he could never really hate. And there is about all this still the curious suggestion of an initiation scenario: just as in many initiation rituals Becket the neophyte went through ordeal, in this case at the king's hands, the king being an unconscious initiator. Becket was enclosed from secular society in his abbey—a liminal place if ever there was—while the king and his baronry were lodged in the castle where the jural-political meetings also were held. Becket then underwent a "ritual of reaggregation," as Van Gennep might have called it, in which he returned to society as an initiated defender of the church—

though his vision of the church does not seem to have coincided with that of his fellow bishops, nor even with that of Pope Alexander—who saw the field of church-state relationships as a cockpit of perennial intrigue, *raisons d'état et d'église* (hardly severable), balance of power, administrative strategies, and so on. For Becket the church seems to have been connected in some way with the virtues of *caritas* and *humilitas*, as the many traditions relating to his almsgiving, personal penances, and ceremonial feet-washings of the poor before dawn at Canterbury seem to indicate. Yet he was no St. Francis—he was a combative, masterful man, skilled in arms, as his exploits before Toulouse in Henry's service demonstrated, a brilliant administrator as chancellor and archbishop, skilled in canon law and civil law. He put these propensities and gifts at the service of the church, yet could not do so wholeheartedly until he had identified himself with the root paradigm of martyrdom. In many superficial respects he remained worldly, but his rich robes literally covered a verminous hair shirt, discovered on his body after his death. Once he knew that he would have to die to get his own way and the way of the church, with which he seems to have identified his own, he achieved a peace and certitude of mind and consistency of action which never failed him until the bloody climax. Writers have argued over the centuries: was Becket "humble" or "proud"? Was his end, like a Japanese *hara-kiri* suicide, an attempt to shame King Henry in an unanswerable fashion, a final pride? Or was he truly a sacrificial lamb, unresistingly slain at the altar? Many icons have sentimentally portrayed him as dying thus meekly despite the eyewitness accounts which tell of an almost arrogant provocation of the king's knights on that last dark afternoon. After all he hurled Reginald Fitz-Urse to the ground in his full armor, before, almost ironically, offering himself to the sword that sheared off his skullcap. My own view—developed in my books on African ritual symbolism—is that Becket became himself a powerful, "numinous" symbol precisely because, like all dominant or focal symbols, he represented a coincidence of opposites, a semantic structure in tension between opposite poles of meaning. Becket was at once lion and lamb, proud and meek. The energy of his pride gives drama and pathos to his self-chosen role of lamb, just as, I have argued, the orectic or sensory pole of dominant symbols gives life and color to the virtues and values at the other pole. Martyrs were, after all, the warriors of the church; like Icelandic heroes they died indomitable, proclaiming their faith in the face of torture and a variety of sticky ends. The intriguing feature of Becket's end was that while formally it was a lamb's fate, psychologically it was a lion's. The Icelandic saga genius saw this and portrayed Thomas like some Gunnar, Skarphedinn, or King Olaf who half-deliberately places himself in an untenable position, refusing aid or chance of escape, and dies in full heroic integrity, knowing that his death will be "worth at least a song."

But let me conclude this presentation by following David Knowles's account of Becket's last day at Northampton. Northampton was the real break in Becket's life; the murder ratified it. Knowles's synoptic and scholarly narrative shows clearly Becket's contradictory yet oddly consistent character, shrewd yet bold, humble and angry. I shall supply exegetical notes and cross-refer to other writers on appropriate occasions.

Knowles writes that after saying St. Stephen's mass, "still wearing some of the priestly vestments under a cloak, preceded by his cross, and carrying secretly the sacred Host to serve as Viaticum [holy communion given to those in danger of death] should the worst befall [Becket] took horse for the castle" (1951:77–79). His cross, incidentally, "was a solid piece of work, for the four knights, six years later, had thoughts of braining him with the haft" (p. 77). The Icelandic saga of Archbishop Thomas bluntly states that "Thomas took for his protection the body of Our Lord [i.e., the Host, the consecrated communion bread], both for the sake of natural fear and strong faith in the mercy of God" (Robertson, 1875, vol. 1:209). Becket, knowing that Henry still hesitated to attack directly any aspect of the sacramental system, tried to guarantee his physical immunity from violence by letting it be known he carried the Host under his cassock. In this way, too, he would be protected while he said his say in the uncongenial and menacing company of Henry's drunken baronry. Knowles continues:

Dismounting in the courtyard, as the gate shut behind him [thus shutting out his popular support], Becket took from his [cross-]bearer the archiepiscopal cross. [This same cross-bearer—and the archbishop of Canterbury was entitled to have one wherever he traveled—was a young Welshman who had formerly rebuked him at Clarendon when he had bowed to the king's will.] Some bishops were at the door of the castle, among them Gilbert of London. One of the archbishop's clerks, Hugh of Nunant, later bishop of Coventry, approached him: "My Lord of London, can you stand by while the archbishop carries his own cross?" "My dear fellow," replied Foliot, "the man always was a fool and he'll be one till he dies." Robert of Hereford, Becket's old master, tried to take the cross from him in vain; Foliot approaching from the other side, told the archbishop sharply that he was a fool and endeavoured to wrest the cross from him. [Bishop] Roger of Worcester [a cousin of Henry II, but a supporter of Becket's] rebuked Foliot: "Would you prevent your Lord from carrying his cross?" only to be told sharply that he would live to be sorry for those words. The bishops then fell aside and Thomas entered alone, bearing his cross, and passed through the hall himself; the others followed, and Foliot again remonstrated: "Let one of your clerks carry it." Thomas refused. "Then let me have it; I am your dean [this was true, the bishop of London acted as Canterbury's dean, or senior prelate, on great state occasions]; do you not realize that you are threatening the king? If you take your cross and the king draws his sword how can we ever make peace between you?" "The cross is the sign of peace," answered Thomas. "I carry it to protect myself and the English Church" [1951:77–79].

Full analysis of the social structure and symbolism of this phase and its contextualization in the ongoing process of state/church and intraecclesiastical relations cannot be dealt with here. However, Becket was beyond all compromise while Foliot wanted at any cost to avoid direct confrontation of the clerical cross by the royal sword. He wanted to avoid the scandal of the cross, but most of all he did not want to provoke the royal wrath which had led to the mutilation of bishops before at the hands of some of Henry's ancestors. Today one can hardly avoid the phallic connotations of cross and sword. Perhaps at the unconscious level Becket wished to avoid what is still common in Africa where the priests of the earth—the ecclesia of West African societies— are collectively and symbolically known as "the wife" of the paramount chief, who represented quintessential politico-legal authority. Both Becket and Henry wished to be "husbands" here; Bracket's heavy wooden cross would confront Henry's sword and scepter, holy machismo would challenge kingly machismo. But, as Knowles writes, after the bishops drew away from Becket, whom they thought doomed, leaving him alone with his two clerks and later biographers, Herbert and Fitzstephen, in the inner chamber, anticipating the worst,

a touch of bitter comedy . . . was provided by the entrance of Roger of York [the archbishop who contended with Canterbury for the primacy over all the metropolitans and bishops of England]. He had arrived late to the council, partly to ensure attention, like a queen at the theatre, partly, so the chronicler suggests, to have a secure alibi should he be charged with having worked the archbishop's downfall [it is said that he had been secretly intriguing with the king]. He now entered with his unpermitted cross borne before him [unpermitted because only Canterbury of all the bishops was allowed to have a cross carried before him outside his own diocese], and there were thus two crosses in the castle, as it were two hostile lances at rest (*quasi "pila minantia pilis,"*as Fitzstephen writes, citing Lucan's *Pharsalia*). [History was never more speedily repeated as farce, though Thomas carried his own while Roger usurped the privilege of Canterbury by having his carried.] The bishops were then summoned to council with the king, who had retreated to the upper floor [of the castle] at the news of Thomas' advent [p. 79].

This retreat was a curious matter—and I do not think I have seen it noted in any history of Northampton—for it reverses the Henry/Thomas situation at Clarendon. There Henry was dominant and sure and Thomas hesitant and on the retreat. Perhaps it began when Henry's spies reported to him from St. Stephen's Chapel in the early morning that Becket had celebrated the Protomartyr's mass, for our sources report that "certain king's folk and clerks" rushed out to tell him that Thomas was comparing Henry and his nobles to the persecutors of the first martyr. William Fitzstephen calls this interpretation "malicious," but it was true enough. My own hunch is that Henry then grasped very clearly what Thomas was intent upon, and he knew that in his own time and society he had no defense against the strategy of martyrdom. Thomas had told Henry earlier at a private meeting, also in Northampton, that he "was ready to die for his Lord," and Henry could now see that he meant business. Henry could intimidate the bench of bishops, even if they were, as Knowles says, perhaps the most able group of bishops in medieval England. But he knew Thomas' mettle from the days of their friendship. When he heard that Thomas was coming with cross and Host he may well have gone into a blue funk. Winston writes that "Henry would have no part in dramatizing a confrontation of *regnum* and *sacerdotium*" and that "he feared his own temper" (Winston, 1967:185), but I think that he knew now subliminally that the root paradigm of the martyr's *via crucis* was archetypically in control of Thomas and that he could only use direct force against him at the expense of giving him what he wanted and what would strengthen the church's position at home and abroad—the martyr's crown. I honestly believe that Henry felt panic at that moment. But he soon rallied sufficiently to bully the bishops whom he had summoned to attend upon him upstairs. They told him that Thomas had reprimanded them and forbidden them to judge him henceforth on any secular charge. Angrily, Henry replied that this was a clear violation of Article XI of the Constitutions of Clarendon, which bound the bishops to participate in all of the king's trials and judgments unless these involved the shedding of blood. Still unwilling to go to the lower hall, where the cross awaited him, Henry sent several of his barons to ask whether

Thomas intended to present the accounts of his chancellorship, as had been requested on the previous Friday, and to provide sureties for his debts. More importantly, Henry learned that Thomas had appealed from his judgment that the bishops should pronounce sentence on Thomas—his scheme for dividing them from their official head—to the pope. This was an open rebuff to the Clarendon rules. He sent a deputation down below to Thomas to ask whether he stood by his appeal.

Thomas answered at some length; as for moneys spent as chancellor, he had received formal quittance; as for guarantors, his colleagues and friends were already too deeply engaged to undertake more; as for the appeal it had been lodged against suffragans [i.e., diocesan bishops subject to the archbishop as their metropolitan bishop] who had condemned him against justice and ecclesiastical precedent; he therefore held to his prohibition and appeal, and commended himself and the Church of Canterbury to the Pope [Knowles, 1951:79–80].

This was rank defiance of the monarchy. Thomas had burnt his boats behind him.

It is not possible to dwell here on the ebb and flow of the subsequent events, each rich in symbolism and drama. The upshot was that the bishops did not want to cut the cord which bound them at one and the same time to Canterbury and Rome, and they knew that if they pronounced a criminal sentence on Thomas they would greatly weaken their position vis-à-vis Rome, which had condemned most of the Clarendon clauses. Meanwhile, the passions of the barons had been rising—several suggested the castration of Thomas. Among the bishops, Thomas' arch enemies, London, York, and Chichester, tried to find a way of getting rid of Thomas while keeping their own hands clean. Smart old Foliot finally thought up a way: they would lodge an appeal to the pope which would accuse Thomas of having perjured himself and forced them to disobey against their oath; they might thus obtain Thomas' deposition. Henry promptly accepted this tactic. But he had no intention of waiting for a papal decision; he wanted action now, if others would do the dirty work for him. One can imagine what Thomas' feelings must have been, sitting in apparent calm in the lower room with his two clerks—rather like a student waiting in the coffee lounge to hear the result of an important oral exam. In the end, Henry sent all the bishops to torment Thomas, having committed them through Foliot to a united attack on him before the pope. Robert of Lincoln, we are told, was in tears, others near weeping. But Hilary of Chichester, who never liked Thomas, had the words. He said that Thomas' obstinacy had put them between the hammer and the anvil, for he had ordered them to make a promise at Clarendon, and then at Northampton he had prohibited them from making that promise. What could they do, then, but appeal to higher church authority—to the Holy Father himself? Thomas replied that two wrongs did not make a right. He now saw that the Clarendon Constitutions were uncanonical—and canon law was the law of God at work in history. Thus no one was bound to keep an oath which he should never have taken. If all fell at Clarendon, all could rise now. The bishops went up to the king, who was shrewd enough then to excuse them from taking part in the trial of Becket, which was still unconcluded. At that, they returned to sit with their Archbishop.

The long day was ending. The barons, unfettered from episcopal restraints, and roaring out the word "traitor," condemned and sentenced Becket—to what, never appeared, but probably to that perpetual imprisonment which he is known most to have dreaded. The whole baronial mob, augmented by sheriffs and lesser men, surged down the stone stairs to pronounce sentence, leaving Henry and a few others above. Thomas did not rise to meet them, but remained sitting holding his cross. No one wanted to be spokesman, but the Earl of Leicester, a not unsympathetic figure, eventually took on the unpopular role—for Becket, like Henry, was not an easy man to outface. Leicester had hardly come to any point when Becket interrupted him and brusquely forbade all present to pass judgment on him. Leicester stammered and stopped, the Earl of Cornwall refused to take over from him, and it was left to the smooth bishop of Chichester to interpolate that the treason was clear and that the archbishop must hear the judgment. Thomas then, with one of those surprising strokes of which he was master, suddenly rose, exclaiming that it was none of their business to judge their archbishop, and strode through the hall toward the door. All hell broke loose. Some barons, roaring "traitor" again, picked up rushes and less reputable debris from the floor to throw at Thomas. In the melee he tripped over a bundle of fagots and there was another howl of imprecation. Hamelin, the king's illegitimate half-brother, and Randolph de Broc (who would later give Becket's killers hospitality in the castle of Saltwood, taken from the Canterbury holdings and given to the de Brocs by King Henry after Becket's flight) joined in the cry of "Traitor!" Now Thomas showed himself as less the meek Christian and more the Norman descended from the Danish vikings of Count Rollo who wrested land from the Carolingian kings. He rounded on Hamelin and spat: "Bastard lout! If I were not a priest, my right hand would give you the lie. As for you [to de Broc] one of your family has been hanged already" (Robertson, *Materials*, 1875, vol. 1:39). Here speaks the London burgess' son, on the defensive among men who counted as aristocrats, violent, illiterate, and savage though most of them. were. Then with his group of attendants he broke out of the room. The gate of the bailey was locked, and the porter was engaged in a private scuffle—everyone that day was overwrought— but a bunch of keys hung by the wall, and the first that was tried opened the door. This was later to form one of the legends of Holy Saint Thomas. The archbishop's horses were standing ready bridled, and he and his entourage rode off across the town, to the cheers of the ordinary people—many of whom he invited to share his supper at St. Andrew's monastery that night, after the model of Christ's parable of the wedding feast, to make up for the many clerics and nobles who had defected from his household out of fear. I have to conclude the narrative here; after Thomas, in disguise and with only three companions, left the church at midnight and rode off into darkness and a violent thunderstorm, we have a new social drama, that of Thomas' odyssey of escape from England, and his exile first at the Cistercian monastery of Pontigny and later in various French refuges, as prelude to the final darkness of the martyrdom. One must note, again, that Henry did not try to prevent Thomas' escape. It is hard to separate love from hate in the relationship between these two men, and harder to define the nature of either.

My intent here has been to show how symbols are dynamic entities, not static cognitive signs, how they are patterned by events and informed by the passions of human intercourse, in friendship, sexuality, and politics, and how paradigms, bodied forth as clusters and sequences of symbols, mediate for men between ideals and action in social fields full of cross-purposes and competing interests. I have used a few decisive incidents which compose a social drama, from the history of friendship that turned sour, to show how personal and state affairs may both achieve a memorable form and generate legend, as well as archives, because of the action of root paradigms in people's heads that become objectivated models for future behavior in the history of collectivities such as churches and nations.

References

Anouilh, Jean. 1960. *Becket of the Honor of God,* tr. Lucienne Hill. New York: Coward-McCann.
Berington. Rev. Joseph. 1793. *The History of the Reign of Henry the Second.* Basil: Tourneisen.
Brown, Paul Alonzo. 1930. *The Development of the Legend of Thomas Becket.* Philadelphia: University of Pennsylvania Press.
Churchill, Winston, 1956–1958. *A History of the English-Speaking Peoples.* London: Cassell. Vol. 1.
Eliot, T. S. 1935. *Murder in the Cathedral.* New York: Harcourt, Brace.
Foreville, Raymonde. 1943. *L'Eglise et la royauté en Angleterre sous Henry II Plantagenet, 1154–1189.* Paris: Bloud and Gay.

Fry, Christopher. 1961. *Curmantle*. London: Oxford University Press.

Hutton, Rev. W. H. 1899. *St. Thomas of Canterbury: An Account of His Life and Fame from the Contemporary Biographers and Other Chroniclers*. London: Nutt.

Jones, Thomas M., ed. 1970. *The Becket Controversy*. New York: Wiley.

Kern, Fritz. 1970. *Kingship and Law in the Middle Ages*. New York: Harper Torchbooks. First published 1956.

Knowles, Dom David. 1951. *The Episcopal Colleagues of Archbishop Thomas Becket*. London: Cambridge University Press.

———. 1970. *Thomas Becket*. London: Black.

Magnússon, Eiríkr, ed. 1875. *Thómas Saga Erkibyskups*. In *Materials for the History of Thomas Becket*. Ed. Rev. James C. Robertson. London: Her Majesty's Stationery Office.

Milman, Henry Hart. 1860. *Life of Thomas à Becket*. New York: Sheldon.

Mountfort, Will, and John Bancroft. 1963. *Henry the Second, King of England*. London: Tonson.

Mydans, Shelley. 1965. *Becket*. New York: Doubleday.

Pollock, Frederick, and Frederic Maitland. 1895. *History of English Law before the Time of Edward I*. Cambridge: Cambridge University. Press.

Robert of Gloucester (1260–1300). 1845. *The Life and Martyrdom of Thomas Becket*. London: Percy Society.

Robertson, Rev. James C. 1859. *Life of Becket*. London: John Murray.

———, ed. 1875–1883. *Materials for the History of Thomas Becket*, vols. 1–5. London: Longmans, for Her Majesty's Stationery Office.

———, ed. 1965. *Materials for the History of Thomas Becket*. London: Kraus Reprint.

Tennyson, Alfred. 1884. *Becket*. London: Macmillan.

Turner, Victor. 1969. *The Ritual Process: Structure and Anti-structure*. Chicago: Aldine.

Winston, Richard. 1967. *Thomas Becket*. New York: Knopf.

CHAPTER 3

Hidalgo: History as Social Drama[1]

The Mexican Revolution of Independence in 1810 provides a vivid illustration of a root paradigm at work in a series of social dramas. It also provides an opportunity to investigate certain properties of the social setting of political action such as "field" and "arena."

In reality, the revolution was a war against colonizing Spain, corresponding, though with crucial differences, to the American Revolution or War of Independence against England. Some historians, like Hugh Hamill, call this phase the "Hidalgo Revolt" or "Insurrection," after Miguel Hidalgo, the priest of the parish of Dolores, in the *intendencia* of Guanajuato, who publicly inaugurated Mexico's long process of political change from the Spanish colonial system to today's governmental structure under the Partido Revolucionario Institucional, the PRI. Others would play down the names of individuals from a purist Plekhanovite distaste for the "great man" or "cult of personality" view of history. Others again would not talk of a revolt, but of the first phase of a valid revolution which has continued until now, with many lets and hindrances. But anthropologists, so it is said, must seize the facts from the stream of opinions and conjectures. Myths and symbols, both of the popular and high culture, are for them an important part of the facts. At any rate the Hidalgo uprising, the first phase of the Independencia, is of interest in that it is precisely the limen between the colonial period of Mexican

[1] First presented at the Department of Anthropology, Brandeis University, in April 1970.

history, the slow and apparently monotonous course of three centuries (though recent historical work is correcting the impression of monotony) following the short and dramatic first period of the Conquest, and the third period when Mexico became, in the blood and turmoil of colonial and civil wars and revolution, a nation. Hidalgo rose in arms against viceregal rule in 1810, and Agustin de Iturbide became short-lived emperor of a politically independent Mexico in 1821. The years between 1810 and 1821, even between 1808 and 1821, made up a complex and dramatic liminal period in which slow processes that had been going on for centuries were succeeded by a series of rapid social dramas which made explicit many of the contradictions hidden in those processes and generated new myths, symbols, paradigms, and political structures. Hidalgo was fifty-seven, no stripling, when he announced the insurrection on September 16, 1810, in the atrium of the parish church of Dolores. He was less than a year older when he was executed in Chihuahua the midyear of 1811. Yet he began Mexico's *rite de passage* to nationhood in the short social drama which he recognized as a people's uprising, and he became not only the borrower and maker of myths and symbols but also a symbol himself. In Mexico the great murals by José Orozco, David Siquieros, Diego Rivera, and others, portraying episodes of Hidalgo's half year of at first successful and then desperate battle, are common signs in many cities and townships. The cultural landscape itself is signed with Hidalgo's name. An entire state and many towns, suburbs, parks, and streets bear that name, while every year at midnight on September 15 the president of the republic repeats from the main balcony of the National Palace in the Zócalo of Mexico City the supposed words of his *Grito* at Dolores, literally, his "Cry," his proclamation, "Mexicanos, viva México!" Statues of Hidalgo abound throughout the land in plazas and parks; the late *doyen* of Mexican historians, Justo Sierra, says that "his purpose was dictated by his love for a country that did not exist outside this love; thus it was he who engendered it: he is the father of his country, our father" (*Evolución politica del pueblo mexicano*, 1957:150). Some historians, inevitably, like the conservative Mariano Cuevas, have tried to debunk the Hidalgo myth, but without great success. No one nowadays really cares too much that he had many illegitimate children by several mistresses and housekeepers or that he failed to prevent his Indians from indulging in indiscriminate massacre, looting, and rape at Guanajuato and Valladolid. The conceit that led him to rejoice in the title and uniform of "Captain-General of America" is forgiven, and his final public repentance for having allowed so much slaughter is forgotten. The symbol has swallowed up the man, and it is a symbol of communitas, of Mexico regarded in the mode of fellowship rather than structure.

Clearly the events of Hidalgo's five months of freedom after the Grito (he was captured on February 21, 1811) can be described as a sequence of social dramas and analyzed in terms of the social drama/social field relationship. A number of obstacles to this kind of treatment exist, however, some personal, some perhaps objectively insurmountable. The first is that my knowledge of the Hidalgo Insurrection is as yet based on secondary historical sources, mostly in English. The second is that I suspect that the full range of data required for a characterization of the nature of the significant social field and political arenas through which the process of the Hidalgo Insurrection passed is not now and never will be available. For example, Hamill (1966:121) tells us that no one knows precisely what Hidalgo said at his most famous public moment, the Grito of Dolores, which initiated the Mexican national ritual mentioned above. The three principal contemporary accounts, by Jésus Sotelo, Pedro García, and Juan de Aldáma, fail to agree, even about where the Grito was delivered —was it from the window or the entrance hall of Hidalgo's house?—and all give different versions of the speech. Aldáma, for example, does not mention any climactic conclusion, while Sotelo records that Hidalgo finished by "raising his voice with great valor . . . [and saying]: 'Long live, then, the Virgin of Guadalupe! Long live America for which we are going to fight!' " But for no one does he shout: "Viva Méjico," as I once heard the former President Gustav Dias Ordaz proclaim rather quietly (on television) from the porch of the parish church at Dolores Hidalgo. Dias Ordaz' many critics say that he went to Dolores not so much out of patriotic piety but from fear of a reprisal, if he "cried" in Mexico City, for the shootings of at least ninety students at Tlatelolco by his orders and the imprisonment of eighty faculty and students without trial during the protests in 1968.

Yet with all these stumbling blocks it may still be instructive to make a programmatic statement as to how a historically minded anthropologist might begin to go about collecting the data which would enable him to make a preliminary characterization of the field in which the Independencia began. True, many of the *insurgentes*, the first heroes of the first Mexican Revolution, have become, in popular thought and regard, mythical heroes not too dissimilar to those Dawn Beings of the Australian aborigines or Clan Ancestors of the Trobrianders, who are believed to have emerged from holes in the ground. The comparison would be not inapposite, for these insurgent heroes came from the earth of Mexico, they were almost all Americans not Spaniards, children of the earth of the New World. They were either criollos—American-born persons of Spanish descent, Indios (indigenous Americans), or mestizos, persons of mixed Spanish and Indian descent and born in the New World. But since the Independencia took place fairly recently, in terms of historical time, there are many kinds of historical documents and other records which give us far richer objective evidence than an Africanist like myself would expect, having become inured to the study of mostly oral traditions and the fading memories of old people. There are also, from the period, various sources of statistics, though perhaps they are not to be relied upon too much.

I chose to study the Hidalgo Insurrection because of its initiatory character—in several senses—and because I found it personally interesting after my trips through part of Hidalgo country in Querétaro, Dolores, Guanajuato, Celaya, and Guadalajara. I also think it might be fruitful as providing a sort of intermediary form between a social drama (with its conservative implications; one writer, Kenneth S. Carlston [1968:425–434], has even commented that I should have used instead the term "constitutive conflict" for social drama) and a revolutionary process. This was an abortive revolution; nevertheless since processual units, even the least of them, leave symbolic deposits in social time, the precise nature of the failure of the Hidalgo Insurrection is of theoretical interest, and its symbolic deposit in actual historical time had potent effects on subsequent dramas and revolutionary processes. It was a failure for Hidalgo the man, but a success in establishing a new myth containing a new set of paradigms, goals, and incentives for Mexican struggle.

My historical sources for the Hidalgo Insurrection are not numerous: Hamill, Leslie Simpson, Luis Villoro, J. Patrick McHenry, Eric Wolf, Justo Sierra. I have relied heavily on Hamill's book for the facts of the insurrection. The main point is to show how, if we had enough facts, we could analyze them in social dramatistic terms and yet remain within the anthropological fold. The arenas of the action of this drama spread in physical terms from a small town to a wide region; its ultimate field setting is not only the whole of New Spain (far greater than, though including, modern Mexico), but also takes in much of western Europe and the young United States and includes, importantly, the general criollo soldiers' ferment from 1810 to 1824 in Latin America. It begins concretely with a handful of conspirators in the Literary and Social Club of Querétaro, who included Father Miguel Hidalgo, Juan Aldáma, and Captain Ignacio Allende, a criollo officer in charge of the local militia; the heads of all three would later rot side by side impaled on poles on the top of the great granary of the Alhóndiga in Guanajuato where Hidalgo had won his most decisive victory. These heads were at first engaged in little more than discussing the fascinating doctrines of the Encyclopedists and of the French Revolution, and perhaps of the application of certain Jesuit doctrines (for example, those of Francisco Suarez) to the problem of wherein political sovereignty resides, the crown or the people, and who are the people, the criollos or the Indians or both? Later, after Bonaparte had kidnapped the Spanish king (who then abdicated in favor of the Crown Prince Ferdinand) and had placed his own brother Joseph on the Spanish throne instead, the worthies of the Literary and Social Club began in real earnest to hatch out a plot, to seek to apply their theories in the political arena. This was the

Chart 3. The Independencia: Some key dates

1765–1772	Galvez, visitor-general, De Croix viceroy, attempted to reform New Spain on centralized Bourbon model
1763–1788	American revolution
June 24, 1767	Galvez expelled Jesuits. Popular uprising in protest. Galvez hanged 85, imprisoned 674, banished 117 Indians and mestizos in reprisal
1788	Charles III of Spain died. Godoy effective ruler of Spain
1789	French Revolution
1795	Godoy made treaty with Bonaparte
1808	Bonaparte kidnapped Charles IV and Crown Prince Ferdinand
1808	Creole City Council of Mexico refused to recognize Joseph Bonaparte as king of Spain
Sept. 13, 1808	Spanish *audiencia* proclaimed Garibay viceroy, recognizing Junta Central of Seville as provisional government of insurgent Spain
Sept. 16, 1810	Grito of Dolores of Miguel Hidalgo
Sept. 28, 1810	Fall of Guanajuato to Hidalgo and Allende
Jan. 17, 1811	Defeat of Hidalgo by Calleja at Bridge of Calderón
March 21, 1811	Hidalgo and Allende betrayed and captured by ex-insurgent Elizondo near Saltillo
July 30, 1811	Hidalgo shot after four-month trial
1812	Liberal constitution of Cadiz in Spain
Dec. 22, 1815	Morelos shot
1820	Liberal government in Spain under Colonel Riego
Sept. 27, 1821	Iturbide proclaimed himself emperor of an independent Mexico under "plan of Iguala." Temporary coalition of conservatives and liberals
1822	Iturbide deposed
1824	Iturbide shot, federal republic established

point of crisis. The plot they came up with was a rather touchingly naive one. Every year there was a big fiesta, accompanying the major pilgrimage to a famous statue of the Virgin at San Juan de los Lagos, which about thirty-five thousand Indians usually attended. This was a two-week affair lasting from December 1–15. One of its main commercial aspects was a horse market where good mules and burros could also be had, which the conspirators hoped would form the nucleus of an insurgent cavalry. But in studying the relationship between religious symbols with their mobilizing efficacy and politically immature mass movements, it is perhaps more important that the main attraction at San Juan de los Lagos (to the west of Guanajuato) was (and indeed, still is) the allegedly miraculous image of La Virgen de Candelária, whose statuette was used in 1623 by an Indian woman, Ana Lucia, wife of the church's caretaker, to save the life of a little girl acrobat (Volatina) who fell on the points of a number of knives. December 8 (the universal feast of the Immaculate Conception) was the day dedicated to the Virgin of Candelária, a day on which many pilgrims—mostly Indians—came to San Juan de los Lagos. On this day an armed force under Captain Allende was to "pronounce" for independence in the name of Ferdinand VII, regarded then by the criollos as the legitimate sovereign of Spain. It was confidently expected that the populace would join up, jump on the steeds conveniently assembled, and, like the first stone of an avalanche, set Mexico rumbling into revolution. Hidalgo and his friends were well aware that for some years past there had been similar political discussion groups in other towns; they hoped these would emerge as rallying points for a struggle for independence from Bonapartist Spain, once Querétaro gave them an example and a lead. It is interesting that Hidalgo seems already to have seen the possibilities of rallying the rural masses round an emblem of Our Lady. According to Hamill, he might well have seized a banner with a picture of the Virgin of the Candelária on it instead of the banner he actually did take up, that of Our Lady of Guadalupe. Spanish property was to have been swiftly seized to finance the incipient movement.

What I find interesting at this early stage is the close association of religious symbols with political action in Mexican history. Hamill has written that "the religious factor would have been called on [by the conspirators] to play a sanctifying if not dominant role in the initial stage of the Insurrection. With the eloquent priest Hidalgo suddenly taking advantage of the aroused emotions of the worshippers before the image of the Virgin, it would have been an easy matter to incite them to seize the Spanish merchants and their goods" (1966: 114). Hamill also speaks of a "crusade" aspect in the "Hildago Revolt," in spite of the fact that the peninsular Spanish enemies of the Indians were also devout Catholics. By the irony of history the Castilians had become "Moors"! Actually Our Lady of San Juan de los Lagos was the subject of a devotion encouraged by the Franciscan order, which, with the Dominicans and Augustinians, provided the first missionaries to work in Mexico. Yet the Franciscans had opposed the initial growth of the devotion to Our Lady of Guadalupe which had been championed strongly by the secular clergy led by Montufar, the second archbishop of Mexico. Ultimately, as Robert Ricard has said:

The cult of Our Lady of Guadalupe and the pilgrimage to Tepeyac— the hill near Mexico City on which the "Brown Virgin" of Guadalupe is said first to have appeared to the Aztec Indian catechumen Juan Diego about ten years after the Spanish Conquest, and the hill, incidentally, on which the pre-Hispanic goddess Tonantzin had been worshipped before Cortés arrived—seem . . . to have been born, grown up, and triumphed with the support of the episcopate, in the face of . . . the turbulent hostility of the Friars Minor of Mexico [1966: 191].

The Franciscans argued that they had gone to great lengths to convince the Indians that one did not worship or venerate the material image, but rather God or the saint the image represented, whereas the miraculous painting of the Brown Virgin had become, with episcopal encouragement, a focus for idolatry. Indeed, Padre Francisco de Florencia, who wrote of Our Lady of San Juan in the eighteenth century, stated that the Virgin Mary shows her face in images to remind us to look beyond them to her whom our faith recognizes and whom our will venerates, in each material representation.

Hidalgo, it must be remembered, was of the secular clergy, and it may well be that he would not have seized a banner with a picture of the Virgin of Candelária on it had the revolt gone according to plan, for this devotion, though immensely popular and drawing pilgrims from such faraway places as Mexico City, Puebla, San Luis Potosí, and Guanajuato, did not have the Mexico-wide character of the cultus of Our Lady of Guadalupe. Hidalgo shared with many other American criollos a sense of national identity and a feeling for human universals, but in his case, by taste and temperament he appealed to concrete, sensorily perceptible, and dramatic symbol vehicles as centers of national unification rather than to abstract ideas of popular sovereignty, as did for instance, the Dominican criollo revolutionary Fray Servando Teresa de Mier and others. Such thinkers were influenced by Deism and the French Enlightenment. Hidalgo understood the mobilizing power of symbols that contained at one pole of their meaning orectic and sensory designations—as did the complex image of the Brown Virgin with its appeal to the ideas of motherhood, mother country, mother earth, and the indigenous past, as Eric Wolf has shown in his celebrated article on this focal Mexican devotion. Mere imageless concepts such as "popular sovereignty" could not rouse and then channel the energies of the popular masses. And local cult symbols such as Candelária had regional rather than national appeal. That is why I am dubious about Hamill's view that it was only chance that prevented Hidalgo using as his banner Candelária rather than Guadalupe. The Querétaro conspirators had already decided that their revolt would escalate to the national level; Hidalgo may not have worked the matter out in a cold-blooded, strategical way; but he did know that if he were to wave a religious banner it would have to be one symbolizing the widest possible corporate unity and continuity to be found in Mexico.

Whatever may have been the case we cannot now know, for government spies, then as now in colonial systems, were active and unmasked the Querétaro plot. Even before this became known Hidalgo had updated the insurrection to October 2 and changed its venue.

Denunciations of the plotters, some in the form of anonymous letters, inundated the Spanish authorities. Captain Arias, one of the conspirators, turned traitor and exposed the October 2 rising. On the other hand, Riaño, the intendant of Guanajuato under the Spanish administration, Hidalgo's good friend, was reluctant to take action against the priest, although he knew of his insurrectionary role. This delay may well have cost the Spaniard his life, for he was one of the first to be slain when Hidalgo's Indians overran Guanajuato a month later. The stage was now set for the Grito de Dolores which we have already described. The events immediately leading up to it have become one of the great myths in Mexican political socialization, for they are retold in every Independence Day speech and every grammar school history text. Even today the Mexican five-centavo piece is called Pepita, from Josefa Ortiz de Dominguez, who was initially responsible for warning Hidalgo that the conspiracy had been discovered in Querétaro and whose head is displayed on the coin. The moment of fate and truth came when Pepita's messenger Perez, with Aldáma, one of the leading conspirators, rode furiously to Dolores to warn Hidalgo and Allende, who was staying with him, that the plot had been discovered. While the others were arguing whether to flee into exile Hidalgo and Allende firmly declared that they would start the rebellion at once. It is said, and this may be mythical, yet true enough for that, that while Hidalgo was pulling on his boots he interrupted Aldáma's excited argument in favor of flight by saying masterfully: "All right, gentlemen, we are lost. There is no help for it but to go and seize *gachupines*" ("spurs," a colloquial term for Spaniards. It also meant "screw, *coger*, the Spaniards").

Some have called Hidalgo's action "brilliantly spontaneous," others "irrational," and yet others, including Hamill, "logical," in view of the fact that no agreeable future lay in surrender or flight, while time was of the essence and reason counseled immediate positive action by a determined leader (Hamill 1966:120). Considering the careful planning that had been undertaken by the conspirators, for example, Hidalgo's manufacture and storing of arms and ammunition, I would be inclined to agree that Hidalgo's call to action, though precipitate, was perfectly rational. But it was also true that the conspirators' hand was forced by the government and that Dolores was not the best place to start a revolution. It would have been better to have declared a concerted uprising in several large centers of population, such as Querétaro, and Allende's home town, San Miguel el Grande. But the fact that the plot was sprung on a Sunday perhaps offset this disadvantage, for Sunday was the traditional market day in Dolores, when large numbers of Indians and mestizos could be expected to attend mass there before buying and selling. Indeed, by eight o'clock in the morning, according to Aldáma's account, there were already more than six hundred men on foot and on horseback in town from the nearby ranches. It was to these that Hidalgo made the eloquent first plea for insurgent action, but most historians now agree that although Hidalgo was already convinced that independence should be its major goal, he was careful at this time to stress that the revolt was to protect the kingdom, whose legitimate sovereign was Ferdinand VII, from the French. Ferdinand at that time enjoyed considerable popularity with the Mexican masses, while the French were greatly feared. It is likely, too, that the priest at this time also climaxed his speech with the slogans "Long live religion!" and "Death to bad government!" These, at any rate, soon appeared on the crudely printed leaflets passed around by members of Hidalgo's movement. It is likely, too, that Hidalgo promised to abolish the tribute levied on Indians by the colonial authorities. It seems to have been only after this harangue, and after the capture of Dolores which immediately followed it, that Hidalgo, leading his little band, snatched up the banner bearing the image of the Virgin of Guadalupe when they passed through the hamlet of Atotonilco at noon on the same day.

Allende's city, San Miguel, like Hidalgo's parish, fell to the insurgents on the same day at dusk. The local criollo militia, already subverted by Allende, went over to the rebels, while the peninsular Spaniards all surrendered and were locked up. On this day, too, in which so many "essences" were "concentrated," the first hint of mass violence was manifested when Spanish stores and homes were stormed and looted. But at this stage Allende, whose emphasis was always on a criollo takeover, though with Indian support, still had enough authority in his own city to quell disorder, and then, with Hidalgo, to set up an insurgent treasury and organize a citizens' junta of local criollos. But he was also more or less compelled to agree, through the pressure of Hidalgo's growing host of Indian peasants and workers, to concede that the cura of Dolores would be the supreme director of the insurrection. On the evening of September 19, Hidalgo's army reached the outskirts of the rich town of Celaya, and the priest delivered an ultimatum to the *cabildo*, or municipal council. In this he was already beginning to take a tough line and threatened to execute Spanish hostages if Celaya did not surrender. The *regidores*, or magistrates, felt obliged to capitulate in the face of Hidalgo's already large army, and the insurgents entered the town on September 21 and plundered it.

It was at Celaya that Hidalgo took the title of "Captain-General of America," but it has to be remembered that this was done in connection with a systematic attempt to organize the army for a significant extension of the revolution. Lieutenants and emissaries were also appointed. Hidalgo, who, as we have seen, was already aware of the value of a dominant symbol of unification in the Guadalupe banner, may well have thought that a focus of leadership was also required. Unfortunately, Hidalgo was not a military man and should, perhaps, have left the organization and training of his army to Allende, a competent soldier; if he had been content to have become what Bertrand de Jouvenal has called a "rex," a transcendental figure embodying the highest common values of a community, and had not aspired also to be a "dux," a pragmatic organizer of concrete groups for the achievement of limited political goals, independence might have been won for Mexico several decades before it actually occurred. But Hidalgo was perhaps by this time neither rex nor dux, but a prophet rendered charismatic by the roused and militant communitas of the insurgent people. Rex and dux are both terms that might have been applied to, and also structural positions that might have found cultural expression in a situation in which the American criollos had remained firmly in control of the direction of events. But as successive large increments of Indians were added to the army, so did the influence of Hidalgo grow and that of Allende and his outnumbered criollo followers wane. It is possible that the religious, even prophetic side of Hidalgo's nature responded only too vigorously, if somnambulistically, to the ardor of his Indians and their violence in shaking off three centuries of Spanish oppression. Certainly the unconscious and irrational components of the insurrection rapidly came to flood out those of conscious calculation. But in this, perhaps, lies the secret of its compelling power over subsequent Mexican history and its potent influence on Mexican art and literature, what some have called its "existential" character.

If we can provisionally label the kind of revolutionary actions manifested in the insurrection, by analogy with Freud's usage, as a "primary process" as Dario Zadra has suggested, we have a clue to the nature of similar processes elsewhere. A primary process does not develop from a cognitive, conscious model; it erupts from the cumulative experience of whole peoples whose deepest material and spiritual needs and wants have for long been denied any legitimate expression by power-holding elites who operate in a manner analogous to that of Freud's "censorship" in psychological systems. Indeed there may well be an empirical relationship in certain revolutionary situations between the overthrow of a political authority at the social level and liberation from repressive controls at the psychological level. As well as violence, there may be creativeness, in the sense that a whole hidden cultural structure, richly clothed in symbols, may be suddenly revealed and become itself both model and stimulus for new, fruitful developments—in law and in administration, as well as arts and sciences. Similar primary processes in the French communes and Événements of 1968 are discussed in Ari Zolberg's paper "Moments of Madness," 1971. One characteristic of such a primary process is that it has a seeming "inevitabilty" of development. It should not be envisaged, as most cultural processes may be, as the product of established principles and norms, whether taken singly, conjointly, or in conflict. Rather it arises from deep human needs for more direct and egalitarian ways of knowing and experiencing relationships, needs which have been frustrated or perverted by those secondary processes which constitute the homeostatic functioning of institutionalized social structure. For this reason a primary process has an urgency and momentum which frequently sweeps away persons and groups who attempt to curb its excesses by the application of ethical and legal sanctions based on established principles and values. Men caught up in a primary process are mad to establish the kingdom (or republic) of heaven on earth, and they proceed compulsively to eliminate whatever they feel to represent obstacles to this desire. The longer this desire for communitas has been pent up, the more fanatical will be the form taken by the primary process when it is at last unpent. I mentioned a "seeming inevitability of development," but it should not be forgotten that a primary process will not take place in a social vacuum but in a prestructured social field full of the complex residues of previous primary and secondary processes. A primary process has some resemblance to an epidemic. Left to itself each process would tend to run its course, complete its trajectory. But epidemics are combated by doctors and revolutions by establishments. Of course, I do not, thereby, imply that revolutions belong to the pathology of society. Indeed some might be said to have clear therapeutic value. I am only stressing that primary processes, such as revolutions and other kinds of compelling social movements, seem to have an etiology and momentum of their own, which cannot be adequately explained in structural functionalist terms, and that such processes have the Gestalt-like character of tending toward appropriate and exhaustive closure and climax.

The criollo plans of Allende and Aldáma were swept away like paper boats on the popular flood of primary process released by Hidalgo's Grito. After Celaya came Guanajuato. A week after the Grito at least twenty-five thousand rebels, mostly Indians, left Celaya to attack this rich mining center, governed by Hidalgo's former friend, the intendant Riaño. It seems almost as if this was the point at which Hidalgo definitely severed the main links with his old life as a criollo priest, for now he saw Riaño as nothing more than a *gachupin* enemy and Guanajuato as the site for a great fiesta of blood. It was more as the leader of a jihad, like the Mahdi in the Sudan, than as a parish priest, that Hidalgo turned his horde loose on the Alhóndiga, the great granary of the city, when Riaño rejected his ultimatum and turned the granary into a fortress. It was a fortress in which were gathered, significantly, not only the peninsular Spaniards of Guanajuato, but also many criollos, a class whose members were already having misgivings about the character of Hidalgo's aims. On September 28 the insurgents stormed the Alhóndiga, massacred most of its defenders, and for two days sacked the city, raping and killing. It is recorded that Allende, weeping and cursing, tried to curb his Indian followers with the flat of his sword, while Hidalgo repeatedly declaimed that they should go unpunished for all that they had done or would do.

The primary process converts factual events into symbols for posterity. Thus the granary-fortress of the Alhóndiga became a symbol for Mexicans, both like and unlike the Bastille of revolutionary France. Riaño's death in its doorway also became a symbol, as did the heroic deeds of three Indian miners on Hidalgo's side who "pulled stone slabs on their backs to shield them from the rain of bullets, and ran, in a crouch, to the doors where they started a fire. Flames licked up the heavy wooden beams and soon devoured the doors" (McHenry, 1962:81). This feat opened the way for the insurgents who entered and struggled for the money and bullion they found there amidst the bloody corpses of their foes and friends. Allende's anger and tears at the slaughter of Mexican criollo middle-class citizens, and Hidalgo's commitment to the slaughter, which he began to describe as the reconquest of Mexico which would annul the Spanish Conquest bloodily completed by Hernan Cortés almost three centuries before, also became symbols of the tragic and creative energy of Mexico's revolutionary discovery of herself. It was Octavio Paz who, in his *Labyrinth of Solitude*, invited us to see the opposite figures of this history as "all part of a single process" (1961:147). His remarks referred to such revolutionary pairs of opposites as Zapata and Carranza, Villa and Obregón, Madero and Cárdenas, and other heroes of the 1917 revolution. But they are also applicable to the heroes of Hidalgo's Insurrection, and, indeed, of the total process of the Independencia.

Here we are concerned with the heroic dyad of Hidalgo and Allende. In many ways the Independencia foreshadowed the revolution. Hegel would have been delighted with the dialectical triad formed by the struggles for independence, reform, and revolution. The first and last of these were dominated by the primary process, the second by the secondary or "structuring" process. Octavio Paz has compared the protagonists of the reform with those of the revolution and declared that the former possess "a certain dryness" which makes them "respectable but official figures, heroes of Public Office, while the brutality and uncouthness of many of the Revolutionary leaders has not prevented them from becoming popular myths" (1961:147–148; see also the *corridos* or heroic ballads). The "thesis" of the Independence shares this mythopoeic quality with the revolution, and the powerful military clerics, Hidalgo, Morelos, and Matamoros, as well as the dedicated warriors, Allende and Guerrero, engage both the popular imagination and the creative rage of artists like Orozco and Rivera quite as much as do the heroes of the "synthesis," the revolution of sixty years ago. The Mexican archetypal man, the mestizo ("mixed blood"), is often portrayed by mural painters as born in fire, out of this joyous and deadly struggle between opposing principles, white man and red man, European and American, Christian and pagan, Catholic and free thinker. Mexican history has been a long exemplification of Blake's rule: "I must destroy the Negation, to redeem the Contraries." The negation, for Mexico, was the hierarchical political structure based on alien Spanish overlordship and subsequently on all other forms of foreign intervention and political and economic domination, French, North American, and other; but the contraries were the Spanish and Indian traditions which marry in the mestizo culture of Mexico. At least this is both the myth and the aspiration. As Justo Sierra, the famous late-nineteenth-century historian who was himself also a creator of myths, was never tired of pointing out: "The Mexicans are the sons of the two peoples, of the two races . . . to this we owe our soul." The three great popular upheavals we have noted are the national social dramas by which conscious recognition, at first in symbolic and later in ideological terms, was given to this fact already latent in the colonial period. Justo Sierra refers not so much to a mestizo "body," the product of genetic mingling, as to a mestizo "soul" (alma = "soul," "being," "human being," "strength," 'frame"), the product of more than a century of violent cultural confrontation. This pan-Mexican mestizo emphasis, so different from that of the South Africa I once knew, is probably one of the reasons why "movimientos" based on Indian, "tribal," or pre-Columbian grounds or assumptions are so blatantly unsuccessful in modern Mexico. Hidalgo was at the radix, the humanistic origin, of this process toward cultural mixture, or rather synthesis, so different from the South American situation broadly conceived.

We have now followed Hidalgo to Guanajuato and to the storming of the Alhóndiga. It appears that Hidalgo had some difficulty in appointing a new intendant to replace Riaño, for he had already begun to alienate the million or so criollos of New Spain, many of whom held office in local government. To provide a sound monetary basis for the insurrection, Hidalgo also set up a mint in Guanajuato to rival the one in Mexico City. Next he appointed officers to his own corps and lieutenants to represent the rebellion in other parts of the country. Some of these were brilliant appointments, especially that of José María Morelos y

Pavon, another warrior priest—formerly Hidalgo's student at San Nicolas College in Valladolid (now Morelia), who became one of the martyr-heroes of Mexico. A state (Morelos) and a major city (Morelia) have been named after him. All the officers belonged to that small section of criollos who supported Hidalgo.

Royalist propaganda, from the moment news of the insurrection reached Mexico City, had been directed at wooing the criollos, both first-generation criollos, known as "European criollos" and those descended from Spanish-born ancestors two or more generations back through intervening persons more or less Spanish in descent by cultural definition. These were known as "American criollos." Persons only one generation from Spain or married to *gachupin* spouses were particularly vulnerable to loyalist and royalist persuasion, for many of their close kin and affines were "peninsulars." The slaughter and imprisonment of peninsulars by Hidalgo's reconquering hordes made a bad impression on them.

It was in this background of increasing criollo resentment against Hidalgo that the insurgent leader forces advanced upon Valladolid. In this center of an earlier criollo plot against the Spaniards, Hidalgo was opposed by another old friend, Manuel Abad y Queipo, the bishop-elect of Michoacan, a liberal cleric. This bishop excommunicated Hidalgo and Allende along with two other insurgent leaders before the surrender of the city. Excommunication was soon followed by charges of heresy and apostasy against Hidalgo by the Inquisition. It is doubtful, however, whether the political use of these religious devices had much effect on Hidalgo's Indian followers, but it may well have deterred urban criollos from committing themselves to his support. Both sides shared the same religion, and the insurgents insisted that the aims of their movement did not threaten the future of established religion in Mexico. They argued: "This business of ours is a purely political matter, without affecting Our Holy Religion in the slightest." But the politicization of religion by the Spanish establishment with its criollo supporters seems to have had some effect in preventing the further spread of middle-class support for the insurgents. It is possible that Hidalgo might have succeeded had all the criollos remained neutral, leaving a direct confrontation between Indians and Spaniards, but many criollos used their influence with the Indians, not only to prevent the latter from joining Hidalgo, but also to turn them actively against the insurrection. They argued that Hidalgo was using Indians merely as cannon fodder, and that in any case the rabble that the priest had roused were merely "Chichimecas," the northern barbarians who had in the past despoiled the high culture of the central Mexican plain. Since many criollos were employers of Indian labor and could reduce their peons and servants to penury and starvation, it is clear that, as political scientists say, they were in a position to use "influence" and "persuasion" against the insurrection.

The last episode (social drama) of what historians like Hamill commonly call the first phase of the Hidalgo Insurrection came when Hidalgo set forth from Valladolid to Mexico City. By October 29, exactly six weeks after the Grito, the insurgents were at Toluca, obstructed only by a range of low mountains and 2,500 colonialist troops from seizing the great prize, once grasped by Cortés when it was still Tenochtitlán—Mexico City. But the defenders, under Colonel Torcuato Trujillo, were disciplined soldiers supported by regular artillery, and although they were forced to retreat, they inflicted many casualties on the undisciplined ranks of Hidalgo's army, killing two thousand men and badly injuring many more, so that thousands of Indians and *castas* (mestizos) deserted their chief. This Pyrrhic victory of the Monte de las Cruces dispirited rather than heartened Hidalgo's forces. Meanwhile, a second and larger colonialist army under General Felix Calleja, the "Butcher Cumberland" of New Spain, had collected at San Luis Potosí and had advanced as far as Querétaro. Hidalgo, left with about half the force of eighty thousand he had taken with him from Valladolid, dallied at the village of Cuajimalpa for three days and tried in vain to enlist further Indian support from the villages of the valley of Mexico. Just previously some of his Indians had tried to steal the Virgin of Remedios from her shrine in Totoltepec but had been thwarted by the royalists. Curiously, this manifestation or "refraction" of the Mother of God had heartened, according to legend, the troops of Cortés during the Noche Triste when they were badly defeated by the Aztecs. Another story tells of how a Spanish soldier, fleeing across the Puente de la Mariscala, north of the city, had hidden the image, a "saddle Virgin," under some maguey plants, until it was rediscovered in 1540 by an Aztec cacique, Juan Cuautli, when he was out hunting. It must have seemed to Hidalgo's Indians that Our Lady of the Remedies still sided with the Spaniards and that Remedios opposed Guadalupe in another modality of the perennial Mexican dichotomy. In any case Hidalgo led his forces away from Mexico City. Many reasons have been proposed for this. Some say that Las Cruces had depleted the insurgents' supply of ammunition, others that the defenders had placed land mines at every entrance to the city. Hidalgo's apologists declare that he spared the capital of New Spain out of humanitarian considerations. It is doubtful whether one can fully believe the testimony published by the colonial government and the Inquisition after Hidalgo's later capture, but it is there alleged that Hidalgo repented bitterly of the massacres committed by his followers in Guanajuato and wished to spare the citizens of Mexico City a similar fate. Political confessions, extorted by those in authority, must always be regarded with caution. It is, I suppose, possible that the criollo side of Hidalgo's personality came uppermost at this hinge of fate, for it must be remembered that his own father was a *gachupin*, born in Spain, and he may have been unwilling to have committed symbolic parricide. But to my mind, it is more likely that, knowing of Calleja's advance, and having experienced the power of military organization which had enabled a small, disciplined army to inflict heavy losses on his huge, untrained following, Hidalgo decided that it would be more prudent to withdraw for the moment and give his horde some sound military preparation. Allende's arguments, so forcefully expressed at Guanajauto, may have seemed more convincing to the caudillo after Las Cruces. If he had entered Mexico City, he may have reasoned, his Indians might well have dispersed in search of loot, and thus have fallen easy prey to the army of the ruthless and able Calleja. Nevertheless, this was Hidalgo's first real faltering, and it symbolized that the limits of the insurrection's initial momentum had been reached. The primary process had been "sicklied o'er by the pale cast of thought." Hidalgo did not even gain Allende's friendship, destroyed at Guanajuato, by this step, for the Allende faction, according to the captive Garcia Conde, began referring to Hidalgo about this time as "that knavish priest." It is possible that had Hidalgo advanced, he might have taken the capital and won the support of enough of its inhabitants, Indian, mestizo, and criollo, to have repelled Calleja, but it is also possible that the citizens had failed to be attracted to the insurgent cause and that Hidalgo knew it. Of course, in the colonialist press at the time, there were not lacking articles comparing Hidalgo's retreat with Attila's from Rome. There St. Peter had cowed the barbarians, here it was Our Lady of the Remedies.

I must now sketch briefly the tragic last phase of the Hidalgo Insurrection. On the way north to Querétaro the insurgents were attacked at Aculco by Calleja and lost almost all their artillery, baggage, and livestock—as well as eight women from their mobile brothel. It was at this battle that the criollo militia fighting for Calleja seemed to have decided not to defect to the insurrection and to remain loyal to the Spanish cause. After Aculco, Hidalgo and Allende divided forces, the former returning to Valladolid to reorganize and recruit, the latter to Guanajuato to manufacture new munitions. Hidalgo vented his resentment against the Spaniards by ordering the secret execution of some sixty of them at Valladolid without trial. Later he was to order the death of 350 more gachupines in Guadalajara. It was no longer a question of seizing the Spaniards, but of slaughtering them. He seems to have thrown in his lot completely with the Indians and eschewed the criollo middle position, the creative liminality which was perhaps at the source of his earlier prophetic and charismatic leadership of a movement that, however unconsciously, was authentically Mexican. No Mexican popular movement since the Conquest has ever succeeded that was either European or Indian; it had to be a New World synthesis of both, or nothing, at least in principle or myth if not always in reality.

When Hidalgo heard that his lieutenant Torres had entered Guadalajara on November 11 he was delighted and himself entered that beautiful city (famed for its beautiful but masterful women) two weeks later, to the accompaniment of martial music and later, at the cathedral, of a *Te Deum* sung with a full orchestra. The local criollo authorities knew how to please a man whose musical soirees at Dolores were well known. Good news came to him here, too, of the early successes of his lieutenant Morelos who was now besieging Acapulco, and of Cura Mercado who had just taken San Blas near the mouth of Santiago River. But the writing was on the wall with the fall of Guanajuato to Calleja, who immediately hung or shot sixty-nine citizens, chosen by lot for this doom in reprisal for Hidalgo's killings.

The sour note already twice sounded by Calleja grew menacingly loud when that tough commander began to advance on Guadalajara with six thousand soldiers, well armed and led, half of whom were cavalry. Hidalgo and Allende, characteristically, differed on how to meet the enemy. Hidalgo, who had been joined during his stay at Guadalajara by many more thousands of Indian insurgents, was all for risking everything on a single throw and hurling his seventy thousand irregulars against the enemy. Allende, made cautious by Las Cruces and Aculco, advised that the insurgent capital should be evacuated and the army divided into six or more parts, each of which was to attack the royalist troops in turn. But Hidalgo won the argument by saying that these measures would result in loss of enthusiasm and morale and would provoke mass desertions. He had yet to learn the lethal lesson learned by Spartacus and Wat Tyler that communitas does not of itself win battles. Structure is more efficiently destructive.

So it was that Hidalgo, splendidly appareled in uniform and mounted on a brave steed, led his huge, unwieldy army out of Guadalajara to the fateful Bridge of Calderón, eleven leagues east. There Calleja, with his smaller but well-disciplined force, persistently took the offensive, yet the struggle was in doubt until a royalist cannon ball struck an insurgent ammunition wagon. The resulting explosion not only killed many Indians but set the dry grass and scrub of the battlefield on fire. A strong wind fanned the flames and blew them in the face of the insurgents. Here the lack of discipline among the rebels counted against them and they panicked. Their flight became a rout; Calleja swept the field. At least one thousand insurgents were killed, as against Calleja's losses of fifty—though his second-in-command Manual de Flon,[2] the conde de la Cadena, was killed at the end of the action. All Hidalgo's artillery and baggage—prepared optimistically for an immediate advance on Mexico City after what the generalissimo thought would be a sweeping victory—was seized by the royalists. Hidalgo and the other leaders were forced to flee. It was, in effect, the end of that first phase of the Independencia known as the Hidalgo Insurrection. Yet historians, for example Hamill, have argued that even if the accident of the explosion had not occurred and Hidalgo's forces had won—and had then gone on to take Mexico City—the rebels would have had no hope of ultimate victory, since they had alienated the criollos and provoked the vast majority of them into military resistance. Indeed, in this respect, they have gone on to say, the insurrection had already failed before the battle of the Bridge of Calderón as a result of the massacre at Guanajuato.

It is always depressing to chronicle a retreat—as Tolstoy found in *War and Peace*, even when one has no sympathy with the defeated—for it triggers off human fears and anxieties of a universal kind. I will therefore telescope the tale of the depressed fortunes

---

[2] Flon was a prominent criollo, related by marriage to Viceroy Gálvez and also to Hidalgo's friend and victim Antonio Riaño, who fell at the storming of Guanajuato.

of the insurgent cause into a few paragraphs. Cut off not only by Calleja but also by the success of other royalist generals [3] from retreat to the center and south, the rebels withdrew to the north, where the movement had already scored some successes in Zacatecas, southern Sinaloa, and San Luis Potosí where Hemera, a lay friar in the order of San Juan de Dios, had seized the important mining city. For a time, they still believed that they could retrieve their fortunes, especially by the acquisition of money and artillery at Zacatecas. Allende, too, profited temporarily by the disgrace of Hidalgo at the field of Calderón. Two days after the defeat, at Pabellón on the way north, he and other escaped leaders stripped Hidalgo of his command, though they allowed him to remain as puppet-chieftan on account of his charismatic appeal. Allende now became generalissimo, but it availed him little, for the news of Calderón preceded the *insurgentes* to Zacatecas. The city remained cool and sullen during their week's stay, and Allende decided to head for the far north to establish diplomatic contact with the United States, in hopes of buying arms and enlisting mercenaries from the northern republic—perhaps in some respects the model for Allende's attempt to produce a middle-class settler revolution. Meanwhile in the central provinces the astute Viceroy Venegas, the fifty-ninth viceroy of New Spain, a career soldier who had seen active service in the peninsular war against the tyrant Napoleon Bonaparte, by using the "carrot" of selective pardon and the "stick" of ruthless reprisal as tactical means to gain strategic ends, had greatly strengthened the royalist position in the major centers of population and power. But the torch of the Independencia still burned bright among the Indians and *castas*, and those two other legendary heroes of the Independencia, Father José Morelos y Pavon, with remnants of Hidalgo's army, and Vincente Guerrero and his guerrillas in the hills of the Mixteca country near Oaxaca in the south, continued to harass the Spanish government and their criollo allies. Ultimately, of course, Guerrero's action in achieving a

[3] For example, José de la Cruz in Michoacan.

rapprochement with the former royalist commander Iturbide led
to independence from Spain in 1821. A few years later both had
departed from this world by the usual assassination route!

With the deposition of Hidalgo from the spearhead position
of military command, the insurgence lost its mythic, primary
processual character and faded into the light of a common day in
which it had little hope. Thus it comes as no surprise to learn that
its first leaders were betrayed—as so many Mexican politico-
mythical heroes, like Emiliano Zapata, for example, a century
later, have been betrayed by a Judas within their own camp—by
an ex-insurgent on March 21, 1811. This completed Hidalgo's six
months of glory and misery, and he was captured for trial near
the desert oasis of Baján—a site more fully known, by the irony
of history, as Nuestra Señora de Guadalupe de Baján. Hidalgo's
flare-up of glory and smoke of misery began and ended with
Guadalupe.

It can be seen that history repeats the deep myths of culture,
generated in great social crises at turning points of change. Many
Mexican revolutionaries have indeed walked a *via crucis*—like
Christ, men of the people, or men of religion, they have preached
a message, achieved initial success, been disgraced or frustrated or
physically suffered (there is room for many sad variations here),
have been betrayed by a friend or alleged supporter, executed
or assassinated by major political state authorities, and have then
experienced a curious resurrection in legislation, a political canon-
ization, expressed in public statuary, popular and elitist art, forms
of school socialization, novels, annual commemorations, and other
modes of social immortalization. Here I would refer back to what
I have said earlier about primary public processes generating
myths, about the role of myth in providing axiomatic frames
for ethical and legal subsystems to function within, and about the
way religious myths—and their episodic components—constitute
dramatic or narrative process models which so influence social
behavior that it acquires a strange processual inevitability over-
riding questions of interest, expediency, or even morality, once

it truly gains popular support. This, I know, is an intuitive statement; nevertheless it should be possible to work the matter out in more rigorous terms. What seems to happen is that when a major public dramatic process gets under way, people, whether consciously, preconsciously, or unconsciously, take on roles which carry with them, if not precisely recorded scripts, deeply engraved tendencies to act and speak in suprapersonal or "representative" ways appropriate to the role taken, and to prepare the way for a certain climax that approximates to the nature of the climax given in a certain central myth of the death or victory of a hero or heroes—or the death-victory in the Mexican case—in which they have been deeply indoctrinated or "socialized" or "enculturated" in the vulnerable and impressionable years of infancy, childhood, and latency. Thus I find it impossible to understand Emiliano Zapata's gullibility when he was invited to his final rendezvous with a known traitor and turncoat, unless he intended to fulfill the prophecy he had often made that he would "die for the people." Previously he had avoided similar traps; this time he was, as the Icelandic sagas put it, "fey." Another way of putting it would be that "collective representations" had displaced "individual representation."

The Christ myth is here the model, not in a cognitive and bloodless way, but in an existential and bloody way. Even the Emperor Maximilian bowed to this myth, when he eschewed flight from Mexico and stayed behind for certain martyrdom —for what? Not for the Hapsburg or Napoleonic cause, but to "fulfill the prophecy," or fulfill the model presented to him by so many symbols of the Mexican cultural scene—symbols in which the processual myth that ends in the *via crucis* is presented. By this death Maximilian avoided total disgrace in Mexican eyes and in an offbeat way became a sort of martyr-hero for his adopted country. To be bloodily killed by the establishment, after betrayal by a traitor to one's own cause as Guajardo betrayed Don Emiliano Zapata, and after proclaiming a message that includes support for the impoverished and exploited—these are the ingredients of a career that, following an archetypal myth, becomes itself a myth generative of patterns of and for individual and corporate processes. But in a way characteristically Mexican the Christian myth of sacrifice without using force against the authorities is here paradoxically fused with the myth of the epic hero, who engages in armed struggle against the foreigner or against an establishment founded by foreigners and yet proves curiously vulnerable to treachery and bad faith, often the treachery of a fellow or follower suborned by the promises of the foreigner.

In the Allende-Hidalgo case, the betrayer was a Lieutenant-Colonel Francisco Ignacio Elizondo, who began as a royalist, changed sides when Mariano Jiménez, the insurgent leader, captured the city of Saltillo for the rebels, and after the battle of Calderón made a deal with the deposed governor of Texas, José Salcedo, and secretly returned to the royalist fold. Elizondo, through Jiménez, persuaded Allende to spread out his remaining 1,500 men along the route to Baján, so that the norias, or draw wells, would have time to replenish themselves between thirsty contingents. He would then meet each group with a guard of honor at Our Lady of Guadalupe's oasis of Baján. (Elizondo was not motivelessly malignant; he had petitioned Allende at Saltillo for promotion to the rank of general and had been summarily turned down.) It was just after this that the retired criollo militia officer decided to pick off the retreating *insurgentes*. As Hamill writes:

On the morning of March 21, . . . Elizondo deployed his picked troop of 342 cavalry into two concealed companies of fifty each and an honor guard lining both sides of the dust trail. Coming around a low hill just before the oasis, out of sight of the following carriages, each capsule—and, finally, the whole army—was methodically taken prisoner by the hidden troops after they had passed innocently through the ranks of the honor guard. Too late, Allende realized the trap. Attempting to resist, he fired vainly at Elizondo. His rashness cost the lives of his son Indalecio and his lieutenant Arías, who were shot inside the carriage while he and Mariano Jiménez were over-powered and tied up. Hidalgo's escort of twenty dragoons, realizing the hopelessness of the situation, their own reinforcements being far to the rear, admonished the ex-commander not to resist. Convinced, the Cura put up his pistol without firing. The Hidalgo Revolt had now reached its definitive end. Elizondo was even more successful than Calleja; the latter had destroyed the horde, while Elizondo had destroyed the leaders [1966:209].

I am not now going to discuss the subsequent trials and execu-tions of the leaders of the insurgents by the royalists, who method-ically "processed" their prisoners before executing them. The roy-alists claim that some of them, including Hidalgo himself, recanted and repented of their deeds before death. Patriotic Mexicans deny this and claim that since the Spanish party controlled all docu-ments bearing on the trial their testimony is spurious. Whatever may have been the case, on the morning of July 30, 1811, the day after he was degraded from the priesthood, Hidalgo went be-fore a firing squad in the courtyard of the former Jesuit College in Chihuahua which had been his prison since April. His last act was to distribute some candies among his embarrassed execu-tioners. After the *fusilamiento* Hidalgo's head was cut off and placed beside the heads of Allende, Aldáma, and Jiménez, all shot in June, in four separate metal cages, to rot on the corners of the Alhóndiga granary roof of Guanajuato, stormed by the insurgents less than a year before. Note once more the curious cyclical symmetry; not only had Hidalgo gone from Guadalupe to Guadalupe; he had returned to the Alhóndiga. But the myth created by the sequence of events in the social drama of the in-surrection proved to be the first phase in a process that was not cyclical but irreversible and that changed Mexican society and culture forever.

It is one of the many ironies of Mexican history that formal in-dependence from Spain came ten years after Hidalgo's execu-tion—under the leadership of the conservative Iturbide, who had been mainly responsible for Morelos' defeat and capture. Whereas the first insurgents had overtly couched their rebellion in terms of loyalty to the Spanish monarchy represented by Ferdinand VII, the Iturbidistas couched theirs in terms of opposition to the liberal regime resulting from the Spanish Constitutionalist rebellion against Ferdinand. Independence was made by an uneasy alliance between the wealthier criollos, on the one hand, and the ordinary criollos, plus nearly all the mestizos and the Indian masses, on the other. The unstable character of the independence movement accounts for its later polarization into liberal and conservative factions in the civil war and the war of French intervention in the middle of the century.

The Hidalgo Insurrection, even in the sketchy presentation just given, can be treated as an extended case history consisting of a sequence of social dramas and taking place in a series of arenas in an expanding social field. However, it cannot be treated adequately in this way because my own knowledge of the primary sources on the insurrection is still exiguous and also because I do not think that enough total information is available for us to characterize the structure and properties of the social field in terms that would be satisfactory to modern anthropologists. We just do not know enough, for example, about the structure and organization of the so-called "Indian" followers of Hidalgo, whom Frantz Fanon might have numbered among his "damnés de la terre" not only at Dolores at the outset, but also at other points along his route of triumph and defeat, to be able to say whether the historians are really correct in calling it "an unruly, undisciplined mob." Each village or regional contingent may well have had its corporate discipline, but there may also have been traditional oppositions on tribal, linguistic, local, factional, or other grounds—and we know nothing of the networks, coalitions, and quasi-groups that may have been formed in connection with the insurrection. All these are matters which anthropology has only recently turned its attention to, and the kinds of systematically collected data which could give us plausible answers to political anthropological questions do not exist.

However, we can scrutinize the historical data with eyes sharpened by anthropological investigation in modern Mexico. For example, some of Robert Hunt's comments on political factionalism today in San Juan in Oaxaca ("The Developmental Cycle of the Family Business," 1966) and on the relationships between agricultural and commercial classes—with the commercial route up the status and power ladder as a common mode of mobility for the mestizo class—may throw light on the probable lines of criollo and mestizo political cleavage within and between the insurgent and royalist camps at the time of Hidalgo. Programmatically, I can say what kind of research framework should be used and what sorts of data should be collected, on the grounds that this approach has been useful in Africa and in comparative studies drawn from anthropological literature.

The main topic of this chapter has been to examine the roles of symbol and myth in social processes—here the process of the Revolución de Independencia. Thus I will content myself with defining "political field" as the "totality of relationships between actors oriented to the same prizes or values," including in "relationships" the "values, meanings, and resources" listed by Marc Swartz in his Introduction to *Local-Level Politics* (1968), and including in "orientation" (1) competition for prizes and/or scarce resources; (2) a shared interest in safeguarding a particular distribution of resources; and (3) a willingness to uphold or undermine a particular normative order. Among the categories of "actors" were Spaniards, European criollos, American criollos, mestizos and Indians. In New Spain, in Hidalgo's time, American criollos competed with Spaniards and European criollos for top-level positions in the state, the army, and the church; mestizos and Indians were in conflict with Spaniards and many criollos for access and rights to land. On the other hand, criollos who competed with one another over office and authority had a shared interest in preserving many features of the system for distributing resources. Again, many criollos as well as Spaniards were willing to uphold the colonial regime; they were even able to persuade or influence many mestizos and Indians to participate in this orientation. *Per contra,* a limited number of American criollos, many mestizos, and many Indians shared a willingness to undermine the normative order constituted by the state-church system of Spanish Mexico. "Prizes" includes not only command over rights as symbols of victory or superiority, such as titles, offices, and rank. The point about a political field is that it is constituted by purposive, goal-directed group action, and though it contains both conflict and coalition, collaborative action is very often made to serve the purposes of contentious action. It should also be noted that the resources actors commit and expend in field processes, such as social dramas, change as events succeed one another in the particular field under study or in other fields in which the same actors concomitantly operate. This means that the geographical boundaries within which the action takes place tend to expand, contract, or demarcate zones of greater and less intensity, or to surround scattered enclaves of action rather than one single region, as goals, resources, prizes, values, and so on, are brought into or removed from the arenas through which the action passes. Thus in the Hidalgo case, the Grito of Dolores led to uprisings in a number of discrete regions and towns—the effective political field in its spatial manifestation resembled in its distribution on the map a scatter of droplets rather than a single large globule. Yet there was clearly a flow of information between the droplets—here Kurt Lewin's advice, "look for the channels of communication" in the social field, is most apposite. Clearly information is needed on the Spanish colonial system of roads, transportation devices, posts, and diligencies, and the network of *posadas* or stopping places set up along the more frequented routes. The roles of mestizos, Indians, criollos, and Spaniards, in this set of interlocking systems, would also have to be examined. We learn from the historians that the inhabitants of Mexico City heard very quickly about the massacre in Guanajuato and that news of Hidalgo's defeat at Calderón preceded him to Zacatecas. Military couriers also played an important part in these transmissions of information. It should be remembered that even

during revolutionary processes many systematic, repetitive interactions continue; not everything is swept up into the wave of
unique, indefeasible events that constitutes the revolutionary history proper. Thus many institutionalized activities of the colonial
regime other than political and legal machinery must have persisted—agricultural routines, markets, the distribution of com-
modities, the urban sanitary systems (such as they were at that
period), postal and transportation services, and others. All these
would make up part of the frame of the field and would also
constitute some of the prizes to which both the revolutionary and
royalist actors were oriented—the regular conditions of public
existence, the control of which is the concern of much of politics.

I have mentioned the term "field" and briefly mentioned some
of its features. I would like also to say a little about the term
"arena," more particularly since my usage now differs quite con-
siderably from that put forward by my good friend Marc Swartz
(1968), although it is quite close to that of Frederick Bailey,
Ralph Nicholas, Frederik Barth, and others. Marc Swartz sees
arena as what he calls

a second space . . . a social and cultural area . . . immediately adjacent to the field both in space and time (It is a social and cultural
space around those who are directly involved with the field participants but are not themselves *directly* involved in the processes that
define the field. . . . The contents of the second space, the "arena,"
depend upon relations with participants in the field but it includes
more than the field. . . . In addition to the actors who populate it,
the "arena" also contains the repertory of values, meanings and resources these actors possess, together with the relationships among
them and with the members of the field. Values, meanings, and resources possessed by the field participants but not employed by them
in the processes which constitute the field are also part of the arena
[1968:9].

Personally, I rather doubt whether we have to give another name
to this second space. If I understand Marc Swartz he seems to
mean that an actor in his primary or focal field is influenced sig-

nificantly by the fact that he is also a participant in a number of other fields. Yet this is not quite what he is saying; participation in multiple fields connotes active participation, whereas Marc Swartz's "second space" suggests that those who are active in a field are inactive or passive in its arena. I would rather regard this batch of active involvements in several fields as determinative of ego's relation to the resources of his community and of the proportion of those assets he is willing to commit to or expend in the field under study.

Thus before the Grito of Dolores, Miguel Hidalgo was active in several fields, several sets of relations between actors oriented to the same goals or prizes. Not only was he a member of the field constituted by the Querétaro conspiracy, but he was also probably (according to the historian of Mexican Freemasonary, José Maria Mateos) a member of the first Masonic Lodge in Mexico City. Allende was also said to have been initiated into this lodge, which contained many criollo regidores, or councilmen in the Ayuntamiento or Municipal Government of Mexico City. Here the ideas and values of the French Revolution were freely discussed. Another field in which Hidalgo played a leading role was in the development of local cash-crop growing and industries by and for Indians. When he was cura of Dolores, Hidalgo tried to start a pottery works, a silkworm industry, and a tannery, to be manned and managed by Indians. He also encouraged Indians to cultivate vineyards and olive groves despite Spanish attempts to restrict wine and olive oil manufacture by New Mexicans. Legislation designed to protect peninsular industries and preserve Spanish colonial markets made difficulties for Hidalgo. But in this field of relationships and goals, Hidalgo persisted. It is interesting that on January 10, 1810, just eight months before the Grito transformed much of Mexico into one revolutionary field, Hidalgo was dining in Guanajuato with his friends, Riaño the intendant, and Abad y Queipo, the bishop-elect of Valladolid, to discuss Hidalgo's Indian-run wine industry. The cura invited both to come watch the grape-pressing process in September. They cheerfully agreed to see this marvel of criollo-Indian collaboration for bringing greater economic self-sufficiency to the region of Dolores—and ultimately perhaps to the whole Bajio—but, as we have seen, certain events intervened which brought Hidalgo to call instead on Riaño in company with his Indians and, later, on Abad y Queipo! I do not mention this to point up, as a novelist might, the tragedy of Hidalgo's Indian comrades killing his Spanish friend, nor of his clerical friend excommunicating him, but to show how events in Field A, the insurrection, were influenced by Hidalgo's relationships in Field B, Indian industry, in Field C, his relationships in provincial educated society, and, of course, Fields D, the Querétaro conspiracy, and E, the Mexico City Masonic Lodge, also provided goals, ideas, symbols, resources, values, and meanings which shaped events and relationships in Field A. The other fields do not merely constitute a second space around the action of Field A; Hidalgo's actions in them actively influenced his and others' actions in Field A. We have to do, of course, not only with overlapping and interpenetrating fields, but also with overlapping and interpenetrating action sets, the persons and relationships between them made visible in each field. Some fields, too, like the Querétaro conspiracy, are organized and purposive and the action sets move in specific directions; others like the insurrection contain organized elements and action sets, but much is arbitrary and accidental, like the firing of Hidalgo's ammunition wagon at Calderón, while conflict between opposing interests and world views is characteristic, again not in any tidy way, but in innumerable small encounters, confrontations, and coalitions of disparate kinds of dissenters from establishment positions.

Historians, too, would not look at the Hidalgo Insurrection in this way. They would try to appraise from the documents and archival materials of variable quality what they would consider to be the best possible account of the facts, the unique successive events, choosing some records and rejecting others, giving due weight to the perspective or angle from which eye-witness observations were made and the biases inherent in contemporary interpretations of those observations. We are deeply indebted to them for their work of sifting and screening in terms of rigorous scholarly criteria. But as anthropologists we are interested in interdependencies, concatenations of facts, events, relationships, groups, social categories, and so on. We are interested in orientations toward prizes and values which bring actors into field relations with one another and from nodes of intersection between fields. It is not the successiveness of isolated facts but the successiveness of connected facts, the successiveness of bundles or systems of relations, that engages our attention—Hidalgo's complex web of relations with his Indian operatives and managers, Hidalgo's relations with his Dolores parishioners in yet another sociocultural field, that of parochial values and aims, his field connections with bishops, intendants, house radicals, liberal *hacendados*, and others in the field of local gentry and intellectuals, sympathetic and unsympathetic, his "Tchekhovian dimension." I am not speaking here, of course, of ego-centered personal networks, but of definite, objective fields, in each of which Hidalgo participated in varying roles, but always and everywhere, we are assured by historians, with eloquence, charm, forcefulness, and—dare one say it?—charisma. Each field provided him with opportunities, resources, concepts, beliefs; yet each imposed on him certain limitations. If one, then, dissents from Marc Swartz's "second space" notion of arena, what sense are we to assign to the term arena? I would be inclined both to put it inside field, speaking crudely, and to make it less abstract than field. Hidalgo's was a Spanish-speaking culture with many elements derived from ancient Rome. I have watched the arena in the Plaza de Toros in Mexico City, the descendant of the gladiatorial and sacrificial arena of Imperial Rome. In the bull ring arena there is visible combat between men and natural forces and competition between men and men, as matadors try to outshine one another in fighting bulls. There is a bounded spatial unit in which precise, visible antagonists, individual or corporate, contend with one another for prizes and/or honor. A political or legal arena may range from an actual battlefield to the setting of a trial or verbal debate— from the field of Calderón to the courtroom of the trial of the Chicago 7. The symbolism and style of contention may vary from arena to arena within the same general field, as a social drama proceeds through its sequence of phases and episodes. Thus in the Hidalgo case the religious symbolism of the banner of Our Lady of Guadalupe in the first arena after the Grito gave way to the military symbolism of the Celaya arena (Captain-General of America); while the criollo bourgeois style of the Querétaro conspiracy (with its emphasis on debating society issues like "where does sovereignty reside, in the monarchy, the constituted authorities of New Spain, or the pueblo?") gave way to the Indian and peasant style of the conquest of Guanajuato. Each arena has its ad hoc symbolism and style, then, as well as representing a deposit or running total of past styles and symbols in synthesis, conflict, or configuration.

In any case, when we examine social dramas or political phase developments, as Swartz and I called the rather more elaborate processual units we discussed in the Introduction to *Political Anthropology* (1966), we have to find a term for those clearly visible settings for antagonistic action characteristic of the critical points of processual change. If we accept Marc Swartz's definition of "arena" as a more inclusive unit than "field," then we have to find another term for our political bull ring, our cockpit of confrontation, encounter, and contention. But why not retain the more familiar usage here?

One might then say (and here I am indebted to a fascinating correspondence with H. U. E. Thoden van Velzen of the Afrika-Studiecentrum for the main features of this formulation) that *an arena is a framework—whether institutionalized or not—which manifestly functions as a setting for antagonistic interaction aimed at arriving at a publicly recognized decision.* The antagonism may be symbolic or actual, an interchange of messages or tokens indicative of challenge, like the Grito of Dolores, by which

Hidalgo threw down the gauntlet to the establishment in Mexico City and in Spanish provincial government— or an interchange of blows and fusillades, as in the successive battles of the Independencia struggle. Opponents may seek power over one another's minds by the use of symbols or over one another's bodies by the use of force—or both methods may be employed, in series or in parallel. But in any case an arena is not a marketplace or a forum, though each of these may become an arena under appropriate field conditions. In an arena even where there is patent cooperation, coalition, and alliance, these are ancillary to the dominant mode of conflict. The second important point to note is that an arena is an explicit frame; nothing is left merely implied. Action is definite, people outspoken; the chips are down. Intrigue may be backstage, but the stage it is back of is the open arena. Of course, culture prescribes the tokens of antagonistic interaction, and it may not be easy for a Westerner to realize that he is in an arena in one of the Burmese villages described by Melford Spiro in *Local-Level Politics* (1968), since real hostility may be masked by soft-spoken elaborate etiquette and other nonviolent or face-saving devices. Yet if one can interpret the cultural symbols of communication correctly one can see a serious struggle for power going on between two factions in this muted arena.

When I try to match the diachronic dimension of my "social drama" or phase development against the dimension of structure and framework—or "fast becoming" against "slow becoming"—I see an arena developing out of the first action phase of "breach of regular norm-governed relations between persons or groups within the same system of social relations" (see above, p. 38). Such a breach is signalized by the public breach or nonfulfillment of some crucial norm regulating the intercourse of the parties. For example, from the perspective of the Spanish colonial authorities, Hidalgo's refusal to accept arrest and, even more, his Grito, constituted a breach of the order which they were committed to maintaining. Here, as in many political breaches, Hidalgo was using the *idiom* of lawbreaking or criminality as a symbol of rejection of the constituted order itself—which in his view was no longer representative, if it ever had been, of what he called, echoing his French and Jesuit models, "the popular will." This breach, symbolized by the Cry, converted what had already been a covert as well as latent "field," that is, an ensemble of relationships between actors antagonistically oriented toward the same prizes or values (in this case control over the state apparatus), into an "arena" or rather into a series of arenas—the beseiged cities and battlefields of the Revolución de Independencia. The field before the Cry was not yet a matter of bold, dramatic, public action; it was a matter of conspiracy, colonial legislation, secret ammunition works and dumps, debates in assemblies, sporadic riots by Indians and mestizos, the voluntary and involuntary exiles of criollos, reactions to the news of Bonaparte in Spain, newspaper articles, and so on. After the Cry, the drama was played out in a sequence of arenas as its plot thickened and action escalated from local to national levels.

The third feature of the arena concept is implicit in the others—the arena is a scene for the making of a decision (van Velzen lays particular stress on this feature). There is a moment of truth when a major decision is made, even if it is the decision to leave things temporarily undecided—as in the battle of Las Cruces when Hidalgo's army approached Mexico City. A deadlock or a truce also constitutes a decision. Usually there is a particular arena in which a decision that may be considered final is reached for the processual unit one is studying. In strong, well-entrenched political systems, the highest appeal court might be such an arena, or the parliament, legislature, or constituent assembly. But for a regime that has lost legitimacy the arena might be the streets of the city where a show of popular force might be enough to evict the *ancien régime*, or a battlefield like Calderón or Gettysburg, or the seizure by force of the administrative area of a city. Whether the new seizers or the old Caesars win or lose is immaterial to the definition here—the arena constitutes the scene of their antagonistic interaction and a decision is arrived at by force, persuasion, or threat of force, which initiates the final phase of a social drama, the process of a group's adjustment to the decisions reached in the ultimate arena. The field includes the myths and symbols of Spain, Bonapartist France, and revolutionary North America, as well as those in Mexico; the arenas were various actual places in Mexico.

If I were, therefore, to make a serious anthropological study of the complete process of the Hidalgo Insurrection, before I considered the successive phases of this processual unit I would seek out whatever information was available on the structure of the field, in what historians have reliably reported on as the "final stage of the colonial period" when the groups and issues of the Independencia were taking observable shape. I would then try to characterize, à la Lewin, the totality of coexisting entities, such as groups, subgroups, categories, members, barriers, and channels of communication, adding many other things, including symbolic systems, such as myths, cosmologies, rituals, and contemporary ideological views about the desirability or undesirability of the extant stratification of categories, groups, subgroups, and so on, at the point of outbreak of the Independencia protest. For example, it is clear that there were two major categories of Spaniards in Mexico, the peninsulars or *gachupines*, and the *blancos mexicanos*, "white Mexicans," or criollos, and that there were many graduations within the criollo category based on wealth, ancestry, occupation, and education—each of these being represented by ideological and symbolic differences and yet sharing common symbols and material interests. Hamill has repeatedly shown that an important cleavage between criollos was between European and Mexican criollos—those like Calleja, Flon, and Riaño who were oriented to Spanish culture and social structure (including the uncritical acceptance of the Divine Right of the Spanish king), and those making up the great majority who had already broken their links with Spain and set deep roots in Mexican soil. Class differences by and large corresponded with this division. Whereas criollos outnumbered peninsulars by about seventy to one, American criollos outnumbered European criollos almost by twenty to one (Hamill's estimate). The European criollos were usually rich; they resented the gachupines mainly because birth in Spain automatically gave an important man precedence over his Mexican opposite number (all the prelates, archbishops, bishops, viceroys, presidents of audiencias, and governors in the capital cities were Spaniards appointed by the king). Many of them also had high positions in the lucrative silver mines, especially at Guanajuato and Zacatecas, and in commerce and the operation of haciendas. They had attractive wives from wealthy families—often European criollo families. Thus they had the edge in any kind of competition even against first-generation criollos with Spanish parents. The million or so American criollos were even worse off with regard to the gachupines. A large percentage was made up of petty municipal officials, artisans, night watchmen, and what Hamill calls "unemployed riff raff," *criollos de plebe*, and formed a significant part of the city mob in Mexico City. But others were small property owners and professional men like Hidalgo and Allende. Some had ranches, others were provincial storekeepers, small businessmen, while others turned their ambitions and hopes for survival to such professions as the law, church, education, and the military, like Allende. Most criollos were members of the bourgeoisie or better-off peasantry, though some were what in South Africa would have been called "poor whites." It would seem that it was a segment of the professional American criollos who sought the support of "Indios" in the insurrection, while the landed and shopkeeping American criollos, together with many European criollos, came to support the colonial regime, at least for a time and more from fear of Hidalgo's peasants than from loyalty to a Spain that was itself displaying distressing signs of liberalism in its opposition to Bonaparte. Nevertheless, it was this American criollo class that was probably the decisive element in the first stages of the Independencia movement, and it was Hidalgo's alienation of its members that cost him the quick triumph he perhaps expected.

For the criollos were dispersed throughout the country, even in the small villages, while the gachupines resided principally in the capital, in Veracruz, and in the main provincial towns. The criollos were thus the dominant educated influence among the rural Indian and mestizo (or *casta*) population. The city dwellers, Spanish and European criollo alike, were absorbed in metropolitan business, state, and church affairs, and in the factionalisms, and sometimes in the salon groups, of the governing classes; they therefore had little contact with the masses. But the American criollos in innumerable small towns and villages became local leaders, since the peasants were kept ignorant by inadequate schooling and suppressed by colonial legislation.

The term "Indio" is highly ambiguous as Hamill and Eric Wolf have pointed out. It cannot, I think, be applied to any kind of tribal group with an indigenous political system and religious and other customs handed down from pre-Columbian times. It seems that contemporary eighteen- and nineteenth-century usage referred to the depressed and underprivileged masses. Many of them were indeed mestizos, just as many American criollos were mestizos. The difference between many criollos and many Indios was more in life style and degree of education, rather than genotypes. The indigenous Indian politicoreligious hierarchy, particularly in the populated Mexica, Otomi, and Tarascan areas, was destroyed by the Conquest. Indian prestige, social standing, and wealth dwindled toward a common peasant basis. Some Indian nobles—but not many—were recognized and given social support by the Spaniards, but these soon melted into the ranks of the developing criollo aristocracy; some, ironically, became "European criollos," when the chips were down! Eric Wolf has cogently indicated:

With the disappearance of the Indian political elite, there also vanished the specialists who had depended on elite demands: the priests, the chroniclers, the scribes, the artisans, the long-distance traders of pre-Hispanic society. Spanish entrepreneurs replaced the *pochteca* (the traders), Spanish artisans took the place of Indian feather-workers and jade-carvers, and Spanish priests displaced the Indian religious specialists. Soon there was no longer anyone who knew how to make feather cloaks and decorations, how to find and carve jade, how to recall the deeds of gods and ancestors in days gone by [1959:213].

Though the Indian peasant of 1800 in customs, speech, dress, and physical appearance might have resembled the ancient Indian, on all counts dilution of pure Indianism had occurred—with the exception of small isolated communities like the Seri, Yaqui, Huichol, Tarahumara, and Comanche.

Nevertheless, as both Wolf and Hamill emphasize, the cultural classification "Indio," including many kinds of miscegenations, did relate to a very real economic category. An Indio had to pay tribute to the crown—but not a criollo. This was a considerable source of royal revenue, therefore it was not altogther disadvantageous to the peninsular government to preserve the tributary class by various cultural devices, such as prohibiting them from wearing Spanish cloths, owning horses, and carrying weapons. They were also to have separate courts and were not allowed to serve in the militia. This must have galled the militiaman Allende, for he had no trained Indian soldiers when he most needed them in the insurrection! Actually, abolition of tribute became a big issue during the Hidalgo affair, with all kinds of symbolic aspects. Between September and October 1810, both insurgents and royalists said that they would end tribute to win Indian support. It was more than an economic matter; it symbolized the end of Indian segregation.

For the specifics of this situation, more study is needed. I mentioned the class structure of Mexico in the early nineteenth century to show that when characterizing a field rather than an arena it is these relations of likeness, such as classes, categories, similar roles, and structural positions, that take prior importance in the sociological analysis. When we come to analyze the successive arenas, what is important for us is to analyze the systematic interdependences in local systems of social relations, going from demography (what are the proportions of Spanish, European criollos, American criollos, castas, and Indians, if possible broken down in terms of age and sex) to class structure and, more importantly here, to residential distribution, genealogical structure, and religious affiliation by parishes as well as by the Catholic/ non-Catholic discrimination. Here, too, corporate groups, factional quasi-groups, and ego-centered networks of leaders become important aspects of arena analysis. On the national level, the field, the category, class structure, cultural universals, likeness, church, state, sect, and party are terms that readily come to mind and influence data collection. At the regional and township level, the arena, corporate groups, alignments cutting across class boundaries, cultural specificities of custom and dialect, commonness, the pattern of local churches and parishes in terms of missionary religious orders and secular clerical control, local government hierarchies, local factionalism have greater relevance analytically. Yet the interdependence of field with arena has also to be grasped and coherently expressed and analyzed.

It is perhaps in arenas that the metaphor of "game" and the strategies of "games theory" so beloved of Frederick Bailey, Frederik Barth, Kenneth Boulding, and the numerous contributors to *The Journal of Conflict Resolution* are most relevant: for arenas are produced in localized areas of social life where there is most social linkage and cultural consensus. But I do not think that man the enterepreneur or man the manipulator—any more than Lévi-Strauss's man the thinker, cognitive man—is an adequate description of or model for man in politics (or man in process, who surely is more than man in politics *pur sang?*). Politics in arenas or elsewhere is not merely a game. It is also idealism, altruism, patriotism (not always the last resort of the scoundrel), universalism, sacrifice of self-interest, and so on. Radcliffe-Brown regarded "values" and "interests" as interchangeable, as different ways of saying the same thing; but from the standpoint of human actors this is not so. People will die for values that oppose their interests and promote interests that oppose their values. And it is this practical result in behavior that we are interested in here.

Certain anthropologists have tried to interpret political action in terms of games theory posed on the premises of interest and power. Games have rules accepted by both sides. Each leader tries to maximize interests and power holdings at the expense of the rival side. In historical practice, it is, as Weber would agree, the educated middle classes that in their competition, whether violent or peaceful, like to introduce rules to which both parties subscribe—for they are rational, entrepreneurial people as regards both means and ends—and their children sometimes become political and sociological theorists. But the politics of class struggle often does not go according to commonly accepted rules, and it was this ungentlemanly element that prevailed at Guanajuato and that estranged the middle-class American criollos from Hidalgo's Indian army—and first began to estrange Allende from the charismatic priest who surrendered in the depths of his being to the Indian notion of playing for keeps. Games theory is an excellent tool for interpreting some kinds of gentlemanly competition, but it is impotent before those social changes that shake the very premises and foundations of the social order. Where there is radical *dissensus* there is no game, and hence no applicability for games-theory models. One side is playing chess, the other side is playing "for keeps." We must go deeper than games to find consistency and order in observed disorder. On the one hand, we can go to the Marxist analysis of the precise structure of the productive forces and productive relations interlinking and separating the categories of human beings involved; on the other, we should look for the symbols that engage their attention, channel their actions, and give meaning to their lives. Pragmatics and symbols are closely allied—often surprisingly so—for symbols whatever else they do concentrate and condense many aspects of human activity in semantic systems attached to a few symbol vehicles, sensorily perceptible formations that manifest symbols proper to human publics. Thus, really to grasp an important aspect of the semantics of Our Lady of Guadalupe, as used by Hidalgo as a banner or center of mobilization for Indians and criollos alike, one has to examine the debate between criollos preceding and accompanying the insurrection about the idea of sovereignty and its proper locus or source. Luis Villoro has traced the progress of this debate in his essay on "Las Corrientes ideologicas en la epoca de la Independencia" (1963:203–241). He shows how ideas under the stimulus of revolutionary praxis assumed new forms and acquired new contents. In 1808 the Spanish metropolis was occupied by Napoleon's troops, but the Spanish people resoundingly took the resistance into their own hands. *De facto*, sovereignty had fallen once more on the people. In New Spain, two parties formed—the Real Acuerdo, the Royalist Agreement, supported by gachupin public officials and merchants; and the Ayuntamiento, or City Government, of the City of Mexico, which voiced for the first time the American criollo middle-class viewpoint.

The effective disappearance of the legitimate monarchy in Villoro's view forced the criollos to formulate the problem of the origin of sovereignty:

Ferdinand VII retains the right to the Crown, but an idea has now been introduced which alters the meaning of his authority; the king cannot dispose of the kingdoms—remember here that the Spanish king ruled over several separate kingdoms, including New Spain— at his own free will, he does not have the power (*facultad*) to alienate them. The abdications of Carlos and Ferdinand are null and void, says Jacobo de Villaurrutia, the only criollo judge (*oidor*) and first ideologue of his class, because they are "contrary to the rights of the nation to whom no one can give a king save the nation itself (thus denying the legitimacy of Bonaparte's puppet and brother), by the universal consent of its peoples, and this only in the case of a king's dying without leaving a legitimate successor to the throne." The lawyer Verdad, another criollo, maintains at this time that though authority comes to the king from God, it does not come from Him directly but only through the people [1963:208].

But at this time the criollo leaders did not take up a radical stance. They argued that if the king should find it impossible to rule, the

nation may take sovereignty upon itself, but on the king's return
the people must abrogate the direct exercise of authority. It was
because of the prevalence among criollos of this view that
Hidalgo, the reader may recall, did not raise the slogan of "Independence" in the Grito, but shouted, "Long live Ferdinand!"
Criollo thinkers at this time seem to have meant by the term
"nation" not the "general will" of the citizens, but the view that
sovereignty devolves upon an already established society, organized in estates, and represented by established governing
bodies, an organic and constituted totality. Thus Juan Francisco
de Azcárate threw doubt on the legitimacy of the "Junta" of
Seville which was then taking the lead in the struggle against
Bonaparte on the grounds that it was set up by the "plebs," by
the common people. For him, as for many of his class, the plebs
are not coextensive with the "people." He asserts: "In the king's
absence or impediment his sovereignty continues to be represented
by the kingdom seen as a whole, and by the classes which form
it—and most specifically, by the senior tribunals which govern
it, administer justice, and by the bodies which convey the public
voice." The criollo Municipal Government of Mexico City fully
endorsed these views. The tale of the relations between the
Royalist Agreement and the municipal government and their
debates about the form that a national congress, representing all
classes, should take would be another complete social drama. But
inasmuch as the symbols and slogans used by Hidalgo and Allende
were partly provided by the myths created in these debates as
charters for the legitimacy of the programs of the factions involved, these debates merit more than a mention. The criollos
were looking for a kind of social contract on which to rest their
notion of a proper junta. They felt that the assembly should consist of deputies from all the secular and ecclesiastical *cabildos*,
local municipal councils, or chapter meetings. In traditional
Spanish democratic thought, these cabildos, close to the people,
were always regarded as the bulwark of democracy and the best
way to resist despotism. They played an important role in the

early days of the colony of New Spain, in the congresses in which they met in close relationship with the Spanish parliament, the peninsular Cortes.

Thus the criollo Municipal Government of Mexico City inaugurates a movement of return to roots that have been hidden by three centuries of despotism. . . . It locates the Social Contract in the moment of the Conquest of Mexico. The rights of the Spanish kings are made to derive from the pact made by the Conquistadores with them—and the Conquistadores are held to be the ancestors of the American criollos. Thanks to this pact New Spain has been included in the Crown of Castile on an equal footing with any of the other Spanish kingdoms, theoretically with the same independence of one another that all enjoy. . . . As Azcarate argued in refutation of the claim to recognition of the Seville Junta: "America does not depend upon Spain, but only on the King of Castile and Leon; if the king is imprisoned and his lands occupied by the foreigner, New Spain must summon the notables of the kingdom to a Junta Assembly provided for by the Code of the Indies. Furthermore, the effective units entering the Junta were to be the municipal cabildos, which were controlled not by Spaniards but by American criollos. The Royal Audiencia and the Viceroyalty were Spanish instruments set up over a nation that had already been fully constituted under the pact between king and conquistadores. There was to be a return to the epoch that preceded monarchical absolutism [Villoro, 1963:211–212].

The criollos are clearly denying the immediate past, the colonial past, in order to reach what they call the *principio*, a term which can be translated as "principle," "beginning," "source," or "basis." All its ambiguities are relevant here: *principio* may be seen as a rational principle underlying sound government or it may be regarded as the historical beginning of a social order. Many revolutionary movements have this dilemma; if one is to get down to the basis of society one has also to go back in time. Thus the paradox of the Mexican revolutionary movement comes into being: to go forward, to achieve progress, one must at the same time go backward, to an age of freedom.

Unfortunately for the moderate criollos, once it became legitimate to seek the basis of legitimacy by going back, some radicals, like Hidalgo, started going back too far. For the moderates, the return to the past only went as far back as the moment of Conquest. For them the "people" were that group formed by "honest men" of a certain education and social standing in each township, men of the cabildos who would now find their place in the national sun. The people emphatically did not include Indians and *castas* (or mestizos). It was not the aborigines, they argued, who made the pact with the crown, but the Conquistadores, the mythical ancestors of the American criollos. At the first meeting convoked by the viceroy, the royalist representative raised this very point, saying that if the criollos were serious about seeking sovereignty in the people, they should pay attention to the *pueblo originario*, the autochthonous people of Mexico—indeed one of the governors present was a descendant of the Emperor Moctezuma! This made several European criollos, including Archbishop Lizana, switch allegiance from the Municipal Government to the Royalist Agreement, the conservative Spanish faction. They feared, correctly, that the regressive movement in search of a principle and an origin would not stop until it reached its real terminus, the effective sovereignty of the broad masses of the Mexican people.

This was the position when the events I have described burst forth on Mexican history.

At the Cry of an educated criollo, Don Miguel Hidalgo, son of a gachupin, the rural Indians, the Indian and mestizo mineworkers, the common people of the Bajío cities respond by revolution. The explosion spreads as fast as the means of communication permit; soon it extends almost to the whole nation. Here we meet with an almost unanimous movement of the popular classes, one which, I believe, is unprecedented in the previous history of New Spain. This revolution is totally different from the attempt at emancipation made by the municipal government members two years earlier. In social composition it is fundamentally a rural revolution, assisted by the mining workers of the silver cities, and the populace, the plebs, of the towns [Villoro, 1963:215].

Criollo leaders of middle-class origin and education now tried to channel and direct this torrent of primary process, this insurgence of communitas seeking maximal expression.

As in other revolutionary movements the theories and historical conceptions of the Mexican Independencia reflect its social composition. Its ideologues, as we have seen, were *letrados*, lettered men, such as lawyers, priests of the lower clergy, members of provincial governments, and journalists. But once they became involved in close, practical contact with the people, especially the masses of Indios, ideas, beliefs, and symbols that would be appropriate to their class tended increasingly to give way to markedly populist sentiments. The thought of the revolutionary criollos became radicalized; it went beyond the specific interests of their class and expressed the general interests of the wider community. Ideas were transformed by the social processual context in which they functioned. It must not be forgotten that it is the radicalization of revolutionary activity in the primary process that makes possible the acceptance of new doctrines and ideological influences—as can be seen in the case of activist lettered criollos—and not the reverse (see Villoro, 1963:215).

Villoro (1963:216) divides the process of radicalization of criollo thinking into two stages: (1) in the first years after 1808, ideas rooted in tradition persist; the theses of the municipal government of Mexico City are repeated and developed. But other viewpoints arise from contact with the new situation; we see the first agrarianist ideas appearing, there are signs of a moderate social egalitarianism, and a trend toward making "indigenism" respectable; (2) in the second stage, the criollo intellectuals become more open to French and Genevan (Rousseauian) democratic ideas, typical of European liberalism. Villoro traces this movement of thought in response to action in much detail. Here we are mainly interested in what he has to say about Hidalgo:

The criollo savant summons the people to liberty. In that very instant, he is raised up as their representative. And the people engulf him, absorb him into their impetus, even convert him into the spokesman of their own longings and aspirations. Every measure he takes in their name, "to satisfy them," to use his own phrase. In appealing to the "common voice of the nation," he probably intended to use that expression in the same sense as the other famous criollos, from Azcárate to Quintana Roo. However, the "nation" which in *reality* acclaimed him was no longer the "constituted bodies," nor the representatives of municipal governments, but the Indian peasants—who proclaimed him "Generalisimo" in the plains of Celaya, the broad masses who from now on were to support him. *In practice*, the "voice of the nation" is tantamount to the "will of the popular classes." To legislate in their name, Hidalgo, *in practice*, elevated the ordinary people to sovereignty, without making any distinction in his heart between estates or classes. Thus his revolutionary praxis gave new meaning and content to the political formulations of the criollo literati. Before any theory had evolved, the people had established itself as the origin of society. The decrees of Hidalgo (e.g., abolishing slavery) do nothing more than express this effectual, actual sovereignty. [In the terms I used in *The Ritual Process*, they converted existential into normative communitas. V.T.] The abrogation of the tributes that weighed on the people, the suppression of slavery and racial (casta) discrimination, are indications of the disappearance of social inequalities. In addition, the first agrarian measure is dictated: lands are restored to the indigenous communities. Rumors spread of even greater radicalism. Many attribute to Hidalgo the intention of distributing all the land in Mexico among the Indians and of seizing the products of the ranches and estates (*fincas*) to divide them up equally among the people [1963:220–221].

Revolutionary experience also radicalized the historical perspective we spoke of earlier. Some criollo radicals now tended to reject the whole juridical order of the colony, regarding that period as three centuries of unmitigated despotism, ignorance, misery, and exploitation. The colonial period was regarded—by Hidalgo and Morelos particularly—as a gloomy interval between phases that did not share its negative quality. It was either a period of imprisonment or serfdom, or a time of sleep. Some regarded it as a mere episode interrupting the course of a different and better life. Even in the eighteenth century a reappraisal of the pre-Cortesian civilizations had begun. The revolutionary intelligentsia fed on their findings. Fr. Servando Teresa de Mier, the great radical Dominican, revived the arguments of the expelled Jesuit Clavigero in defense of the indigenous civilizations and challenged the basic legitimacy of the Conquest. He and his followers came to assert that the entire *colonia* was a fraud, an extraneous and illicit domination, a usurpation of natural rights (see Villoro on Mier, 1963:217–218). It is this attitude that exactly informed Hidalgo's policies toward the gachupines at Guanajuato and Guadalajara. Killing them was a just reprisal. Radical criollos now boldly renounced their own past—which was post-Conquest—threw in their lot with the Indians, "the ancient and legitimate owners of the country," as Mier called them, "whom an iniquitous Conquest had been unable to deprive of their rights" (Villoro, 1963:225). What, then, became of the criollo Magna Carta, the "American Constitution" established between Spanish king and Mexican Conquistador? Was it to be abandoned before the more primordial rights of the Indians? Evidently Hidalgo thought so, but Allende did not. Nor did the many criollos who turned against Hidalgo explicitly.

Yet there was a strange affinity between criollo and Indio, an affinity that really does receive ideological expression in this myth of the cancellation of the Conquest. It was not the product of a romantic movement, such as in Europe influenced Rousseau, Goethe, and the early Marx and Engels. It did not try to restore the remote past, with its grisly deities and their blood lust, Huitzilopochtli, Coatlicue, Chacmool, and the rest. It did not seek in the native civilizations for values to supplant those of the

Colonia. What the radical criollos sought would perhaps be approved of by both Hegel and Lévi-Strauss. They felt, in an intuitive way, that their epoch of early Independencia was similar to the pre-Cortesian one. As good Christians, and this would be the feeling of Mier, Hidalgo, Morelos, and Allende, they might well say that both periods, the pre-Cortesian and post-colonial, were untainted by the colonial lapse from grace. In a sense the convergence of indigenous and postcolonial periods was purely negative; they met because both were marginal to the order both denied. But from their encounter was generated a curious and significant symbolism. The Conquest negated indigenous society; Independence, in Hegelian terms, was the negation of that negation. The new indigenous revival reversed indigenous subjugation in the Conquest. Hence the term favored by Hidalgo "Reconquest" with further echoes from the time of the reconquest of Spain from Moorish domination. Morelos conferred on himself the title "Commissioned by the Reconquest and New Government of America." Anastasio Bustamante popularized the idea of a war which replicated in reverse the adventure of Cortés and his companions, even down to the smallest incidents. Many other instances exist of this precise reversal.

But these ideas coexisted with the moderate criollo view. Both can be regarded as different degrees of depth in an ongoing process. But once Hidalgo had announced that the ultimate origin or *principio* was the liberty of all the people, the average criollo could not ignore this formulation. He had to look for pre-Cortesian origins, and when he did this he could not ignore the revelation of the people as dominantly made up of Indians and half-Indians and the fact that these were the authentic social basis of independent Mexico. The nation itself had to be constituted anew—the radical criollo ideologues thus became vulnerable to all kinds of novelty—openness to deep antiquity and openness to new political doctrines, coming from Europe and the United States.

It is not possible in this chapter to work out the full implications of criollo vulnerability to extra-Mexican influences. My intent here is only to examine how abstract ideas such as "who are the people?" and "what is sovereignty?" are caught up into the semantic system associated with such sensorily perceptible symbol vehicles as Our Lady of Guadalupe, and are then made vivid foci of mobilization for the popular masses.

First, though, I should point out that the same tendency to regress to some past, whether pre- or post-Cortesian, can be seen in religion as well as politics. But in religion it is not to the past of Aztec deities. Indeed, to get a firm hold on the masses their educated leaders could not realistically appeal to the religious system of the dominant pre-Cortesian political authority in Central Mexico, the Aztecs. For the Tarascans, Otomie, Zapotecs, and Totonacs, to name but a few coherent cultures, did not accept a single cosmology any more than they accepted a single political authority. Their descendants maintained this sense of cultural autonomy even when they felt their over-all unity as Indians of political importance. But in religion, nostalgia concerned itself with producing a more purified conception of the church. After all, the church had deeper roots than the Spanish state, and if one were going back there, one would go back to the early days of the church, the prehierarchical and pre-Roman ones, long before Spain, let alone New Spain. It all began quietly—and politically—enough with Hidalgo's protest against excommunications (like his own) which were launched for purely political motives, and he located their cause in the worldly interests of the clergy and in the distortion of religion by political authority and power. Later, Mier, Dr. Cos, and, especially Morelos, would point to the damage caused by the attitude of the high (Spanish) clergy to the church itself and to the necessity of separating religion from all earthly interests. They quickly stressed notions of ecclesiastical reform. Even Allende proclaimed the advantages of putting in order and reforming the ecclesiastical estate, and particularly that of the religious orders, by reducing them to the primitive rigor and strictness of their patriarchs and founders. Dr. Cos claimed that the pride and worldly power of the higher clergy had challenged Christians to react like the early Christians who had direct communion with the ordinary people, while ecclesiastical dignitaries were democratically elected by the assembly of the faithful. In reply to those who asserted that America would fall into heterodoxy if it broke away from the Spanish church, Dr. Cos retorted: "Religion will emigrate from Spain to live among Americans in all its pristine purity and splendor; the Early Church will be reborn; the priest will truly be revered, as now he is not revered" (quoted in Villoro, 1963:219). In brief, a new church would be founded in America, that is, in Mexico, purified from worldly corruption, reviving the early days of Christianity. Teresa de Mier carries on this line of argument:

He examines the origins of Caesaro-Papalism with its temptation to realize the Kingdom of Heaven in terms of a mundane society, to identify Augustine's City of God with his Terrene City. He champions a popular religion, poor, without privileges, presided over by tolerance and respect for the rights of others, and free from the influence of reactionary ideologies. In the natural ideal of equality and liberty for all men, he sees a correspondence with the pure doctrine of the gospels [Villoro, 1963:219].

In brief, he tries to unite doctrinally the need to purify Christianity spiritually with the new ideas of liberty and equality proposed by the thinkers of the French Encyclopedia and the French Revolution.

I have mentioned earlier the importance of multivocality in dominant ritual symbols. All these radical criollo ideas I have just mentioned in connection with religion and politics—both being "Brotherhood" in William Blake's phrase—seem to have been involved with one another in Hidalgo's selection of the banner and image of Our Lady of Guadalupe as the supreme mobilizing emblem of his movement. Our Lady of Guadalupe had spatial continuity with the Aztec mother of the gods, Tonantzin. Her cult began only fifteen years after the Aztec Lady's cult had been forcibly discontinued by the Conquest. Moreover, according to the tale known over all Mexico by 1810, the Queen of Heaven had visited with a simple Indian catechumen, Juan Diego, not with a Spaniard, still less with a Spanish religious. That Juan Diego, unlike Bernadette in France, was never canonized, made him even more an object of sympathy and identification for Indians, who saw him as one of their own and not as a gachupin. At a deeper social level, it has been pointed out that when secular structural power is in the hands of a single group, and where both groups in Mexico as well as Spain regard masculinity and patriliny as the sources of authority, legitimacy, office, economic wealth, and every kind of structural continuity, the unity, continuity, and the countervailing "power of the weak," the sentiment of ultimate wholeness of the total community, is often assigned to female, especially to maternal symbols, as Radcliffe-Brown hinted in his famous paper on "The Mother's Brother in Africa" (1961). Mary-Tonantzin stood for the common people, for the ultimate legitimacy of the politicojurally despised and rejected in the sight of God. The Conquest had effectually destroyed the Aztec gods, who, in any case, had never compelled the allegiance of all the Mexican indigenous peoples. Indeed some feared the Aztec gods like the plague and even today have recourse to the Virgin of the Remedies rather than to Our Lady of Guadalupe. Nevertheless, when Father Hidalgo, in the old Mexican tradition of priest-philosopher-leaders, like Quetzalcoatl of Tula of the Toltecs, took up the banner of the Brown Virgin of the oppressed many-centuries-dominated Indians, he was seizing a sign of wholeness and prophetic pan-Mexicanness that his opponents could not really counter, something that gave ritual power to his empirical, rational messages.

His instinct was a good one; Our Lady of Guadalupe also held an appeal to criollos. These people too were indigenous Mexicans, like the Indians, and not a few were genetically mestizos. Their future, as I have argued, was to some extent to replicate the pre-Hispanic past. Our Lady of Guadalupe was the nearest thing to which Indians who had rejected the specific paganism of the

Aztecs could come in their totality to an Indian goddess. But the universal Christian aspect of all refractions of the hyperdulia due to Our Lady in any form had an obvious appeal to those who considered themselves American, even if not Indian; for Guadalupe was metropolitan Mexico, and not Spain, Italy, Poland, or any other country that had produced Marian devotions as a result of the visions of the poor and afflicted. Indian "thesis" and "criollo-Indian" synthesis, structurally bracketing Spanish-colonial "antithesis," were united in devotion to a feminine principle that had become instead of a peace symbol a war symbol because the male king figure had been overthrown by history, giving the power of the weak the opportunity to become converted into the power of the strong. Again, criollo social patterns and life styles did not replicate the supposed pre-Hispanic past; they reflected back on that past and on those whom criollos considered its living representatives—the Indians—features of culture and structure they had acquired during their three centuries in the New World, including some of their own styles of piety, which matched and synthesized with some of the religious styles of the Indians. Our Lady of Guadalupe I would regard, therefore, not only as an Indian symbol but also as a joint criollo-Indian symbol, which incorporated into its system of significance not only ideas about the earth, motherhood, indigenous powers, and so on, but also criollo notions of liberty, fraternity, and equality, some of which were borrowed from the atheistical French thinkers of the revolutionary period.

It would further be possible to consider, in precise terms, the relationship between symbols and each successive stage of the social drama or political phase development. Light can be shed on ritual and political symbols by considering them not as atemporal abstract systems, but in their full temporality, as instigators and products of temporal sociocultural processes. Our Lady of Guadalupe *lives* in scenes of action, whether of regular annual, cyclical devotion by members of different regions, occupations, or religious groups, or as a multivocal symbol of popular powers in times of major social crisis. *Per contra*, Hidalgo, Morelos, Guerrero, Juarez, Zapata, Villa, and others have been transformed into symbols by the primary processes that made them historically visible when they were living men. Studies of the relations between processes and symbols at any given time and in their cumulation over time are at present the main focus of my field and historical research.

References

Carlston, Kenneth S. 1968. *Social Theory and African Tribal Organization*. Urbana: University of Illinois Press.

Cuevas, Mariano. 1952. *Historia de la nacion mexicana*. 3 vols. Mexico City: Talleres Tipograficos Modelo. First published 1940.

Hamill, Hugh. 1966. *The Hidalgo Revolt*. Gainesville: University of Florida Press.

Hunt, Robert. 1966. "The Developmental Cycle of the Family Business." In *Essays in Economic Anthropology*, ed. June Helm. Seattle and London: Proceedings of the American Ethnological Society, 1965.

McHenry, J. Patrick. 1962. *A Short History of Mexico*. New York: Doubleday, Dolphin Books.

Paz, Octavio. 1961. *Labyrinth of Solitude*. New York: Grove Press.

Radcliffe-Brown, A. R. 1961. "The Mother's Brother in Africa." In *Structure and Function in Primitive Society: Essays and Addresses*. London: Cohen and West. First published 1924.

Ricard, Robert. 1966. *The Spiritual Conquest of Mexico*. Berkeley: University of California Press.

Sierra, Justo, ed. 1957. *Evolución politica del pueblo méxicano*. Mexico City: Universidad Nacional Autonoma de Mexico. First published 1900–1902.

Simpson, Leslie Byrd. 1967. *Many Mexicos*. Berkeley: University of California Press.

Spiro, Melford. 1968. "Factionalism and Politics in Village Burma." In *Local-Level Politics*, ed. M. Swartz. Chicago: Aldine.

Swartz, Marc. ed. 1968. *Local-Level Politics*. Chicago: Aldine.

——, V. Turner, and A. Tuden, eds. 1966. *Political Anthropology*. Chicago: Aldine.

Turner, Victor, and M. Swartz. 1966. Introduction to *Political Anthropology*, eds. M. Swartz, V. Turner, and A. Tuden. Chicago: Aldine.

Turner, Victor, and M. Swartz. 1969. *The Ritual Process: Structure and Anti-structure*. Chicago: Aldine Press.

Velzen, H. U. E. Thoden van. 1970. Personal communication.

Villoro, Luis. 1952a. "Raiz del indigenismo en México," *Cuadernos Americanos* 61 (1):36–49.

———. 1952b. "Hidalgo: Su violencia y libertad," *Cuadernos Americanos* 2 (6): 223–239.

———. 1963. "Las Corrientes ideologicas en la epoca de la independencia." In *Estudios de historia de la filosofia en Mexico*, publication of La Coordinacion de Humanidades. Mexico City: Universidad Nacional Autonoma de Mexico.

———. 1967. *El Proceso ideologico de la revolución de Independencia*. Mexico City: Universidad Nacional Autonoma de Mexico.

Wolf, Eric R. 1958. "The Virgin of Guadalupe: Mexican National Symbol," *Journal of American Folklore* 71:34–39.

———. 1959. *Sons of the Shaking Earth*. Chicago: University of Chicago Press.

Zolberg, Aristide R. 1972. "Moments of Madness: Politics as Art." *Politics and Society*. Winter:183–207.

CHAPTER 4

The Word of the Dogon[1]

The school, and indeed the family, of the late Professor Marcel Griaule have made outstanding contributions not only to West African ethnography, but also, and definitively, to the study of African systems of thought. *Ethnologie et langage*,[2] written by Griaule's daughter, Madame Calame-Griaule, is in many ways the keystone of the arch of three decades of studies by the Griaule group among the Dogon of the Bandiagara cliffs in the southwestern region of the Niger Bend. Many aspects of the expressive culture of the Dogon have been elaborately exhibited and finely analyzed, notably of late by Madame Germaine Dieterlen,[3] but Madame Calame-Griaule cogently argues that the Dogon term *sɔ:*, a multivocal concept which she translates by the French multivocal term "parole," provides in its various senses, contexts, and usages the master key to the understanding of Dogon culture. To employ another pertinent metaphor, *sɔ:* is the Archimedean point where she places the fulcrum of her work to raise this particular "African world" to full intelligibility. The "word" is the clue to the "world."

In this as in other respects, the daughter is inspired by the father. Madame Calame-Griaule inferred from his *Dieu d'eau* the notion of "a Word (*Verbe*) of divine origin, cosmic, creative, and fertilizing, viewed from the angle of myth and, one might say, of metaphysics" (Calame-Griaule, 1965:10). But for M. Griaule the

[1] First published as a review in *Social Science Information* 7, no. 6 (1968): 55–61.

[2] G. Calame-Griaule, *Ethnologie et langage: La parole chez les Dogon* (Paris: Gallimard, 1965).

[3] G. Dieterlen, *Les Âmes de Dogon* (Paris: Institut d'Ethnologie, 1941); *Le Renard pâle* (Paris: Institut d'Ethnologie, 1963).

Dogon sɔ: was something rather more than this. It represented the "spirit of order, organization and universal reorganization which contains everything, even disorder. It is at the same time something else that we do not understand, something consisting both of the unknown and of what we are beginning to perceive; and this would be covered for Christians by the name Word [*Verbum*]." [4] Madame Calame-Griaule replies to the question implicit in Griaule's study by approaching the Dogon notion of speech from a phenomenological standpoint and exhibiting in their full richness of classification and context the manifold modalities of sɔ:. Although she conducted her enquiries in French she had entirely adequate control of Dogon, particularly of the Sanga dialect, and could follow the discussions and asides of her informants. These Sanga speakers varied greatly in personality and in the scope of their knowledge of Dogon esoterica. But the author felt that this focus on a single area and dialect presented no serious obstacle since Dogon culture has a remarkable unity in its basic conceptions of the nature of speech, while other parts of the territory had been well studied by members of the Griaule school. It is one of the major advantages of such a sustained project by many scholars of diverse interests that each investigator can erect on the collective foundation his own edifice of specialized study without having to restate laboriously the ensemble of Dogon findings in his published account. Nevertheless one difficulty remains of which I am myself acutely conscious. It is that one can fashion out of the narratives and commentaries of various informants—as both Madame Calame-Griaule and I have done—a relatively consistent and harmonious picture of a cosmology, a ritual system, a syntax of relations between symbols, and so on, but the reader is seldom able to get behind the author's presentation to the informants' original statements or the dialogues and conversations in which they were proffered. It may well be that a bias is introduced into the investigator's account by a tendency to select as representative of a culture only those accounts or sections of accounts that

[4] Marcel Griaule, "L'Alliance cathartique," *Africa* 18, no. 4 (1948): 251.

appear to be internally coherent and consistent—in terms of his own unconscious canons of coherence and consistency. Or his bias may lie the opposite way: he may, again perhaps unconsciously, feel that a technologically simple and preliterate culture has no coherence, and thus tend to emphasize the illogicalities and absurdities in his informants' accounts, justifying these, it may be, by some currently fashionable sociological theory.

Such difficulties may be partly circumvented by publication not only of vernacular texts of informants' statements but also of the full context of the conversations. In *Dieu d'eau* the context of situation was dramatically portrayed, but one there missed the vernacular documentation. I have myself both used translators—of varying quality—and interrogated informants in their own language and dialect. In the first case I found that informants were more inclined to weigh their words and to try to make intelligible to the stranger certain facts and connections of their own culture which they may have learned from intercourse with Europeans and Africans of other cultures were considered outlandish or odd. Here the emphasis was on justification, legitimation, and cognitive explanation. But when I conversed with informants in their own tongue (however ineptly, at first, on my part), there prevailed the conventions of what Basil Bernstein has called a "restricted code" of discourse. Many premises and features of culture and social structure were left unstated; use of a common language implied a consensus as to values and beliefs. Shared experience, motives, and feelings were also taken for granted. The translation situation forced informants to think carefully before they spoke about their customs and beliefs and, indeed, compelled them to become aware of principle and regularity where before there was merely an obscure sense of fitness. The vernacular situation was linguistically more condensed and cryptic but had multiple reference to "the contemporaneous state of the [social] field" (to cite Kurt Lewin).

I mention these difficulties solely because it is by speech that we investigate the notions of speech held by another culture. Moreover, the views and speech styles of our informants are to some extent related to their social positions. Thus it may well happen that with regard to a deity venerated by a certain segment or class of society one informant may give a list of attributes or a cycle of myths in most ways opposed to the exegeses of another. Here sex, age, membership in a specific moiety or clan or in a secret society may be of decisive importance in accounting for the discrepancy. Unless we present texts in terms of the circumstances under which they were obtained, from whom they were taken, and the social and psychological characteristics of their narrators, we are in danger of selecting concordant features from disparate accounts and producing a logically satisfactory synthesis which would perhaps be unintelligible to most members of the indigenous culture.

It is clear that Madame Calame-Griaule is well aware of such problems and has taken them into account in making her masterly summation of everything that can be systematically connected with *sɔ:*. I only raise them because it is rare to find an anthropologist who shows us, as natural scientists do, the whole sequence of steps from preliminary observations to the formulation of hypotheses.

Sɔ: for the Dogon roughly represents the whole Saussurean "family" of *language, langue,* and *parole.* More than this it even seems to connote something similar to the *signatura* of the mystic Jakob Boehme, just as the entire Dogon mythico-cosmological system is equivalent to Boehme's *signatura rerum.* In both cases the unmanifest One becomes the manifest Many through a timeless or pretemporal process of seven phases—which then coexist as principles of cosmic structure. In both cases the manifest creation can be reduced to a set of correspondences. The "human form divine," to quote William Blake who is himself indebted to Boehme, for the Dogon as for Boehme—and indeed for many other overt as well as Gnostic religious cosmologies—is the model and measure of all things. As Madame Calame-Griaule writes of the Dogon (p. 27): "Man seeks his reflection in all the mirrors of an anthropomorphic universe where each blade of grass, each little fly is the carrier of a word (*parole*). The Dogon call it, word of the world, *aduno so*: (*parole du monde*), the symbol." Thus every Dogon "symbol" is part of a vast system of correspondences between and often cross-cutting cosmic domains. It does not, as many of the religious symbols of central African peoples do, form an autonomous cultural focus to which are assigned senses that vary with social context; it is a fixed point of linkage between natural kingdoms, animal, vegetable, and mineral which are themselves regarded as parts of "un gigantesque organisme humain" (p. 27). For example, the Dogon establish a correspondence between the different categories of minerals and the organs of the body. The various soils are conceived of as the organs of "the interior of the stomach," rocks are regarded as the bones of the skeleton, and various hues of red clay are likened to the blood. Sometimes these correspondences are remarkably precise: a rock resting on another images a chest; little white river pebbles stand for the toes of the feet. The same "parole du monde" principles hold good in the relationship between the human image and the vegetable kingdom. Man is not only "the grain of the universe" but each distinct part of a single grain is a part of the human body, a heart, a nose, or a mouth. Mary Douglas has demurred at Madame Calame-Griaule's use of the term "humanisme" to describe this "humanisation" of the nonhuman universe ("Dogon Culture—Profane and Arcane," *Africa* 38, January 1968:19). She holds that it "runs counter to the usage of Renaissance scholars who use humanism for the shattering of the primitive, anthropomorphic world-view of mediaeval Christianity." In short, it would be the sharp distinction between cosmos and man, as thesis and antithesis, which for her constituted humanism; man is no longer a "microcosm," but something radically opposed to and alienated from all other modalities of being. It is only when the universe is emptied of hominiform associations that the true nature of its cause-effect relations and functional interconnections can be discovered, according to this view. It is a view that emancipates men from the complex weave of "correspondences," based on analogy, metaphor, and mystical participation, and enables them to regard all relations as problematical, not given, until they have been experimentally tested or systematically compared.

A fascinating historical and diffusionist problem is posed by the close resemblance between Dogon myth and cosmology and those of certain Neo-Platonist, Gnostic, and Kaballistic sects and "heresies" that throve in the understory of European religion and philosophy. One wonders whether, after the Vandal and Islamic invasions of North Africa, and even before these took place, Gnostic, Manichaean, and Jewish-mystical ideas and practices might have penetrated the Sahara to the Western Sudan and helped to form the Dogon *Weltbild*. The Gnostic sequences of "archons," arrayed as binarily opposed androgynous twins, have affinities with Fon and Dogon notions. St. Augustine's *Confessions* indicate that Christianity did not have Manicheanism as its sole powerful rival for men's minds in the fifth century A.D. in North Africa. It is possible that adherents of such persuasions filtered or fled through the centuries to the Niger region and as bearers of a more complex culture exercised influence on the beliefs of its inhabitants. Archeological and historical research may throw more light on this problem.

Words are in truth inadequate to describe the skill with which Madame Calame-Griaule has isolated and then recombined the many attributes of Dogon speech. There is, for example, a subtle and finely wrought interplay between the components of speech and those of the personality. The body is the visible portion of man and constitutes a magnet or focus for his spiritual principles, which are nevertheless capable of sustaining an independent existence. The body is made up of four elements: water (the blood and bodily fluids), earth (the skeleton), air (vital breath), and fire (animal warmth). There is a continuous exchange between these internal expressions of the elements and their external aspects. The body has twenty-two parts: feet, shins, thighs, lumbar region, stomach, chest, arms, neck, and head—nine parts (it would seem that as in the case of twins double parts like feet and thighs are reckoned as units) to which are added the ten fingers (each counting as a unit) and the number three standing for the male sex. The resultant twenty-two is thus the answer to an addition sum rather than a sort of Pythagorean archetypal number. More numerical symbolism is involved for there are believed to be eight symbolic grains—representing the principal cereal crops of the area—lodged in the collar bones of all Dogon. These represent the mystical bond between man and his crops. I have no space to discuss the other parts of the personality, the vital force, the eight *kikinu* or spiritual principles, classified by body and by sex. It will be enough to mention that speech is regarded as "the projection through sound into space of the personality of man; it proceeds from his essence, since it is by its means that his character, intelligence, and emotional state are revealed. It is at once the expression of the individual's psychical life, and the source of his social life; it is the channel by which two egos communicate with one another. That is why the Dogon regard it as an emanation of the being, similar to it in each of its parts" (p. 48). The *body* of speech is, like the human body, made up of four elements: water is saliva without which speech is "dry," air gives rise to sound vibrations, earth gives speech its "weight" and significance, fire gives speech its "warmth." There is not only homology between personality and speech but also a kind of functional interdependence, for words are selected by the brain, stir up the liver, rise as steam from the lungs up to the clavicles which decide ultimately whether the speech is to emerge from the mouth.

To the twenty-two parts of the personality must be added forty-eight types of speech, consisting of two sets of twenty-four, each of which is under the sign of a supernatural being, the androgynous twins Nommo and Yourougou (the "pale fox" of Madame Dieterlen's narrative). These are the creations of Amma: one rebelled against Amma and had incestuous relations with his mother—he was punished by being changed into a pale fox; the other, Nommo, saved the world by an act of self-sacrifice, brought humans, animals, and plants to the earth, and became the lord of speech. One wonders again whether the Gnostic and Christian echoes here are more than mere convergence and may derive from remote historical contact. Nommo's speech can be heard and is human; the fox's is a silent sign language made by pawmarks. Only diviners can interpret it. But I must refrain from entering into the fascinating intricacies of this binary system. All I can do is to promise the reader many intellectual pleasures and surprises if he enters the labyrinth with Madame Calame-Griaule as his "delightful guide"!

The book proceeds through accounts and interpretations of the relationship between speech and myth and speech and techniques to the role of speech in social life. In all these realms we find order in process and structure. It is this order that I find problematical, the result of my field experience in central and East African Bantu-speaking peoples. It would seem that it is principally among agriculturally based societies with deep traditions of continuous residence in a single region that one may find cultures of the *signatura rerum* type, where every element is interwoven with every other in a fine tapestry of symbols and ideas. In central Africa, while it is possible to find cultural sectors made up of systematically related components, it is more usual to find discrepant and even contradictory principles, values, norms, and symbolic representations of these. Here, too, there is a paucity of myth. Such societies are descendants of groups that first migrated in a relatively short period of time through various major ecological habitats and were then exposed to several centuries of slave raiding and trading. They became fragmented, broke up, and recombined with the fragments of other societies in new temporary polities. There were conquests, the rise and fall of "kingdoms of the savannah." Slash-and-burn agriculture kept people constantly on the move. Many men were hunters, following the capricious tracks of game. All told, there was little stability, in residence, in social structure, in political type. Perhaps it is partly due to this lability and mobility that there emerged few central African cultures—at any rate in the last few centuries—with anything like the pancultural coherence of the Dogon system. Indeed, so little coherence did I find at the level of abstract culture among the Ndembu that I tended to regard system as mainly the result of concrete interests and interacting wills rather than existing "out there" in a world of beliefs, norms, and values. Rather did I tend to regard the latter as free-floating and disengaged. This very quality allowed them all the more readily to be recombined in *Gestalten* that varied situationally in accordance with the goals and designs of factions and interest groups "on the ground." In short, I saw social action as systematic and systematizing but culture as a mere stock of unconnected items. Order came from purpose, not from *connaissance.*

This viewpoint is obviously extreme and hence false, but it did enable me to focus my attention on social processes, on movement and conflict in concrete relations. Clearly, there is much more order and consistency in Ndembu expressive culture than I granted it at the time, and I have since tried to make some amends for my earlier processual extremism by exhibiting structures of ideas underlying Ndembu ritual. Yet I still feel that if ordinary Dogon villagers were continually aware of the correspondences between everything they would be unable to undertake the simplest manipulations of norm and value—and it is these manipulations that make day-to-day social adjustments possible. Otherwise people would be oppressed by the weight and dazzled by the complexity of their own religious, ethical, and philosophical systems. A certain degree of ignorance is necessary for the activists and men in the street in any society—who make its politics and nudge it into change—just as attaining a high and hidden degree of gnosis is necessary for its thinkers and prophets. But some way must be found to distinguish empirically between the knowers and the doers and the knowledge of the doers and the actions of the knowers and to exhibit these distinctions in anthropological reports. And, of course, in many preliterate societies the knowers are pre-eminently the doers too. The problem here is: how do they segregate their active and contemplative roles—and what are the linguistic concomitants of this segregation?

Madame Calame-Griaule, Madame Dieterlen, and the other members of the school have shown courage and pertinacity in bringing to the fore issues and problems that have long been ignored by anthropologists who have succumbed to the behavorial science seductions. Man truly does not live by bread alone; he is "turned on" by legend, literature, and art, and his life is made glowingly meaningful by these and similar modalities of culture. Madame Calame-Griaule has shown us coolly and lucidly the patterns of thought that live like salamanders in their glow.

CHAPTER 5

Pilgrimages as Social Processes[1]

In this examination of the specific type of ritual symbols associated with religious pilgrimages, I have just begun to make a comparative study of pilgrimage processes, not only as they exist at a given time but also as they have changed over time, and of the relations into which different pilgrimage processes have entered in the course of massive stretches of time. The main focus is on those pilgrimage processes, many of which have consolidated into pilgrimage systems, to be found in the major historical religions, Christianity, Islam, Judaism, Hinduism, Buddhism, Confucianism, Taoism, and Shintoism. In addition, I have begun to collect materials on pilgrimages in archaic societies, such as ancient Egypt, Babylonia, the civilizations of Meso-America, and pre-Christian Europe. Finally, I hope to discover indications of pilgrimage behavior or pilgrimage-like behavior in the nonliterate societies customarily studied by anthropologists.

In previous work I have described my theoretical interests, including the study of "processual units," social "anti-structure," and the semantics of ritual symbols. All these interests converge on pilgrimage processes, as we shall see even in the tentative formulations in this chapter. For pilgrimages are liminal phenomena—and here we shall be concerned with the spatial aspects of their liminality; they also exhibit in their social relations the quality of communitas; and this quality of communitas in long-

[1] First presented at the Department of Anthropology, Washington University, St. Louis, in February 1971, and published as "The Center Out There: Pilgrims' Goal," in *History of Religions* 12, no. 3 (1973): 191–230.

established pilgrimages becomes articulated in some measure with the environing social structure through their social organization. Pilgrimages may also be examined in terms of the extended-case history approach. Satisfactory documents or oral narratives of the personal experiences and observations of pilgrims and of detached investigators enable us to envisage the social process, involving a particular group of pilgrims during their preparations for departure, their collective experiences on the journey, their arrival at the pilgrim center, their behavior and impressions at the center, and their return journey, as a sequence of social dramas and social enterprises and other processual units to be isolated by induction from an appropriate number of cases, in which there is a development in the nature and intensity of relationships between the members of the pilgrimage group and its subgroups. We are also able, by this technique, to raise problems concerning the social and cultural relations between the pilgrimage group and the successive sociocultural environments through which it passes. The detailed accounts of such intrepid pilgrims—to name only three out of hundreds—as Hsuan-tsang (c. 596–664), who left China in 629 to visit in turn the famous Buddhist centers in India; Canon Pietro Casola of Milano, who made the pilgrimage to Jerusalem in 1494; and Sir Richard Burton, who went on the hadj from Suez to Mecca in 1853, disguised as a wandering dervish named Abdullah of Indo-British extraction, seem to be admirably detailed, and when these are related to what is known of the social, political, and cultural circumstances of their times and journeys they should give us useful clues to the nature of the dynamic interdependence between structure and communitas in different religions and epochs. They certainly tell us much about the organization of group activities and social life, the economics and logistics of the journey, the symbolic and social settings at different way stations, and the sacred and profane attitudes, individual and collective, of the pilgrimage groups.

Most of the accounts I have read stress the opposition between social life as it is lived in localized, relatively stable, structured systems of social relations—such as village, town, neighborhood, family—and the total process of pilgrimage. To take an example at random from my growing pile of data, C. K. Yang, in his book *Religion in Chinese Society* (1961:89) comments on the pilgrim mood at the celebration of the birthday of the deified general Ma Yuan (first century A.D.):

For three days and nights, the emotional tension and the religious atmosphere, together with the relaxation of certain moral restrictions, performed the psychosocial function of temporarily removing the participants from their preoccupation with small-group, convention-ridden, routinized daily life and placing them into another context of existence—the activities and feelings of the larger community. In this new orientation local inhabitants were impressed with a distinct sense of community consciousness.

The remarks of Malcolm X in his *Autobiography* (1966) on the dissolution or destructuring of many of his stereotypes after his experience of what he calls the "love, humility, and true brotherhood that was almost a physical feeling wherever I turned" (p. 325) at the culmination of his pilgrimage to Mecca are striking:

You may be shocked by these words coming from me. But on this pilgrimage, what I have seen and experienced has forced me to *rearrange* much of my thought-patterns previously held [this rearrangement is a fairly regular feature of liminal experience] and to *toss aside* [Malcolm X's emphasis] some of my previous conclusions. . . . During the past eleven days here in the Muslim world, I have eaten from the same plate, drunk from the same glass, and slept in the same bed (or on the same rug)—while praying *to the same God* [Malcolm X's italics]—with fellow Muslims, whose eyes were the bluest of blue, whose hair was the blondest of blond, and whose skin was the whitest of white. And in the *words* and in the *actions* and in the *deeds* of the "white" Muslims, I felt the same sincerity that I had felt among the black African Muslims of Nigeria, Sudan, and Ghana. We were *truly* [Malcolm X's italics] all the same (brothers)—because their belief in one God had removed the "white" from their *minds*, the "white" from their *behavior*, and the "white" from their *attitude*. ["White" for Malcolm X, here represents power, authority, hierarchy, "structure."] I could see from this, that perhaps if white Americans could accept the Oneness of God, then, perhaps, too, they could accept *in reality* the Oneness of Man—and cease to measure, and hinder, and harm others in terms of their "differences" in color [pp. 340–341].

This is one of very many quotations one could make from various literatures illustrating the communitas character of pilgrimage. But here I will distinguish between three types of communitas, a distinction I made first in *The Ritual Process*, for it is of decisive importance in considering the nature of the social bond in pilgrimage situations. These types are (1) *existential* or *spontaneous* communitas, the direct, immediate, and total confrontation of human identities which tends to make those experiencing it think of mankind as a homogeneous, unstructured, and free community; (2) *normative* communitas, where, under the influence of time, the need to mobilize and organize resources to keep the members of a group alive and thriving, and the necessity for social control among those members in pursuance of these and other collective goals, the original existential communitas is organized into a perduring social system—this is never quite the same as a structured group whose original *raison d'être* was utilitarian, for normative communitas began with a nonutilitarian experience of brotherhood and fellowship the form of which the resulting group tried to preserve, in and by its religious and ethical codes and legal and political statutes and regulations; and (3) *ideological* communitas, which is a label one can apply to a variety of utopian models or blueprints of societies believed by their authors to exemplify or supply the optimal conditions for existential communitas.

My preliminary survey of pilgrimage data indicates that while the total situation fosters the emergence of existential communitas, it is normative communitas that constitutes the characteristic social bond among pilgrims and between pilgrims and those who offer them help and hospitality on their holy journey. An example comes from Dom Bede Jarett's article on "Pilgrimages" in the 1911 edition of *The Catholic Encyclopedia.*

At first a question of individual travelling [to Jerusalem, Rome, Compostella and other pilgrim centers] a short period was sufficient to develop pilgrimages into properly organized companies . . . clerics prepared the whole route beforehand and mapped out the cities of call . . . troops are stationed to protect pilgrims, and hospices established along the line of travel. . . . King Stephen of Hungary, for example, [established the "King's Peace" and] made the way safe for all, and thus allowed by his benevolence a countless multitude both of noble and common people to start for Jerusalem [as the old chronicler, Raoul Glaber puts it]. . . . Pious journeys gradually harden down and become fixed and definite . . . and are allowed for by laws, civil and ecclesiastical. . . . [Ultimately,] pilgrimages become regarded as part of normal life [pp. 86–87].

Normative communitas reigns. Yet the communitas spirit is still latent in the norm and can be reanimated from time to time. A Hindu example is the great Maharashtrian pilgrimage to visit the shrine of Vithoba Bhave at Pandharpur, southeast of Poona in the Deccan. G. A. Deleury in his book *The Cult of Vithoba* (1960:103) thus describes "the psychology of the Varkaris"— members of a specific Hindu Vaishnavite school of spirituality devoted to the deity who is regarded by them as an avatar of Vishnu, though he is sometimes considered as a combined form of Vishnu and Shiva (*Harihara*).

Although a Varkari is supposed to go on the pilgrimage to Pandharpur every year he

has not the psychology of one who would abide by a rule but of one who fulfils an essential and well-loved promise. [That] is why there is no sanction for the Varkari who would not perform his annual pilgrimages, and it could not be otherwise. The problem does not even arise: the Varkari is too keen on his pilgrimages to miss any of them of his own free will: and it is a proverb amongst Varkaris that if one of them is not seen at the pilgrimage he must be dead or dying.

This characteristic of a freely-taken engagement gives to the pilgrimage a remarkable quality of spontaneousness. It is with all the joy of his heart that a Varkari takes part in it. This spontaneity is not hampered by a stiff frame: although there is a definite organization, it is meant more to canalize the enthusiastic participation of the pilgrims than to impose a totalitarian rule on them. For instance, there is no *hierarchy* [italics mine] among the members of the procession. The pilgrimage has no director; there is no distinction between priests, officiants, clerks and faithful: all the pilgrims are on the same level, and if there is an authority it is not due to any office, but to the spiritual personality of some of the pilgrims acknowledged as *"guru"* by their followers.

Yet, as we shall see, distinctions of caste are maintained during the pilgrimage journey, though in modified form. In pilgrimages, the mere demographic and geographical facts of large numbers of people coming at set times and considerable distances between their homes and the sacred site compel a certain amount of organization and discipline. The absolute communitas of unchanneled anarchy does not obtain here. What we see is a social system, founded in a system of religious beliefs, polarized between fixity and travel, secular and sacred, social structure and normative communitas, which may aspire to an open morality in Henri Bergson's sense, may even imagine it possesses one, but stops short at the cultural bounds of a specific religious world view. Daily, relatively sedentary life in village, town, city, and fields is lived at one pole; the rare bout of nomadism that is the pilgrimage journey over many roads and hills constitutes the other pole. As we shall see, the optimal conditions for flourishing pilgrimage systems of this type are societies based mainly on agriculture, but with a fairly advanced degree of division of craft labor, with patrimonial or feudal political regimes, with a well-marked urban-rural division but with, at the most, only a limited development of modern industry. Today, reports from all over the world indicate that, if anything, larger numbers of people than ever are visiting pilgrim centers. In this case, however, pilgrimage is not integrated, as it was in medieval Europe and Asia, for example, into a wider sociocultural system. My guess at the moment is that during the present transitional period of history, when many institutionalized social forms and modes of thought are in question, a reactivation of many cultural forms associated traditionally with normative communitas is occurring. Social energy is being withdrawn from structure, both preburcaucratic and bureaucratic, and it is cathecting various modalities of communitas. New manifestations of existential communitas are also taking place; but when those who manifest them wish them to persist in community and seek symbols to safeguard their persistence, such symbols tend to be drawn from the repertoire of communitas groups down the ages and communicated to the present era by writing and other symbolic codes. In this way, there is a cross-influence between new and traditional forms of communitas, leading in some cases to the recovery of traditional forms that have long been enfeebled or at a low pulse. More detailed work is needed, however, by way of depth studies of pilgrimage centers that are currently popular. Clearly, such factors as the general and rapid increase of the world's population, the improvement of communications, the spread of modern means of transportation, the impact of mass media on travel, have all had the effect of increasing the numbers of visitors to shrines, many of whom should perhaps be considered as tourists rather than pilgrims per se. Nevertheless, my own observations in Mexico, and the data I shall present, indicate that in the age of Aquarius, pilgrimages like many other liminal or underground, as opposed to mainline, manifestations of the religious, not to mention the esoteric and the occult, are surfacing once again as significant, visible social phenomena, as they have surfaced in the past in periods of destructuration and rapid social change, such as in the waning of the Roman Empire and in the waning of the Middle Ages.

But I shall consider some published definitions of pilgrimage, culled from various sources, for these may give us some clues as to the character of the phenomenon. Some of these have been written by believers in religions having pilgrimages, others by pilgrims themselves, others by historians, including historians of religion. Together they may shed some light on the properties and functions of pilgrimages as sociocultural phenomena and on the attitudes people in different religions or of no religion have held toward them. A "pilgrim," for *The Oxford English Dictionary*, is "one who journeys to a sacred place as an act of religious devotion," while a "pilgrimage" is "a pilgrim's journey." "Sacred," for this source, means "consecrated or held dear to a deity . . . dedicated or reserved or appropriated to some person or purpose; made holy by religious association, hallowed." Authorities discussing the different historical religions are much more specific than this. For example, *The Jewish Encyclopedia* (1964) defines pilgrimage as

a journey which is made to a shrine or sacred place in performance of a vow or for the sake of obtaining some form of divine blessing. Every male Israelite was required to visit the Temple three times a year (Exodus 23:17; Deuteronomy 16:16). The pilgrimage to Jerusalem on one of the three festivals of Passover, Shabu'ot, and Sukkot was called 're'iyah' ('the appearance'). The Mishnah [a digest of laws made by Rabbi Judah, the Patriarch (*c.* 135–220)] says, 'All are under obligation to appear, except minors, women, the blind, the lame, the aged, and one who is ill physically or mentally' . . . A minor in this case is defined as one who is too young to be taken by his father to Jerusalem. While the appearance of women and infant males was not obligatory, they usually accompanied their husbands and fathers, as in all public gatherings (Deuteronomy 31:12) [vol. X, p. 35].

The element of obligatoriness in the ancient Israelite pilgrimage is found again in Islam, where, according to A. J. Wensinck in *The Encyclopedia of Islam* (1966), the central Muslim pilgrimage, the hadj, (probably derived from an Old Semitic root, *h-dj*, meaning "to go around, to go in a circle") "is a journey obligatory on every Muslim, man or woman, who has reached the age of puberty and is of sound mind. . . . [It must be performed] at least once in his or her life provided that they have the means to do so (p. 33).

The notion of making a pilgrimage to perform a vow or obtain a blessing is also clearly conceptualized in North China in connection with mass religious gatherings for "celebrating the birthday or other event in connection with a god" (Yang, 1961:86). There are two major types of devotional acts at the pilgrimage shrine, known as *hsü yüan* and *huan yüan*. *Hsü yüan*

was the making of a wish before the god with the vow that, if the wish should come true, one would come again to worship and offer sacrifice. *Huan yüan* was worship and sacrifice to the god as an expression of gratitude *after* the wish had come true, whether it was recovery from sickness, the bringing of prosperity, or the begetting of a male heir. One might [also] thank the god for the fulfillment of wish during the past year, and then make a new wish for the coming year [Yang, 1961:87].

It is necessary to discuss this matter of pilgrimage as obligation and pilgrimage as a voluntary act involving a vow, or, as they say in Ibero-American, "a promise" (*promesa*). Even though obligation is stressed in several religions, as in connection with the Pandharpur Hindu pilgrimage mentioned earlier, in ancient Judea, and in modern Islam, many categories of people were exempt from this duty, such as women, minors, and the sick under Mosaic law, non-Varkaris at Pandharpur, women who were unable to travel with their husbands or relatives within the prohibited degrees in Islam. In addition, in Islam dispensations could be granted on grounds of illness or infirmity, unusual insecurity on the route (wars or banditry), or lack of the necessary funds to provide for one's family during absence as well as for the expenses of pilgrimage. Even for those on whom obligation rested the obligation was a moral one; there were no sanctions behind it. Nevertheless, it was important that even where there was obligation, it should be voluntarily undertaken, the obligatory should be regarded as desirable. Thus, B. Lewis writes of the hadj in medieval Islam:

Every year, great numbers of Muslims, from all parts of the Islamic world, from many races and from different social strata, left their homes and travelled, often over vast distances, to take part in a common act of worship. These journeys, unlike the mindless collective migrations familiar in ancient and medieval times, are *voluntary* and *individual*. Each is a personal act, following a personal decision, and resulting in a wide range of significant personal experience. . . . [The *Hadjdj* was] the most important agency of voluntary, personal mobility before the age of the great European discoveries. . . . [It] must have had profound effects on the communities from which the pilgrims came, through which they travelled, and to which they returned ["Hadjdj," *Encyclopedia of Islam*, 1966:37-38].

Christian pilgrimages tended at first to stress the voluntary aspect and to consider sacred travel to Palestine or Rome as acts of supererogatory devotion, a sort of frosting on the cake of piety. But a strong element of obligation came in with the organization of the penitential systems of the church. When this became authoritatively and legally organized, pilgrimages were set down as adequate punishments inflicted for certain crimes. As Bede Jarett writes (1911:85): "The hardships of the journey, the penitential garb worn, the mendicity (the beggardom) it entailed, made a pilgrimage a real and efficient penance."

Thus when one starts with obligation, voluntariness comes in; when one begins with voluntariness, obligation tends to enter the scene. To my mind this ambiguity is a consequence partly of the liminality of the pilgrimage situation itself—as an interval between two distinct periods of intensive involvement in structured social existence out of which one opts to do one's devoirs as a pilgrim, and partly of the patrimonial and feudal orders of society in which pilgrimage systems seemed to have a stabilizing function in regard to both local and international relations within a system of shared religious values. Such orders of society, though relatively stable in themselves, occupy a historical and logical limen between societies based as Sir Henry Maine would have said (*Ancient Law*, 1861) on status and those based on contract. In

the former case, in the early law of Europe, as in the law of tribal
society, most of the transactions in which men and women are
involved (to quote Gluckman)

are not specific, single transactions involving the exchange of goods
and services between relative strangers. Instead, men and women hold
land and other property, and exchange goods and services, as members of a hierarchy of political groups and as kinsfolk and affines. People are linked in transactions with one another because of pre-existing
relationships of status between them. As Maine said in a pregnant
phrase: ". . . the separation of the Law of Persons from that of
Things has no meaning in the infancy of the law . . . the rules belonging to the two departments are inextricably mingled together, and
. . . the distinctions of the later jurists are appropriate only to the
later jurisprudence." We can only describe the Law of Things, i.e.,
the Law of Property, in these types of society by describing also the
Law of Persons, or status; and we can only discuss the law of status
by talking about ways of owning rights over property [1965:48–49].

In our modern industrial society rights of ownership are rarely
unrestricted, but the restrictions usually arise through voluntary
contractual arrangements (such as granting leases, mortgaging,
pledging), through testamentary restraint on inherited things (and
testamentary disposition again involves a voluntary act), or
through a mass of regulations and bylaws defining property zones
for special users, licensing vehicles for special purposes, and soon.
But in tribal and prefeudal societies these sorts of restraints, and,
of course, the corresponding rights, derive from status and kinship, and are consequently much more closely interwoven in the
social structure. In the medieval period, both in Islamic and Christian lands, the notion of voluntariness and contract became
established with the diversification of social and economic life.
Indeed, the feudal oath of fealty was a kind of contract whereby
a man vowed before witnesses to be another's vassal and tenant
and to serve him in many ways in return for armed protection and
a measure of physical security. But such voluntariness swiftly
became obligation, and indeed the oath itself was partly an ack-

nowledgment of the obligation of fidelity to the lord. Furthermore, the status of vassal and tenant then tended to be inherited, to become what anthropologists would call an *ascribed* or *ascriptive* status. In pilgrimage we see clearly displayed this tension and ambiguity between status and contract and an attempt to reconcile them in the notion that it is meritorious to *choose one's duty*. Enough room is left to the individual to distance himself briefly from inherited social constraint and duty, but only enough room so as to constitute, as it were, a public platform in which he must make by word or deed a formal public acknowledgement of allegiance to the overarching religious, political, and economic orders. Yet even here appears the thin edge of the contractual wedge that will lead eventually to a major loosening up of the structure of society. Pilgrimages represent, so to speak, an amplified symbol of the dilemma of choice versus obligation in the midst of a social order where status prevails.

Yet medieval pilgrimages, though generically framed by obligation and institutionalized in a great system of obligation within that frame, represented a higher level of freedom, choice, volition, structurelessness, than did, say, the world of the manor, village, or medieval town. They were *Yin* to its *Yang*, cosmopolitanism to its local particularism, communitas to its numerous structures. Islam tended to emphasize pilgrimage as a central institution more than Christianity did and gave communitas almost the role of a mandala center, geographically represented by the black stone by the Kaaba at Mecca, turning liminality into its opposite. Here I cannot refrain from quoting B. Lewis again on the *hadj* in medieval Islam:

The needs of the pilgrimage—the commands of the faith reinforcing the requirements of government and commerce—help to maintain an adequate network of communications between the far-flung Muslim lands; the experience of the pilgrimage gives rise to a rich literature of travel, bringing information about distant places, and a heightened awareness of belonging to a larger whole. This awareness is reinforced by participation in the common rituals and ceremonies of the pilgrimage in Mecca and Medina, and the communion with fellow-Muslims of other lands and peoples. The physical mobility of important groups of people entails a measure of social and cultural mobility, and a corresponding evolution of institutions [1966:37].

And here follows an interesting comparison from the perspective of communitas/structure, with on the one side the stratified, rigidly hierarchic society and intense local traditions within the comparatively small area of Western Christendom, and on the other the situation in medieval Islam.

The Islamic world has its local traditions, often very vigorous; but there is a degree of unity in the civilization of the cities—in values, standards and social customs—that is without parallel in the medieval west. "The Franks," says Rashid al-Din "speak twenty-five languages, and no people understands the language of any other." It was a natural comment for a Muslim, accustomed to the linguistic unity of the Muslim world, with two or three major languages serving not only as the media of a narrow clerical class, like Latin in Western Europe, but as the effective means of universal communication, supplanting local languages and dialects at all but the lowest levels. The pilgrimage was not the only factor making for cultural unity and social mobility in the Islamic world—but it was certainly an important one, perhaps the most important [p. 37].

One must comment here that even if Christian pilgrimages did not have the immense scope of the hadj, they had similar effects in bonding together, however transiently, at a certain level of social life, large numbers of men and women, who would otherwise have never come into contact, due to feudal localism and rural decentralization of economic and political life. Indeed, some of the major pilgrimage centers, such as Compostella near the northwest corner of Spain, attracted huge crowds of pilgrims from every country in Europe. But if one can speak of a catchment area as a metaphor for the geographical area from which the majority of pilgrims are drawn to a particular shrine, the catchment areas of European pilgrim centers were certainly much smaller than Mecca's. Europe was the continent of the great regional and protonational pilgrimage centers. We find that, according to Ivor Dowse, *The Pilgrim Shrines of England* (1963), there were in England alone during the medieval period at least seventy-four well-attended pilgrimage sites and shrines, and in Scotland, before the Protestant Reformation, thirty-two (Dowse, *The Pilgrim Shrines of Scotland*, 1964). Furthermore, we find the beginnings of a tendency to arrange pilgrim shrines in a hierarchy with catchment areas of greater and lesser inclusiveness. Thus in England, Canterbury and Walsingham were of the first national importance, though Chichester (St. Richard), Durham, (St. Oswold, St. Cuthbert, and St. Bede), and Edmundsbury (St. Edmund, king and martyr) ran them close, while there were many shrines like St. Walstan's at Bawburgh in Norfolk, St. Gilbert of Sempringham's in Lincolnshire, St. William's at York, and St. Aidan's of Lindisfarne in Northumberland—still an important pilgrimage center—which were mainly local or regional in scope.

A similar pattern of national, regional, district, and intervillage pilgrim catchment areas exists in Mexico today, as we shall see. What seems to have happened there after the Conquest, as in medieval Europe, is that any region possessing a certain cultural, linguistic, or ethnic unity, often corresponding also to an area of economic interdependence, tended to become at once a political unit and a pilgrimage catchment area. But since the communitas spirit presses always to universality and ever greater unity, it often happens that pilgrimage catchment areas spread across political boundaries. At the level of kingdoms, pilgrimage processes seem to have contributed to the maintenance of some kind of international community in Christendom, for French, Spanish, German, and Dutch speakers visited the shrine of St. Thomas-à-Becket at Canterbury, while, as R. L. P. Milburn writes:

> Men may leave all gamys
> That saylen to Saint Jamys

So ran the old song declaring that, in the Middle Ages, Englishmen were prepared to face the extreme discomforts of an overcrowded pilgrim ship if only they might reach the famous shrine of St. James at

Compostella and there receive, perhaps, those benefits to body and soul which seemed to spring from a place hallowed by the Apostle [1963:9].

There was in fact a distinct tendency toward the kind of religious unity aimed at by Islam, symbolized by the great pan-European pilgrimage centers such as Compostella. The feeling and tone of a major pilgrimage, is evident in the following translation in poetic form of a quotation in Raymond Oursel's *Les Pèlerins du Moyen Age*. This quotation, by an unknown author (for Oursel does not footnote it, only puts its in quotes), describes the last stage of a pilgrimage to the shrine of St. James the Greater at Compostella. It provides as it were, the ideal model of the kind communitas hoped for on such occasions.

Arrival at Compostella

And the long sought splendour
Burst upon the evening of the trail
Which now had the feeling, the fragrance of farewell.

Into the sanctuary, huge as a ship in full sail
Winged and emblazoned,
Religiously they entered.

The shadows echoed with murmurs
As if the great ship, between sleep and waking
Were drowsing on the mystery of a dream.

Column after column they passed,
Altar after altar,
Unable to think, careful and fragile,
They went on and on,
Twisting the hardened old folds of their pilgrim hats with their
    fingers,

Ashamed.

So dirty
Withered and stiffened
Poor

Before this very great Saint now in his riches
High up there; and how greatly benevolent.

Their footsteps quietened; the nave was rising
To the very heights and infinities of heaven.
They hardly breathed.

They fled along like a flock at bay before the dog,
Frightened, driven, jostling each other—

Two
Three
Four
Ten
A hundred
A thousand
Crowds beyond number!

This was the whole of Christendom in one single being
Advancing up the bedrock pavement
In one irresistible Body
To the place that love and the vow of its heart had centered on.

The cathedral spread over all the loneliness of that holy place,
Her mantle of velvet and night
As a mother veils her child.
And happily she enfolded all her forgiven children
In her great loop of glittering glory.
She gave them for their weariness
The seige throne and grace of fulfilment
And she rocked them with the tender humming of her voice.

[1963:94; translated by Edith Turner]

A further aspect of pilgrimage is suggested by the Buddhist concept of such sacred journeys. It seems that Buddhist usage derived at first from Hindu practice. This makes it interesting that the Pali form of the Sanskrit word for pilgrimage (*pravrajya*, Pali *pabbajja*, literally, "a going forth," "retirement from the world") should be the technical term for admission or "ordination" to the first grade of the Buddhist monkhood. Some Buddhist as well as Hindu holy men, like the palmers of medieval Europe, spent their whole lives visiting pilgrim centers. My point is that there is a *rite de passage*, even an initiatory ritual character about pilgrimage.

I tend to see pilgrimage as that form of institutionalized or symbolic anti-structure (or perhaps meta-structure) which succeeds the major initiation rites of puberty in tribal societies as the dominant historical form. It is the ordered anti-structure of patrimonial feudal systems. It is infused with voluntariness though by no means independent of structural obligatoriness. Its limen is much longer than that of initiation rites (in the sense that a long journey to a most sacred place used to take many months or years), and it breeds new types of secular liminality and communitas. The connection between pilgrimages, fairs or fiestas, and extensive marketing systems will be discussed later in the chapter. The influence of pilgrimage extends into literature, not only in works with direct reference to it, such as Chaucer's *Canterbury Tales*, Bunyan's *Pilgrim's Progress*, and even Kipling's *Kim*, but also the numerous "quest" or "wayfaring tales," in which the hero or heroine goes on a long journey to find out who he or she really is outside "structure"—recently D. H. Lawrence, Joseph Conrad, and Patrick White provide examples of this genre. Even *2001* has something of this pilgrimage character, with a Mecca-like "black stone" in outer space, near Jupiter, largest of the peripheral planets.

As the pilgrim moves away from his structural involvements at home his route becomes increasingly sacralized at one level and increasingly secularized at another. He meets with more shrines

and sacred objects as he advances, but he also encounters more
real dangers such as bandits and robbers, he has to pay attention
to the need to survive and often to earn money for transportation,
and he comes across markets and fairs, expecially at the end of
his quest, where the shrine is flanked by the bazaar and by the
fun fair. But all these things are more contractual, more associa-
tional, more volitional, more replete with the novel and the un-
expected, fuller of possibilities of communitas, as secular fellowship and comradeship and sacred communion, than anything he
has known at home. And the world becomes a bigger place. He
completes the paradox of the Middle Ages that it was at once
more cosmopolitan and more localized than either tribal or
capitalist society.

The topography of certain traditional African societies, topography defined as the representing of certain ritual features of the
cultural landscapes on maps, is important to this study. In many
ways my methodology is Durkheimian; one way is that I begin a
study by regarding social facts or collective representations, like
the ideas, values, and material expressions associated with pilgrimages, as being, in a sense, like things. Just as a physical scientist looks at the physical world as an unknown but ultimately
knowable reality, so the sociologist or social anthropologist must
approach the phenomena of society and culture in a similar spirit:
he must suspend his own feelings and judgments about social facts
at the beginning of an investigation and rely upon his observations, and in some cases, experiment with them before he can say
anything about them. As Durkheim has said, a thing is whatever
imposes itself upon the observer. To treat phenomena as things is
to treat them as data which are independent from the knowing
subject. To know a social thing the observer, at least at first,
cannot fall back upon introspection; he cannot come to know its
nature and origin by seeking it from within himself. He must in
his first approach go outside himself and come to know that thing
through objective observation. But after collecting and analyzing
the demographic, ecological, and topographic facts, I would go

beyond Durkheim's view in laying stress, as Znaniecki does, not only on rules, precepts, codes, beliefs, and so on, in the abstract, but also on personal documents which give the viewpoint of the actors, or on their own explanations and interpretations of the phenomena. These would constitute a further set of social facts. So too would one's own feelings and thoughts as an observer and as a participant.

Anthropologists have sometimes noted that in certain societies a ritual topography, a distribution in space of permanent sacred sites, coexists and is, as it were, polarized with a political one. Thus, among the Shilluk of the Sudanese Republic, E. E. Evans-Pritchard has shown how a system of ritual localities becomes visible and relevant on major national rites of passage such as the funerary and installation ceremonies of kings. These ritual sites and territorial divisions do *not* precisely coincide with major political centers and divisions such as the national capital, provinces and provincial capitals, and villages headed by aristocrats (*The Divine Kingship of the Shilluk of the Nilotic Sudan*, 1948:23–24). Meyer Fortes has gone further, and uses the overlapping transparent diagrams so familiar to generations of anthropology students in his book, *The Dynamics of Clanship among the Tallensi*, (1945:109), to show how Tale clans or maximal lineages are linked by different sets of ties in dominantly political and dominantly ritual situations. He shows, too, how earth shrines are set up *outside* settlements, while lineage ancestral shrines are located *within* them. Moreover, in the ritual field itself certain shrines have become pilgrimage centers for non-Talis, many of whom come from as far away as the Gulf coast of West Africa, a journey of several hundred miles. G. Kingsley Garbett has suggested, following Gelfand and Abrams, how, underlying the divisions between relatively autonomous Shona chiefdoms in Rhodesia, there still exists a set of connections between spirit mediums who are believed to be the mouthpieces of ancient chiefs of the Monomatapa royal dynasty ("Religious Aspects of Political Succession among the Valley Korekore," 1963; *passim*). Whether this system of ritual linkages—and it *was* a system since it was partially reactivated to organize unified resistance to the British in the Shona Rebellion—was itself the attenuated and symbolic successor of a once fully operational political system, as some scholars such as Terence Ranger and J. Daneels suppose, it nevertheless continues to operate, like the Tale cults of the earth and External *Boyar*, as a symbol of "common interests and common values" (Fortes, 1945:81). These earth shrines, too, were closely identified with the indigenous people of the region, the Talis, rather than with the incoming Namoos. I do not propose to multiply citations here, but would like to point to the further distinction made in many west and central African societies between *ancestral* cults and cults of *the earth*, and between *political* rituals organized by political leaders of conquering invaders and *fertility* rituals retained in the control of indigenous priests. Each of these opposed types of cults tends to be focused on different types of shrines situated in different localities, resulting in overlapping and interpenetrating fields of ritual relations, each of which may or may not be hierarchically structured. To simplify a complex situation, it might be said that ancestral and political cults and their local embodiments tend to represent crucial power divisions and classificatory distinctions within and among politically discrete groups, while earth and fertility cults represent ritual bonds between those groups, and even, as in the case of the Tallensi, tendencies toward still wider bonding. The first type stresses exclusiveness, the second inclusiveness. The first emphasizes selfish and sectional interests and conflict over them; the second, disinterestedness and shared values. In studies of African cults of the first type, we find frequent reference to such topics as lineage segmentation, local history, factional conflict, and witchcraft. In cults of the second type, the accent is laid on common ideals and values, and, where there has been misfortune, on the guilt and responsibility of all rather than the culpability of individuals or factions. In cases of homicide, for example, in many parts of West Africa, the whole land may be purified by an earth priest.

Rituals of the second type, those stressing the general good and inclusiveness, become more prominent in the so-called "historical," "higher" or "universal" religions, such as Christianity, Judaism, Buddhism, Islam, Confucianism, and Hinduism, although they do not, of course, in any sense, replace the first type, the locally bonded religious congregations. In addition, individual responsibility is now extended from the domain of immediate kin and neighborhood relations in localized normative systems to that of the generic human "brother" and the "neighbor" who might be anyone in the wide world but whom one should "love." The "other" becomes a "brother," specific siblingship is extended to all who share a system of beliefs. Yet despite this shift, the polar distinction between cultural domains of exclusivity and inclusivity remains. The first domain is topographically and geographically expressed in the focusing of religious activity on localized shrines, situated in churches, synagogues, temples, mosques, and meeting houses, which are themselves parts of bounded social fields, and which may constitute units in hierarchical or segmentary politico-ritual structures. Where, then, in the complex large-scale societies and historical religions are we to look for the topography of the inclusive, disinterested, and altruistic domain? The short answer is in their system of pilgrim centers. The question was first raised for me, in two visits to Mexico, by the observation of great numbers of pilgrims coming from all parts of Mexico on important feast days (and to some shrines every day) at such centers as the Villa de Guadalupe near Mexico City; Chalma, some seventy miles from Mexico City; Acámbaro in Guanajuato; and Naucálpan near Mexico City where the shrine of Our Lady of the Remedies is situated. People came in tens of thousands during the principal fiesta to these and to other centers, by many means of transportation, on foot, riding horses and donkeys, by car, train, and airplane, and, today, overwhelmingly by bus and coach. They came as individuals, in family groups, and in organized parties of industrial workers, bank employees, office employees of the different branches of government, schools, parishes, and business organizations. To the basilica of the Patroness of Mexico, and now also of the Americas, Our Lady of Guadalupe, came pilgrims not only from Mexico and all the Latin-American countries, but also from the United States and Canada, and even from Europe, India, the Philippines, and other parts of Christian Asia. Clearly, too, these throngs came not only for solemnity but also for festivity and trade. At all the pilgrimage centers there was dancing by bright, feathered troupes of traditional performers. Often there were rodeos, bullfights, and fairs with ferris wheels and roundabouts, and always there were innumerable stalls and marquees where almost everything could be had, from pious pictures and religious objects to confectionery, food, clothing, and domestic utensils. Communion, marketing, the fair, all went together in a place set apart.

For an anthropologist nothing social is alien, and here was patently a social phenomenon of great interest and possible significance. I turned eagerly to the anthropological literature on pilgrimages not only in Latin America, but also in other parts of the world, but could glean relatively little. There was little more in contemporary ecclesiastical and religious sources. Here was a great extant popular process, demographically comparable to labor migration, involving millions of people the world over in many days and even months of traveling, rich in symbolism and undoubtedly complex in organization, and yet very largely ignored by the often competing orthodoxies of social science and religion. Why was there this neglect? In the case of the anthropologists, there may have been a combination of causes: the concentration, until quite recently, on the elicitation and analysis of highly localized, fixed, and focused "structures" and "patterns" rather than on patterns and processes on a national or even international scale, coupled with an almost obsessive emphasis on kinship, law, politics, and economics rather than on religion, ritual, metaphor, and myth; on pragmatics rather than symbolics. Religious leaders, on the other hand, have been silenced by their ambivalent feelings about pilgrimages. On the one hand, they seem to regard them as in a way meritorious and pious, but on the other, as suspect, being tainted with primitive and peasant superstitions, and bearing all too clearly the marks of an ancient paganism. Though operational on a wide scale, pilgrimages have somehow brought features of what Robert Redfield would have called the "Little Tradition" into what should have been theologically, liturgically, and, indeed, economically controlled by leading representatives of the "Great Tradition."

It seems that matters were not always thus, for we find that in the Middle Ages, especially in the centuries when Gothic architecture throve, "the age of the towering pilgrimage churches and cathedrals, was, economically speaking, the age of the great fairs" (Otto von Simson, *The Gothic Cathedral*, 1962:164), and that "the church herself had every interest in protecting as valuable sources of revenue the markets and fairs held under its patronage" (p. 165). It is still the case, in Mexico, that priests and the religious of a specific parish associated with a pilgrimage shrine foster the devotion paid to its santo, but since the *Reforma* in the mid-nineteenth century they have had no authority to protect the markets and fairs: the local administrative bureaucracy has these firmly under its own control. The Catholic church in the Middle Ages had, in any case, a greater tolerance for popular tradition than it has today, when it is seeking to modernize its image and thinking. It was Calvin rather than Erasmus who probably did most to foster the modern disapproval of pilgrimages, for he thought that they "aided no man's salvation," and even although the Catholic (Counter Reformation) Council of Trent rather weakly affirmed that "places dedicated to the memories of saints are not vainly visited," the Calvinist version of the Protestant ethic seems to have won the day in northern Europe and North America. Pilgrimages, for Calvin and the Puritans, were mere peregrinations, wasting time and energy that might be better put to the service of demonstrating, in the place where God has called one, that one has been personally "saved," by a thrifty, industrious, and "pure" style of life. Or as Nanak, the first Sikh guru put it in the Indian context, when asked by a Muslim why he did not turn in the direction of Mecca to pray: "There is no place where God is not."

When I began to investigate pilgrimages more closely, I came to see that they might well constitute objectively a connected network of processes each involving a journey to and from a particular site. Such sites were places where, according to believers, some manifestation of divine or supernatural power had occurred, what Mircea Eliade would call a "theophany." In Mexico the most typical theophanies were held to be miracles brought about by images or paintings of Christ, the Virgin Mary, and certain saints. Mexico differs from Europe in that images rather than relics of saints are there the major sacred objects of pilgrimage devotions. This may have been due to the virtual monopoly over the relics of the major saints maintained by the great religious centers (and notably the pilgrimage centers) of Europe and to difficulties involved in the transportation of holy relics across the Atlantic; but there may well have been a pre-Columbian influence at work, in view of the tendency of the Maya, Aztecs, and Tarascans to make vivid and putatively efficacious effigies and paintings of their deities. Less indirect, however, than statuary and paintings known to have been man-made is the celebrated case of the Dark Virgin of Guadalupe, *La Virgen Morena*. The Virgin Mary, in her advocation as the Immaculate Conception, is believed to have appeared in person to an Aztec commoner, Juan Diego, ten years after the Conquest of Mexico by Cortés, and to have imprinted her image, that of a mestiza girl, on the rough cloak or *tilma* of maguey fibers (the century plant) which he was wearing. This miraculous painting is still the central focus of veneration for all Catholic Mexicans, and it is estimated that an average of fifteen thousand pilgrims and tourists come every day to contemplate it in its glass-fronted frame over the high altar of the basilica at Tepeyac. Most of the other images of the Virgin except the original statue of our Lady of Ocotlán are believed to be human artifacts, though many are

held to produce miraculous effects. These two Virgins are linked
to the period immediately following the Conquest and to the two
nations most involved with the conquistadores of Hernán Cortés,
Guadalupe to the Aztecs, Ocotlán to the Tlaxcalans, rivals of the
Aztecs and allies of Cortés.

Mexico shares with medieval Europe its network of pilgrimage
routes and trails, many of which converge from different directions on a single pilgrimage center, while others crisscross as
pilgrims travel to different holy places. Walter Starkie's book on
the pilgrimage trails to the shrine of Santiago of Compostella, *The
Road to Santiago* (1965), and Francis Watts's *Canterbury Pilgrims
and Their Ways* (1917) abundantly document this point. Moreover, in Mexico, as in many parts of Catholic Europe, towns and
municipalities contain several sodalities or brotherhoods (*hermandades*), each of which includes in its annual activities a pilgrimage to the place where its patron saint is most highly
venerated. Thus, Nutini (1968) has shown how in the *municipio*
of San Bernardino Contla in Tlaxcala state, with 10,589 inhabitants, there were forty brotherhoods (*hermandades*) distributed
over the ten territorial subdivisions of the municipality. These
brotherhoods organized annual pilgrimages to seventeen different
pilgrimage centers, located at varying distances and in different
directions from Contla. Since this situation seems to prevail over
much of Mexico, each *municipio* contains a number of persons
who have links of common devotion to sections of many other
municipios who belong to brotherhoods affiliated to the same
patron saint. Periodically all these devotees meet together on the
major feast days of their holy patron. Each local brotherhood or
sisterhood brings its banner to the principal mass, and there the
brotherhoods encounter one another, solemn encounters that are
continued more informally at the time of the commingling of individuals during marketing and fiesta. Since not only brotherhoods but also many other types of groups, and even solitary individuals, come together as pilgrims or to service the needs of
pilgrims, much news about regional and even national affairs cir-
culates on such occasions, commercial relationships are estab-

lished, *compadrazgo* (literally, the spiritual relationship between a child's parents and godparents) are formed, and matches are made, especially such as facilitate trade and local politicking. Ties of *posada* (exchange of hospitality) are also made along the pilgrimage trails of Chalma. Unfortunately, we do not yet have an adequate intensive anthropological study of the total social field of relationships generated by the sacred and secular goals of pilgrims in connection with their saints' feasts.

The Contla study brings us back to the dichotomy made earlier between religious structures firmly attached to localized socio-cultural systems and those concerned with the maintenance of the highest common values of the widest accepted cultural community. For, in Contla, in addition to the brotherhoods which are sponsored on a voluntary basis by associations of people in the various local divisions (sections, *pueblos*, *pueblitos*, and *parajes*) of the *municipio*, there are other religious associations known as *mayordomías* (literally, stewardships), which control its internal religious affairs. Stewardships are organized by *barrio* (an important socioreligious unit) or by locality (*pueblo* or *pueblito*). *Barrio* membership cuts across locality membership. Stewardships by *barrio* are those in which sponsorship of a saint's fiesta rotates in a given order among Contla's ten *barrios*. Above the stewardship system is the religious government or *ayuntamiento*, which is a body of officials elected on a yearly basis by the united assembly of the people of Contla on November 30 of each year. In other words, there is a complex religious structure focused on *local* chapels and shrines, offet by a looser, voluntaristic religious *affiliation* focused on distant shrines. It is interesting to note here that wherever a *municipio* contains or is near a major pilgrimage center, its inhabitants, though they may participate in festive and marketing activities associated with the pilgrimage saints' feast days, tend to go as pilgrims to distant shrines rather than to near ones. Yet these same people participate daily in the local *mayordomía* system. I found this to be the case, for example, at Amecameca, mentioned below.

This brings us to the very important point that, generally

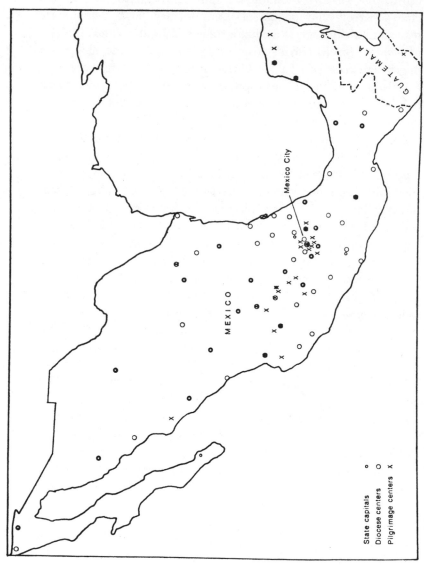

Map 1. Mexico: State, church, and pilgrimage centers

State capitals   ∘

Diocese centers   O

Pilgrimage centers   ✕

speaking, pilgrimage shrines in central Mexico, though not in Yucatán, tend to be located not in the centers of towns and cities but on their peripheries or perimeters or even at some distance beyond them (see Map 1). Thus, the hill of Tepeyac, where the shrine complex of the Virgin of Guadalupe is located, is on the northern rim of Mexico City, the basilica of our Lady of Zapópan, the great pilgrimage center of the city of Guadalajara which has the states of Michoacán, Nayarit, and Jalisco as its main pilgrim catchment area, is situated on the northwestern limits of the city, the basilica of Our Lady of Ocotlán stands on a small hill outside the southeastern boundary of the city of Tlaxcala, while the extremely sacred image of Our Lady of the Remedies is kept in the Church of San Bartolo in Naucálpan, some nine miles northwest of the old Spanish colonial capital of Mexico, but now almost engulfed by spreading suburbia. Of pilgrimage sites dedicated to one or another image or advocation of Christ, that of the Sacromonte is on a hill outside the town of Amecameca in the state of Mexico, while the important basilica of St. Michael of Chalma, which houses a miraculous crucifix, is located at a distance of about seventy miles from Mexico City whence many of the pilgrims come. Again, in contrast to Europe where many traditional pilgrimage centers are great city cathedrals, such as Canterbury, Durham, Chartres, Toledo, Ancona, and Aachen, few Mexican cathedrals attract pilgrims from afar. Of course, the most popular contemporary European Catholic pilgrimage centers are also in peripheral places. One need only mention the shrines of the Virgin at Lourdes, Fatima, Czenstoshowa, La Salette, and Oostacker (in Ghent, Belgium, an offshoot and imitation of Lourdes). This peripherality of the holiest shrines is by no means confined to Christian pilgrimage systems. For example, Deleury writes of the pilgrimage to Pandharpur that

Pandharpur is situated on the *borderline* [my italics] of the region covered by the *"palkhis"* (a palkhi is literally a palanquin carrying a representation of a god's or saint's footprints, *padukas* [not idolatrous, but representing *samadhi*, "the Experience"], and here stands for a group of pilgrims following the same guru or spiritual teacher, living or dead). . . . Not only is Pandharpur not in the center of the Marathi-speaking countries, but it is quite possible that in former times it was situated on the boundaries of Kannada-speaking countries [1960:78; see also Map 2].

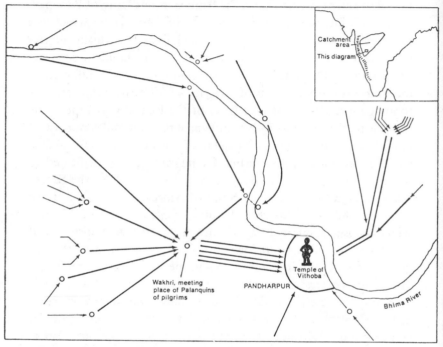

Map 2. Pilgrimage to Pandharpur: Meeting places of Palanquins. Adapted from G. A. Deleury, *The Cult of Vithoba,* Deccan College, Postgraduate and Research Institute.

Again, Mount Kailās and Lake Mānas, two of the holiest places of pilgrimage for Hindus, are located on the further side of the Himalayas in western Tibet. Today, of course, ever since the occupation of Tibet by China, Indians have been denied access to these natural shrines, already regarded as holy in the *Mahābhārata.* Even in good weather they are difficult of access. Marginal though they are, however, they are at the source of the five great rivers of India, including the Ganges, Indus, and Brahmaputra (see Bhagwān Shri Hansa's book *The Holy Mountain*, 1934).

An apparent exception to the peripherality of pilgrimage centers is Mecca, where the black meteoric stone on the Kaaba is regarded by all Muslims as "the navel of the world." The hadj, or pilgrimage to Mecca, 'Arafât, and Mina, is the fifth of the five pillars of Islam. It is still observed annually and continues to exert a profound influence on the entire Muslim world. Despite its centrality for the religious domain, however, Mecca is certainly peripheral to each and all of the many social and political systems into which Muslims have become secularly organized. It is almost as though Islam by a kind of paradox had made sacred peripherality itself central to man's authentic existence, at least in terms of the ideal model it presents to the world. For the journey to Mecca is "a duty obligatory on every Muslim man or woman who has reached the age of puberty and is of sound mind" (Wensinck, 1969:33). The hadj should be performed once in a person's life provided that he has the means to do so. In practice, statistics show that only a small number of Muslims, especially those in countries far from Mecca, are able to perform the pilgrimage. Even so, according to the Meccan press, from 1957 to 1962 there was an annual total of between 140,000 and 180,000 pilgrims, coming for the limited period of the hadj proper, and excluding those who came from the Arabian peninsula itself. These arrived by air, sea, or land transportation from such widely dispersed areas as Egypt, Iran, Pakistan, India, Indonesia, Syria, Sudan, Nigeria, Iraq, and even from the Soviet Union as Malcolm X attests in his *Autobiography*.

These theories about peripherality can be related to other anthropological notions. For example, the marked peripherality of pilgrimage shrines, their location outside the main administrative centers of state or church, and, indeed, the temporal structure of the pilgrimage process, beginning in a familiar place, going to a Far Place, and returning to a Familiar Place, theoretically changed, relates to the well-known work of the Belgian ethnographer van

Gennep on *rites de passage.* Van Gennep demonstrated that many types of rituals, notably initiation rites, have three distinguishable stages, of varying relative duration within and among cultures, which he described as (1) *separation,* (2) *margin* or *limen,* and (3) *reaggregation.* Sometimes he simply called these: "preliminal," "liminal," and "postliminal." He had noticed that rituals are often performed, in societies at all levels of social complexity, when individuals or groups are culturally defined as undergoing a change of state or status. Van Gennep paid particular attention to the correlation between status movement and change of *spatial* position. This was particularly pronounced in initiation rites involving the seclusion of initiands or novices moving from a lower to a higher, and exoteric to an esoteric status role. Novices are often secluded from the scenes of their preliminal activities and social interactions in such wild or hidden sites as forests or caves. There they are given instruction, dominantly through nonverbal, symbolic communication, by the use of masks, arrays of sacred objects, body painting, rock painting, and so on, often accompanied by the telling of recondite origin-myths or other kinds of gnomic utterances, secret languages, and songs in the basic assumptions of their culture. I have discussed elsewhere some widely distributed features of this liminal stage in tribal societies. It constitutes, quite typically, a cultural domain that is extremely rich in cosmological meaning, though often misleadingly simple in outward form. The symbol vehicles may be unimpressive, but the messages they convey are highly complex. The mere fact of spatial separation from the familiar and habitual is an example of this. It may, in various cultures, have punitive, purificatory, expiatory, cognitive, instructional, therapeutic, transformative, and many other facets, aspects, and functions. But basically the process and state of liminality represents at once a negation of many, though not all, of the features of preliminal social structure and an affirmation of another order of things and relations. Social structure is *not* eliminated, rather it is radically simplified: generic rather than particularistic relationships are stressed. Once more, a dichotomy is suggested, similar to that between politico-jural rituals focused on localized subsystems of social groups and structural positions, and rituals concerned with the unity and continuity of wider, more diffuse communities.

Now it can be seen that pilgrimages have attributes both of the wider community, "earth shrine," types of ritual we have glanced at in Africa and of the liminal stage of *rites de passage*. The networks formed by intersecting pilgrimage routes—which are themselves studded with subsidiary shrines and way stations and lined with markets and hostelries—represent at the level of pre-industrial, politically centralized, high-agricultural cultures, the homologues of those reticulating the earth shrines and shrines of nonancestral spirits and deities found in many stateless societies in sub-Saharan Africa with a simple agricultural technology. Here the peripherality of pilgrimage centers distinguishes them from the centrality of state and provincial capitals and other politico-economic units. It further distinguishes them from centers of ecclesiastical structure such as the sees or diocesan centers of archbishops and bishops (see Map 1). This peripherality may be regarded as one spatial aspect of the liminality found in passage ritual. A limen is, of course, literally a "threshold." A pilgrimage center, from the standpoint of the believing actor, also represents a threshold, a place and moment "in and out of time," and such an actor—as the evidence of many pilgrims of many religions attests—hopes to have there direct experience of the sacred, invisible, or supernatural order, either in the material aspect of miraculous healing or in the immaterial aspect of inward transformation of spirit or personality. As in the liminality of initiation rites, such an actor-pilgrim is confronted by sequences of sacred objects and participates in symbolic activities which he believes are efficacious in changing his inner and, sometimes, hopefully, outer condition from sin to grace, or sickness to health. He hopes for miracles and transformations, either of soul or body. As we have seen, in the pilgrim's movement toward the "holy of holies," the central shrine, as he progresses, the route becomes increasingly sacralized. At first, it is his subjective mood of penitence that is important while the many long miles he covers are mainly secular, everyday miles, then sacred symbols begin to invest the route, while in the final stages, the route itself becomes a sacred, sometimes mythical journey till almost every landmark and ultimately every step is a condensed, multivocal symbol capable of arousing much affect and desire (see Map 3). No longer is the pilgrim's sense of the sacred private; it is a matter of objectified, collective representations which become virtually his whole environment and give him powerful motives for credence. Not only that, but the pilgrim's journey becomes a paradigm for other kinds of behavior—ethical, political, and other.

Pilgrimages in all historic, large-scale religions rest initially on voluntarism. For example, B. Lewis writes of the hadj that "these journeys . . . are voluntary and individual [despite the general injunction to all Muslims to make the hadj at least once in a lifetime], each is a personal act, following a personal decision, and resulting in a wide range of significant personal experience" (1966:37). Deleury writes that the pilgrim going to Pandharpur "has not the psychology of one who would abide by a rule but of one who fulfils an essential and well-loved promise" (1960:103). Christian pilgrimages, too, are voluntarily undertaken to fulfill a vow, a promise, or as a self-chosen act of penance. In this way it may be said that they differ from tribal initiations which are often obligatory on all members of a certain age and sex group. Yet in many tribal societies as well there are associations which may be entered voluntarily, if the candidate is willing first to submit to certain ordeals and humiliations and to undergo certain permanent restrictions on diet, dress, and deportment. For example, among the Ndembu of Zambia, while all boys had to undergo the circumcision rites, only whose who chose to be initiated into the Mung'ong'i funerary association needed to do so, though it was thought to be meritorious to endure its exacting ritual trials. Nevertheless, ascription and obligation are clearly dominant over

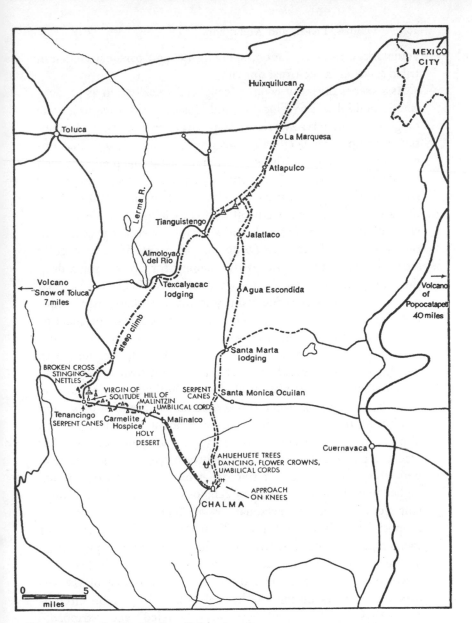

Map 3. Chalma: An Otomi Indian pilgrimage route

voluntarism, free association, spontaneity, and personal choice in tribal societies in the ritual domain.

As societies diversify economically and socially and as particularistic multiplex ties of locality and kinship yield place to a wide range of single-interest relationships between members of functional groups over ever wider geographical areas, individual option and voluntarism thrive at the expense of predetermined corporate obligations. Even obligations are chosen; they result from entering into contractual relations. The individual replaces the group as the crucial ethical unit. No longer is a "particular error atoned for," as Peacock and Kirsch have recently written in their textbook *The Human Direction* (1970:186) by a "particular sacrifice," but "man worships by begging forgiveness for a deep sinfulness within his total self." And, as Max Weber has pointed out, the individual extruded from previous corporate, mainly kin-based matrices becomes obsessed with the problem of personal or individual salvation. The need to choose between alternative lines of action in an ever more complex social field, the increasing weight, as he matures, of responsibility for his own decisions and their outcomes, prove too much for the individual to endure on his own, and he seeks some transcendental source of support and legitimacy to relieve him from anxieties about his immediate and ultimate fate as a self-conscious entity. Yet salvation has a social as well as a personal aspect in all the historic religions, as Durkheim understood in his study of suicide—when he demonstrated that higher suicide rates prevailed in religious groups, such as Protestant sects, that stressed personal responsibility without corporate support for one's own salvation. To understand the nature of this social aspect and its relationship to the voluntarism of pilgrimage it is necessary to take another look at the notion of liminality.

My own observations in Zambia in central Africa of the behavior of novices during the liminal phase of Ndembu circumcision rites suggested that these boys, "leveled" and "stripped," as Erving Goffman would say, of antecedent status, standing, and rank, developed a fellowship, a comradeship, among themselves, based on individual choice of friends rather than on kinship and neighborhood, somewhat in the fashion of modern military recruits in the same barracks room at a boot camp. Like these recruits, too, they came under the strict control of generalized elders, in contrast to their secular situation where subordination was parceled out among several particularistic kin relationships. No longer were they grandsons, sons, nephews, but simply anonymous novices, confronting the general category of initiated elders. Social structure, in brief, was simplified and homogenized. When control was relaxed the novices looked upon each other as equals, each an integral person rather than a social *persona* segmentalized into a series and a set of structural roles and statuses. Friendships made in these circumstances of liminal seclusion sometimes lasted throughout life, even though there was no formal age-set or age-grade system among the Ndembu. As elsewhere, I call this modality of social relatedness "communitas," borrowing the term— though not its meaning—from Paul Goodman, and distinguishing it from "community" which refers to a geographical area of common living. (The term *gemeinschaft,* similar to "community" as used by Ferdinand Tönnies, combines two major social modalities which I distinguish, structure and communitas. By "structure" or "social structure" I do not mean what Lévi-Strauss or his followers mean by these terms, that is, a structure of "unconscious categories" located at a deeper level than the empirical, but rather what Robert Merton has termed "the patterned arrangements of role-sets, status-sets and status-sequences" consciously recognized and regularly operative in a given society and closely bound up with legal and political norms and sanctions. *Gemeinschaft* in that it refers to the bonds between members of tightly knit, multifunctional groups, usually with a local basis, has "social structure" in this sense. But insofar as it refers to a directly personal egalitarian relationship, *gemeinschaft* connotes communitas, as, for example, where Tönnies considers friendship to express a kind of *gemeinschaft* or "community of feeling" that is tied to neither blood nor locality.)

In rites of passage, novices or initiands pass from one position or condition of structure to another. But in the passage from structure *to* structure they may, and usually do, if the rites are collective in character, experience communitas. Liminality, the optimal setting of communitas relations, and communitas, a spontaneously generated relationship between leveled and equal total and individuated human beings, stripped of structural attributes, together constitute what one might call anti-structure. Communitas, however, is not structure with its signs reversed, minuses instead of pluses, but rather the *fons et origo* of all structures and, at the same time, their critique. For its very existence puts all social structural rules in question and suggests new possibilities. Communitas strains toward universalism and openness; it must be distinguished, for example, in principle from Durkheim's notion of "mechanical solidarity," which is a bond between individuals who are collectively in opposition to another solidarity group. Here communitas is asserted for the "part" at the expense of the "whole," hence denies its own distinctive quality. In "solidarity," unity depends on "in-group, out-group" oppositions, on the we-they contrast. The historical fate of communitas seems to have been to pass from openness to closure, from "free" communitas to the solidarity given by bounded structure, from optation to obligation, from W. H. Auden's "needless risk" to the "endless safety." But in its genesis and central tendency, communitas is universalistic. Structures, like most species, get specialized; communitas, like man and his direct evolutionary forebears, remains open and unspecialized, a spring of pure possibility as well as the immediate realization of release from day-to-day structural necessities and obligatoriness. The relationship between social structure and social communitas varies within and between societies and in the course of social change. In tribal societies communitas is often relegated to a mere interval between status incumbencies. Even then it is regarded by the guardians of structure as dangerous and is hedged around with numerous taboos, associated with ideas of purity and pollution, or concealed beneath a mound of ambiguous symbols. In societies of greater complexity and diversity, religions develop which emancipate, to some degree, communitas from this envelopment. These religions recognize some of the anti-structural features of communitas and seek to extend its influence throughout whole populations as a means of "release" or "salvation" from the role-playing games which embroil the personality in manifold guiles, guilts, and anxieties. Here the pioneering communities formed by prophets, saints, and gurus together with their first disciples provide the cultural models and paradigms. Seeking oneness is not from this perspective to withdraw from multiplicity; it is to eliminate divisiveness, to realize nonduality. Thus even the solitary mystic achieves communitas by reaching the root, the "Atman," he believes exists identically in all men, indeed, in all beings, embracing nature as well as culture in communitas. But this theologizing of experience is to reduce what is essentially a process to a state or even the concept of a state, in other words, to structuralize anti-structure.

Pilgrimages seem to be regarded by self-conscious pilgrims both as occasions on which communitas is experienced and as journeys toward a sacred source of communitas, which is also seen as a source of healing and renewal. In this kind of thinking, too, the health and integrality of the individual is indissoluble from the peace and harmony of the community; solitude and society cease to be antithetical.

Some articulate pilgrims of varying religious affiliations have written about their subjective feelings of communitas. An example is the account of a female Nahuatl-speaking Mexican Indian, Luz Jiménez, who once served as a model for the famous mural painter, Diego Rivera. She went every year, from her village of Milpa Alta, on the pilgrimage to the sanctuary of Our Lord of Chalma. This famous shrine was only about forty miles from her home, but to reach it the Milpa Alta pilgrims had to walk or ride across mountains, then infested by bandits and thieves. Her account was recorded by the anthropologist Fernando Horcasitas in Nahuatl, the language of the Aztecs, and translated by him into Spanish. I translate into English her description of how various groups of pilgrims halted for a meal at Agua de Cadena, about halfway through their journey:

There in Agua de Cadena they used to dismount from the horses to heat up the food. Many of the menfolk collected firewood and made large fires to warm the food. It was indeed a lovely sight! Here, there, and everywhere we could see food being eaten. The better-off brought chicken, turkey and *tamales*. But many of our fellow-creatures had nothing, not one tortilla nor a single piece of bread. But everywhere they received some food. Pilgrims called to them, "Please come and eat your tortilla!" Another would say, "Come along, hurry, here is another tortilla, with meat!" Others again gave them *tamales*, until all who had no food were filled [1968:57].

Notice the stress here on dining together, commensality as a symbol. This also appears in the other personal documents of communitas.

Many readers will have seen the lyrical passages in *The Autobiography of Malcolm X* where Malcolm describes his experiences in Cairo, Jedda, and Mecca as the first Black Muslim to go on the hadj. I quote almost at random:

Love, humility, and true brotherhood was almost a physical feeling wherever I turned. . . . All *ate* as One [commensality is here stressed too], and slept as One. Everything about the pilgrimage atmosphere accented the Oneness of Man under One God. . . . Never have I witnessed such sincere hospitality and the overwhelming spirit of true brotherhood as is practised by people of all colors and races, here in this Ancient, Holy Land, the home of Abraham, Muhammad, and all the other prophets of the Holy Scriptures [1966:325, 330, 339].

It is sadly likely that Malcolm X's discovery through pilgrimage of what he calls the "true brotherhood" of men of "all colors and races," in sharp contrast to his previous antiwhite stance, and his announcement of this in the United States, led swiftly to his assassination by racist fanatics.

Another interesting document of pilgrimage experience comes

from an article by the late Irawati Karve, formerly professor of sociology and anthropology at the University of Poona ("On the Road: A Maharashtrian Pilgrimage," 1962). She had decided to take the road to Pandharpur as a member of a *dindi*, a subdivision of the *palanquin* group mentioned earlier, making the pilgrimage to the shrine of Vithoba Bhave. Her personal situation was complex and interesting. She was at once a seasoned social scientist, a liberal, something of a feminist, an author of novels and poetry in English, and a Brahmin! She was steeped in the Western rationalist tradition but had strong nationalist sympathies. She records how deeply she was moved by the communitas she experienced among her fellow pilgrims, so moved, in fact, that she could not endure their division into caste-bound *dindis* within the *palkhi* or *palanquin* group, the salient religious unit of the pilgrimage. If she had been content to accept the standpoint either of her own caste or of detached anthropological observation, perhaps she would not have been so evidently stirred up and involved. But then, as is so often the case, we would have been deprived of a lot of the truth of the situation. Thus she writes:

Just as I had become friendly with the Brahmin group, the Maratha women had also taken me to their hearts. . . . After I had taken my meal with them [which none of the other Brahmin women had done —taboos against commensality with subcastes other than one's own are strong in Hinduism], I felt that they were more friendly. Many of them walked alongside of me, held my hand, and told me many things about their life. Towards the end, they called me "Tai," meaning "sister." A few of them said, "Mark you, Tai, we shall visit you in Poona." And then one young girl said, "But will you behave with us then as you are behaving now?" It was a simple question, but it touched me to the quick. We have been living near each other for thousands of years, but they are still not of us, and we are not of them [p. 19].

These remarks raise the important point that though pilgrimages strain in the direction of universal communitas, they are still ultimately bounded by the structure of the religious systems within which they are generated and persist. Thus, it is highly unlikely that if one of Malcolm X's companions during the circumambulation of the Holy Kaaba had suddenly proclaimed loudly that he was a Christian, a Jew, a Hindu, a Buddhist, or an atheist, he would have been so warmly welcomed into the "brotherhood" around him! For, just as ancestral shrines are polarized with earth shrines in West Africa, so are localized mosques, temples, and churches polarized with pilgrimage shrines in the major historic religions to form a single system and share a common cultural content, though one pole stresses the model "structure" and the other "normative communitas." However, until now communitas lives within structure, and structure within communitas. Total or global brotherhood or communitas has hardly yet overlapped the cultural boundaries of institutionalized religious structures. Communitas itself in time becomes structure-bound and comes to be regarded as a symbol or remote possibility rather than as the concrete realization of universal relatedness. Thus pilgrimages themselves have generated the kind of fanaticism which, in the Middle Ages, led to their Christian reformulation as Crusades and confirmed the Muslim belief in the spiritual necessity of a jihad or holy war, fought for custody of the pilgrimage shrines of the Holy Land. When communitas becomes force rather than "grace," it becomes totalism, the subordination of the part to the whole instead of the free creation of the whole by the mutual recognition of its parts.

Yet when communitas operates within relatively wide structural limits it becomes, for the groups and individuals within structured systems, a means of binding diversities together and overcoming cleavages. This was well understood by Deleury, who, like Karve, pointed out that on the Pandharpur pilgrimage the members of the various castes were not mixed together, but the members of each *dindi* belonged to one subcaste (*jati*) only. In his view, however, this was not in opposition to the anti-hierarchical ideal of the pilgrimage, clearly stated by the hymns and sermons sung by all on the road. On the contrary, he writes, it was

a solution of the problem of the distinction of castes and of their life together. The idea of a group composed of individuals coming from different castes with different cultures, traditions, and customs could only be an artificial juxtaposition and not a true community. . . . The Varkari solution is a *happy compromise* between the *reality* of the distinctions between castes and the ideal of a social community to unite them. . . . The hardships of the way contribute to bind the various groups together and the good will of all prevents hurt and spares the feelings. Slowly but truly a *palkhi* consciousness (embracing all its sub-caste divisions) grows through the willingness and kindness of all [Deleury, 1960: 105].

Here we see how the Pandharpur pilgrimage, like the Muslim hadj, remains within an established religious system. It does not lower defenses between castes, just as Islam does not allow those beyond the *Umma* (the comity of Islam) to visit the holy places of Mecca and Medina. Nevertheless, it may be said that, while the pilgrimage situation does not eliminate structural divisions, it attenuates them, removes their sting. Moreover, pilgrimage liberates the individual from the obligatory everyday constraints of status and role, defines him as an integral human being with a capacity for free choice, and within the limits of his religious orthodoxy presents for him a living model of human brotherhood and sisterhood. It also removes him from one type of *time* to another. He is no longer involved in that combination of historical and social structural time which constitutes the social process in his rural or urban home community, but kinetically re-enacts the temporal sequences made sacred and permanent by the succession of events in the lives of incarnate gods, saints, gurus, prophets, and martyrs. A pilgrim's commitment, in full physicality, to an arduous yet inspiring journey, is, for him, even more impressive, in the symbolic domain, than the visual and auditory symbols which dominate the liturgies and ceremonies of calendrically structured religion. He only *looks* at these; he *participates* in the pilgrimage way. The pilgrim becomes himself a total symbol, indeed, a symbol of totality; ordinarily he is encouraged to meditate as he peregrinates, upon the creative and altruistic acts of the saint or deity whose relic or image forms the object of his quest. This is, perhaps, akin to the platonic notion of anamnesis, recollection of a previous existence. However, in this context it would be more properly regarded as participation in a sacred existence, with the aim of achieving a step toward holiness and wholeness in oneself, both of body and soul. But since one aspect of oneself consists of the cherished values of one's own specific culture, it is not unnatural that the new "formation" desired by pilgrims should include a more intense realization of the inner meaning of that culture. For many that inner meaning is identical with its religious core values.

Thus social and cultural structures are not abolished by communitas and anamnesis, but the sting of their divisiveness is removed so that the fine articulation of their parts in a complex heterogenous unity can be the better appreciated. Some might say that pure communitas knows only harmonies and no disharmonies or conflict; I am suggesting that the social mode appropriate to all pilgrimages represents a mutually energizing compromise between structure and communitas; in theological language, a forgiveness of sins, where differences are accepted or tolerated rather than aggravated into grounds of aggressive opposition.

Thus, in order fully to understand pilgrimages in Mexico it would be necessary to take into account the contemporaneous structure of Mexican society and culture and to examine its historical vicissitudes and changes. For this structure and culture invades the social organization and symbolism of Mexican pilgrimages today just as much as the present and past caste structures of Hinduism permeated the pilgrimage of Pandharpur. Pilgrimages may be studied synchronically and diachronically, as they are today and as they were in various yesterdays. The historical aspects of pilgrimage are described in a brilliant study of the genesis, growth, and adventures of a pilgrimage devotion in northeast Brazil in the late nineteenth century, in its full social setting. It is Ralph della Cava's *Miracle at Joaseiro* (1970). A synchronic study of pilgrimages would entail, in the first place, the making of an inventory of all the shrines and localities classified by Mexicans themselves as centers of pilgrimage (*peregrinación, romería*). Then, in each case, it would be necessary to seek to establish the scope and range of a shrine's catchment area, that is, the geographical regions and social groups and classes which provide it annually with pilgrims. Within this geographical area will be found regions of greater and less concentration. For example, in the case of the most renowned Mexican pilgrimage shrine, that of the Virgin of Guadalupe, pilgrims come not only from every state of the Mexican republic, but also from the United States, Catholic Canada, Spain, El Salvador, Cuba, Guatemala, the Philippines, every South American nation, and indeed, from all over the Catholic world, including Rome itself. Near the other end of the scale, we find pilgrimages on a regional basis, such as the black Cristo of San Román near Campeche, whose shrine is visited mainly by pilgrims from the state of Campeche and by sailors and fishermen from along the adjacent Gulf Goast. Even below this pilgrimages exist which hardly involve more than the inhabitants of a dozen villages, such as the miraculous crucifix of San Juan, near Uruápan in Michoacán. Here the crucifix, rescued from the village of Paricutín when the volcano of that name erupted from a farmer's field, is said to be performing miracles in its new setting, having saved the inhabitants of Paricutín from the flames and lava of the opened-up underworld.

It seems that pilgrimage centers can almost be arranged into a ranking order of importance. Since, however, they are open in principle to any Catholic anywhere who has a personal devotion to the pilgrimage *santo*, one finds that any center can draw individual devotees from any part of Mexico. Nevertheless, the older centers have become the objects of organized pilgrimages, where the typical units are not individuals but such groups as parishes, sodalities, and confraternities, and parties drawn from such secular groups as trades-unions, cooperatives, branches of government, and private firms. Time brings and consolidates structure. To cater for the needs of these groups, elaborate market, transportation, catering, recreational, and lodging arrangements have been developed, each social class, ethnic category, and cultural region having its own distinctive type of travel and accommodation.

A synchronic study would concern itself with the central organization of pilgrimages and also with the organization of pilgrimage parties, as they travel from their points of origin to the center and back again. It would also have to concern itself with the fixed symbols which mark the pilgrimage routes from beginning to end, from the local church or chapel or domestic shrine devoted to the pilgrimage *santo*, in the home, village, or ward of the pilgrims, through the holy places encountered on the way, to the cluster of shrines, stations, rosary walks, holy wells, caves, sacred trees, and other features of sacred topography that prepare the way for the pilgrims' encounter with the most sacred image, that of the Christ, Virgin, or saint, which is the ultimate goal of the journey. As one approaches the holy of holies the symbols become denser, richer, more involuted—the landscape itself is coded into symbolic units packed with cosmological and theological meaning.

The Israeli scholar Shlomo Deshen of Tel Aviv University, who has published extensively on the sociology of religion, briefly outlined the pilgrimage structure of Israel today, which principally concerns Oriental and North African but not European Jews. What he says about Israel, *mutatis mutandis*, also applies to modern Mexico. He writes that

there are dozens of small pilgrimages rooted in localized personalities peculiar to specific "ethnic" [by "ethnic" he means "culturally distinctive"] groups and locales. Each of these events attracts up to 3,000 people. In recent years these memorial celebrations seem to have become increasingly popular. There is a gradation from memorial celebrations in domestic settings which are very common, to the popular pilgrimages on a large scale to the graves of such saintly rabbis as Shimon bar-Yohai in Meiron (Galilee), in May, which attracts normally between 50–70,000 pilgrims who attend for about 24 hours, and to Elijah's cave on the Carmel slopes—there seem to be motives of mystical nationalism connected with this pilgrimage [personal communication, 1970].

In Mexico, too, and beyond, into Texas, New Mexico, and other regions formerly part of Old Mexico, there is just such a gradation. This extends from fiestas dedicated to local miracle-working images on appropriate days of the liturgical calendar, or to popularly, though not pontifically, "canonized" saints, such as the gentle Pedrito, a Chicano *curandero* or medicine man (discussed by V. Romano, O. I., in "Charismatic Medicine, Folk-Healing and Folk-Sainthood," 1965:1151–1173), whose grave near San Antonio, Texas, is fast becoming a notable pilgrimage center; to regional celebrations, such as the two novenas devoted around Epiphany to the Three Kings or Magi of Tizimín, in Yucatán; and, centrally, to the mystical nationalism of the several feasts for the Dark Virgin of Guadalupe.

It might be instructive to consider briefly the topography of the catchment area of an important regional pilgrimage, medial between the national and local kinds, to the shrine of Our Lady of Ocotlán near Tlaxcala City, capital of Tlaxcala state. Here there are two major categories of pilgrims: those coming regularly or intermittently from parishes outside the bishoprics of Puebla and Tlaxcala—which until recently were united under a single bishop, the bishop of Pueblo; and groups coming according to a regular schedule from within these two bishoprics (Carlos M. Aguilar, *Nuestra Señora de Ocotlán, Tlaxcala*, 1966:234–241). The schedule for these inner-circle pilgrims reveals very clearly the communitas quality that lurks even within tight calendrical arrangements of pilgrimages. We found that sixty-four parishes took part in this annual cycle of pilgrimages. A parish (*parroquia*) often includes several villages (*pueblos*) and hamlets (*pueblitos*).

It is often, but not always, coextensive with the administrative unit known as a *municipio,* which may itself be divided into such units, depending on local nomenclature, as *barrios, pueblos, aldeas,* and *parajes.* The pilgrimage group is usually a brotherhood (*hermandad*) which may be associated with the whole parish or with one or more of its component territorial units. Its *raison d'être* is to provide a party to visit one of several pilgrimage centers once a year—only one parish brotherhood (that from the *pueblo* of San Juan Totolac in Tlaxcala state) visits Ocotlán twice in the liturgical year. It is not obligatory to go on a pilgrimage; an individual may go to fulfill a promise (*promesa*), a pledge or vow, made to the patron of the shrine in return for supernatural help believed to have been given in his own or a relative's affliction. A *promesa* may also be made in order to obtain a spiritual or temporal remedy in the future. The pilgrim may go to pray for help in need or to be cured of an ailment. He may go to offer thanks for a benefit received, or to obtain grace merely through visiting the shrine, touching holy objects there, and then rubbing his hands on his body or those of his children. Nevertheless, the fact that there is a regular annual pilgrimage ensures continuous interaction between the outlying parishes and the spiritual center of the region. Pilgrimages are, in a way, both instruments and indicators of a sort of mystical regionalism as well as of a mystical nationalism. On the greater feast days at Ocotlán, such as Quinquagesima Sunday in February, the Feast of the Patronage of Tlaxcala in July, and the Feast of the Immaculate Conception on December 8, pilgrims travel on an individual basis and assemble in tens of thousands from places far beyond the two inner bishoprics. But it is interesting to see how even in this organized inner core of corporate, structured units forming the central catchment area there is evidence of a leveling, equalizing tendency at work, of what I have called "normative communitas" (*The Ritual Process,* 1969, chapter 4).

To show this, we made a map of this inner catchment area (see Map 4). The southernmost parish, Chila de la Sal, is about 85

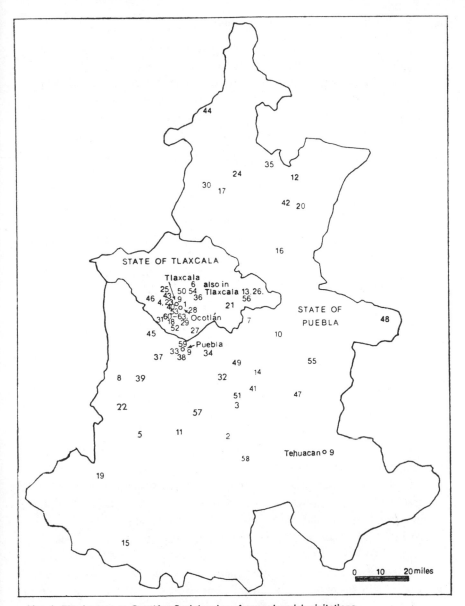

Map 4. Pilgrimages to Ocotlán: Serial order of annual parish visitations

miles from Ocotlán, the northernmost is about 80 miles, the most easterly nearly 75, while the westernmost, Huejotzingo, is only 16 miles from the shrine. This proximity is due to the orographic fact that the mighty volcanoes Popocatepetl and Ixtaccihuatl present formidable eastern barriers to pilgrims coming from the states of Mexico and Morelos—who in any case seem to fall more naturally, in terms of ecology and cultural tradition, within the catchment areas of the great pilgrimages centered upon Our Lady of Guadalupe and Chalma. Historically, too, the pilgrims from the inner circle seem to come mostly from within the limits of the pre-Columbian Tlaxcalan "republic," once allied with Cortés against the Aztecs. Here is perhaps an instance of what was formerly mystical nationalism, when Tlaxcala was an independent state. Pilgrims go almost pointedly to the ancient heartland near the city of Tlaxcala, although the major episcopal and hence church-structural center is now Puebla, historically and essentially still a Spanish and creole city. It was built after the Conquest according to a Hispanic city plan. One might almost regard the Virgin of Ocotlán as the Tlaxcalan answer to the Virgin of Guadalupe. Both, in fact, are said to have had similar miraculous origins, for the Virgin of Ocotlán appeared to a Tlaxcalan peasant named Juan Diego, about ten years after the Virgin of Guadalupe revealed herself to the Aztec Juan Diego, at Tepeyac. Shortly after the vision the Virgin's image was discovered by Franciscan missionaries, embedded in the trunk of a huge *ocote* pitch pine tree (whence Ocotlán), and Tlaxcalans believe that it is this statue of *ocote* wood which is today placed above the high altar in the basilica. But whereas the Guadalupan devotion was fostered by the secular clergy, according to Robert Ricard, author of *The Spiritual Conquest of Mexico* (1966:190), the Tlaxcalan devotion was encouraged from the beginning by the Franciscan order—which, indeed, has promoted the first growth of other important regional devotions, such as the cults of Our Lady of Zapópan at Guadalajara, Our Lady of Izamal in Yucatán, and of Our Lord of the Sacromonte at Amecameca. Much has yet to be written in terms of cultural dynamics about the complex interrelations between the secular church, the various missionary orders, each with its own subculture and style of organization, and the different indigenous Mexican peoples. The political anthropology of these relations also remains to be written.

To return to the map of the inner catchment area: the parishes sending pilgrim groups to Ocotlán were mapped and allocated numbers according to their order of departure for the shrine in the annual pilgrimage roster. There was a marked tendency to alternate near and far parishes, and those coming from south, north, and east. For example, if one considers successive pilgrimage journeys, one finds that in forty-three cases out of sixty-four these came alternately from the cardinal points and from the central area immediately around Ocotlán. If, for example, one considers the first fifteen journeys in the calendar year in terms of near and far parishes, the sequence runs: near, far, far, near, far, near, far, far, near, far, far, far, near, far, far, far. The last two sequences of three "far" parishes represent swings from east to south to north. Even when pilgrim groups come successively from the inner circle of parishes round Ocotlán, they come alternately from different compass directions. These data show how there is an attempt—here, probably, conscious and deliberate—to avoid the creation of solidary blocs of pilgrimage groups coming from the same subregion in successive waves. The same tendency may be observed in the rotation of market days in intervillage systems in Mexico today. A homogenizing and mixing process goes on, even at this level of the conscious ordering of pilgrim groups, in contrast to the segmentary *barrio* organization within villages and *municipios*.

On a grander scale the same is true of the Guadalupe pilgrimage system's organization. Here the major ecclesiastical units are dioceses, though parishes from all Mexico also send groups throughout the year. I was lucky enough to purchase, in Mexico City, runs of three magazines specializing in Guadalupan affairs for periods of approximately fifteen years, though with some serious lacunae. These are: *La Voz Guadalupana,* closest to the clergy; *Tepeyac,* the one with most quantitative information; and the popular devotional magazine *Juan Diego,* firmly and patriotically dedicated to the cause of the Aztec commoner whose cloak became the canvas for the miraculous painting. These various sources yielded much information about the kinds of pilgrimage groups that pay official visits to the basilica. From a partial processing of the data, the following list of pilgrim groups —taken from *Tepeyac*—visiting the basilica from January 13 to 31, 1951, is characteristic. On January 13, the parishes of Teoloyucán and Átlacomulco in the state of Mexico; on the 14th, the personnel of the Ejidal Bank, the personnel of a drugstore, the Union of Fishermen, and the personnel of a hotel; on the 16th, a group of neighbors from Peralvillo in the Federal District; on the 19th, the parishioners of Calítlahuaca, Mexico State; on the 23rd, the alumni of an engineering school; on the 25th, the parishioners of Tultepec, Mexico State; on the 26th, the guild (*corporación*) of the "Children of America"; on the 27th, the Congress of Catholic Schools, hopefully edified on this occasion by a sermon from the archbishop of Mexico; on the 28th, coachline workers, personnel of the Bank of Mexico, parishioners of Tultitlán, Mexico State, personnel of a printing and paper company, and of a candy and chocolate factory; finally, on the 31st, pilgrim students back from the 1950 Holy Year observances at Rome, under the leadership of the Society of Jesus. The lists include professional groups, such as architects, doctors, pharmacists, engineers, schoolteachers, and lawyers, as well as businessmen, bankers, journalists, and writers. In May 1951, there were pilgrimages by "Spanish bullfighters" and "nutrition students"! Diocesan parties, led by their own bishops, usually go on the same date each year: thus, the diocese of Zacatecas reaches the shrine at Tepeyac every September 10, that of León on October 15, of Aguascalientes on October 29, of Saltillo and San Luis Potosí on November 7, the Archdiocese of Oaxaca on May 12, and so on. The magazine *La Voz Guadalupana* also mentions that many family pilgrimages take place annually. These inventories of groups are supplemented by information about individual pilgrims. Sometimes their motives for visiting the Virgin of Guadalupe are given: for example, in November 1952 the matador "El Pito" went to thank her by offering her the prize he had won, with her aid, in the arena, probably the ears or tail of the slain bull! An air hostess attributed to a miracle by Our Lady the foiling of a "scandalous attempt" to rob the passengers and crew (thus jeopardizing their lives) of a Mexican Airlines plane on its way from Mexico City to Oaxaca. It is clear that mass media of communication and modern means of transportation have been absorbed into the pilgrimage system here as elsewhere, for example, at Lourdes and Mecca (see Rev. J. A. Shields, *Guide to Lourdes*, 1971:38, fn. 2, and Malcolm X, 1966:321). Indeed, the communitas character of pilgrimages and their capacity to evoke the loyalty of the most diverse types and groups of people to common aims—in contrast to many sectarian religious activities— are probably well adapted to the communications media of mass culture and large-scale societies, industrial perhaps even more than feudal. For example, during the eighteen days of the great fiesta of the Three Kings at Tizimín in Yucatán from December 31 to January 17, trains of twenty-four cars each leave Mérida Central Railroad station at short intervals every day, bearing their bulging loads of pilgrims, while from as far away as Mexico City motorists drive their automobiles to be blessed at the shrine! For the Three Kings were themselves great travelers in Mexican opinion and well knew the hazards of the public highways! Perhaps one of the most bizarre and at the same time heroic involvements with modern transportation is rather cryptically related in the August 12, 1947, issue of the popular newspaper *Excelsior*, cited in *Tepeyac:*

the widow Encarnación de Guerra of Copán, Honduras, is beginning a pilgrimage to Guadalupe on foot. . . . It is a penance precisely because she had lost a leg in a car accident [the paper rather characteristically does not mention whether she had an artificial limb!]. In

January of this year the Guerra family made a pilgrimage to the Sanctuary of the Cristo of Esquipulás in Guatemala, and the car in which they were traveling crashed into a deep ravine. The result of this catastrophe was the death of six of the seven passengers. After a long stay in a North American hospital, the lady, now a widow, recovered. For her deliverance from death, and as a result of a previous promise, she committed herself again to the mercy of the Guadalupana [the Dark Virgin]. Given the difficulties of a journey under these conditions, it is easy to imagine that the penitent has not designated a fixed date for her arrival at the end of the route. But her travels have already begun. The distance from Copán to Mexico City is more than 1500 kilometers.

It is not recorded whether the gallant, one-legged, and undeniably tragic lady ever made it to Mexico City, but it is certainly proverbial in Mexico that once one starts on a pilgrimage one should never turn back. For example, a major folk belief about the Chalma pilgrimage—which, on foot, is quite an arduous undertaking—is that if one complains about the journey and starts to return home, one will be turned into a stone. The same fate will befall couples who commit adultery on the way. But pious pilgrims say that if one kicks such transformed humans lavishly littering the road all the way to the shrine of Our Lord of Chalma they will finally be forgiven and changed back into men and women. And so every pilgrim kicks a few stones toward the shrine as he goes along. According to Ruben Reina (1966:176) the pilgrims traveling to Esquipulás in Guatemala have the same belief in punitive petrification. And it was to this shrine that the lady was traveling when she had her accident. Pilgrimages even have their perils for Americans, for, as one pilgrim remarked to John Hobgood on the road from Ocuilan to Chalma: "You know, there is even a stone they call *El Gringo de Chalma*. He was an American who laughed at our customs and was changed into a stone" (1970b:99).

A final example of synchronic arrangement in pilgrimage systems is provided by the annual fiesta, just mentioned, of the

Three Kings in eastern Yucatán. Here the major unit of pilgrimage is not the brotherhood or sodality (*hermandad*), but the religious guild (*gremio*). Robert Redfield has discussed the *gremio* briefly in *The Folk Culture of Yucatán* (1941:71, 161, 299), but has not commented on certain of its features that once more manifest what I have called the communitas bias of pilgrimages. The *gremio* or guild, which is more elaborately developed in Yucatán than in the rest of Mexico, seems to have been introduced by the Spanish as a direct copy of the European medieval guild. Otto von Simson writes of the European guild that there was "an intimate interconnection between religious and economic elements in the corporate life of artisans and merchants. It was usual for medieval guilds to place themselves under the protection of a patron saint and to join in the regular observation of certain devotional practices" (1962:167). We were assured by several citizens of Tizimín that "originally" (they did not know precisely when), the *gremio* in Tizimín was a "corporation" of workers in a particular trade or craft (*oficio*), and that it was obligatory to join it. Today the *gremios* are exclusively religious in function and organize the religious aspect of the great fiesta. Affiliation to *gremios* is voluntary, and many of their members come from outside Tizimín—in contrast to the *hermandades* or "brotherhoods" of central Mexico which draw their membership from the local people only. The governing body of the *gremio* is made up of a president, a secretary, and treasurer, and a variable number of committee members (*vocales*), any of whom can be strangers to the parish. One elected official is known as the *anfitrion* or "host," a curious term, for it is derived from the Amphitryon of classical legend who was cuckolded by Zeus. He has to be a permanent resident of Tizimín. In some *gremios* the "host" voluntarily takes on his role, to fulfill a promise (*promesa*) made to the three Holy Kings. His main duty is to give a banquet on the day of the fiesta, in which the members of his *gremio* traditionally take part—sometimes the feasters amount to as many as six to eight hundred people at a time. This means that from the time of his appointment, the host must acquire and fatten up pigs, turkeys, and other delicacies for the banquet. Two or three days before the *gremio*'s great day, female members or wives of members come to help with the preparation of the meal. The contributions of the members in cash, kind, and services all help to make the banquet possible. According to Redfield (1941:299) members are both men and women, and a term of membership consists of three years; some *gremios* are divided into sections, and it is possible that some of these have become independent *gremios* since Redfield's time, thus accounting for the increase in numbers of *gremios*, from nine to twelve. Redfield further suggests that all the members of a section sometimes came from the same town or village or from Mérida, the capital city of Yucatán. This arrangement recalls the corporate organization at Ocotlán and Mérida and indicates the centralizing function of Tizimín for Yucatán—and indeed far beyond, for Campeche, Quintana Roo, and even parts of Guatemala and Honduras, in fact for the old Maya *oikoumene*.

The *gremio* offices may be held more than once—again in contrast with other systems of religious government, for example, of the *mayordomia* type—at the local level. Sometimes, however, they remain under the control of a single family.

Variation also characterizes the names of the *gremios*. There are several criteria of nomenclature. Sometimes sex and civic status is determinative of the title, as in the Gremio de Señoras and the Gremio de Señoritas, though men may belong to these; sometimes it is occupation, as in the Gremio de Agricultores (the farmers' guild); other *gremios* are named after religious personages or figures, such as the Gremio of Leo XIII, and the Gremio of the Holy Kings. It was hard for us to discover in a two-day visit just how many guilds there were. Redfield had mentioned nine, but several of our informants, declared there were twelve. They were only able to give us six names though— the five just mentioned plus the traders' guild (Gremio de Vendedores).

All agreed, however, that each guild was responsible for one of the days of the fiesta, and that this was always on the same date every year, so that the members could make preparations well in advance.

As well as being open, varied, and flexible, the guild system of Tizimín betrays its liminal and communitas character or style in the degree to which it is independent of the institutionalized church. Structurally, the parish priest has little to do with the guilds. Certainly, he has no jurisdiction over their affairs, for he belongs to none of them. This is not due to any ecclesiastical rule, but simply because, as one priest, Father "Panchito" Puc, a volatile, elfin figure, but highly intelligent, told us, if he belonged to one he would have to belong to all, and this would be tantamount to belonging to none. In fact, his role is complementary to theirs. The guild has to assist him, for he says their special mass for them, thus providing their religious *raison d'être*. In a sense, its other functions, solemn and festive, devolve from this sacred legitimation. Despite its significance, however, interaction between guild and priest is restricted; the priest's role is sacerdotal rather than pastoral, structural rather than intimate. As in many other aspects of Mexican religious life, the *pueblo*, both as people and as locality, has a high degree of autonomy from the secular clergy. This seems indeed to be especially the case in the pilgrimage domain. Traditional pilgrimages continue to operate— with the help of modern technology—as though the pilgrims had never heard of ecclesiastical modernization or renewal.

The fiesta of the Three Kings lasts for eighteen days conceptualized as two successive novenas of nine days apiece. The first novena stresses the religious, the second the commercial and festive aspects of the total situation, which contains, as pilgrimage celebrations do the world over, three major foci in space/time. These are solemnity, festivity, and trade, all three representing different types of liminal disengagement from day-to-day participation in structural role playing and status incumbency, and three types of voluntaristic activity. In Tizimín, it would seem that the guilds are most prominent during the first novena which culminates on January 8, the principal day of the fiesta. This date is itself an interesting example of how the numerical logic of the popularly controlled feast, in a thoroughly Mayan fashion, has taken precedence over the church's liturgical calendar, where, of course, January 6, Epiphany, is, properly speaking, the Feast of the Three Kings or Magi.

It is, to my mind, plausible that originally there were nine guilds, as Redfield wrote, but that their number has been increased to twelve subsequently as the fiesta has continued to grow in popularity and to acquire something of the character of a trade fair. This is particularly true of the second novena, for it is at this time that the local government maximizes its participation in the running of the fiesta. Redfield (pp. 298–299) has vividly described how the officers of the Tizimín town government appoint a commission from political favorites to hire musicians to play at the *jaranas*, the national folk dances of Yucatán, and at the rodeos and bullfights. To obtain funds for these activities, the commission holds an auction at Christmas and disposes of the various concessions involved in the fiesta: "the *corridas* (bullfights), the *vaquerías* (including the *jarana*, or national dance of Yucatán), the merry-go-round, the 'wheel of fortune' (the ferriswheel), and forty or fifty 'locations' (*puestos*) in the market place at which the buyers are entitled to sell food or drink or operate gambling tables." Redfield reports that although the net profits accruing to the commission are supposed to be handed over to the municipal treasury to pay for public improvements (in accordance, one might think, with the communitas spirit of the whole occasion), it is widely held that a part "remains in the pockets of the commission." And this may not be too wildly far from the truth.

According to our informants, January 8 is the high spot of the fiesta, and attendance begins to decline after this midpoint, which is the culmination of the *fiesta sagrada*, the religious novena. Matters were perhaps different in Redfield's time—in the 1920's and 1930's, during and just after the antireligious regimen of President Plutarco Calles—when the "fiesta of Tizimín [was] . . . a business enterprise so arranged as to make it possible for the genuinely pious also to take part" (1941:299–300). Today, as in other pilgrimage centers, there appears to have taken place at Tizimín a resurgence of the religious component—perhaps because pilgrimage represents a final defense for folk Catholicism against the iconoclastic and rationalizing modernization now going on in the structured church. Perhaps it represents a reaction and an alternative to the depersonalizing and anomic tendencies in modern industrial and bureaucratic organization and may not be unconnected with the "retribalization" processes described by Abner Cohen (1969) and S. N. Eisenstadt in several monographs. The Maya, at any rate, seem to be more than ever proud today of being Maya. And being Maya includes being pilgrims to Maya Christian shrines.

It is possible on the evidence before me to make a few generalizations about the symbolism of Mexican pilgrimage centers. In the first place, the greatest shrines, as opposed to village or *barrio santos*, seem to be devoted to universalized and supernatural father and mother figures, for Christ is almost everywhere regarded as a "Father God" rather than as "God the Son," for example, at Chalma and Sacromonte. Second, they are frequently connected with natural features, such as hills, mountains, caves, wells, and springs. Third, in Mexico, several of the most important Christian centers of pilgrimage are located at or near the major pre-Columbian pagan centers of pilgrimage. Fourth, and as an extension of this tendency to superimpose later upon earlier structures, many centers are composite in character, containing not one shrine, chapel, or other edifice, but several, each constructed at a different period in the pilgrimage's history. Usually, at such centers, too, the approach to a major shrine is demarcated by a sequence of minor shrines; often these take the form of the fourteen Stations of the Cross or the fifteen Mysteries of the Holy Rosary. Frequently, but not always, these structured approaches are up a hill, to represent the soul's ascent through penance and patience. Fifth, Guadalupe has a special, unique place in the system shared by no other center; in its shrine complex there is neither direct nor indirect reference to any other Mexican pilgrimage devotion, whereas at *every* other center there are shrines, paintings, or statues devoted to the Dark Virgin, indicating her position as the dominant symbol of Mexican mystical nationalism, and beyond this, I suggest, of a Catholic communitas extending beyond the boundaries of the present and past Mexican political systems. In some towns, as, for example, Culiacán in Sinaloa state, there is an exact facsimile of the spatial structure of the Mexico City devotion, dedicated to Our Lady of Guadalupe, with a basilica located on a hill outside the town, and a pilgrim's way, flanked by shrines representing the mysteries of the rosary, leading to it, just as there is in the national capital. This recalls the pre-Columbian practice of building cities on a cosmological plan, recently demonstrated for many ancient civilizations by Paul Wheatley (1971); the layout of buildings and quarters on the ground replicates the major modes of cosmological classification, translating a cognitive into a spatial arrangement of parts—as do the divisions of the Aztec and Maya calendrical cycles (see John Ingham, "Time and Space in Ancient Mexico," 1971) Provincial towns, again, in their layout tend to replicate the master plan of the capital. This would be another example at a different cultural level of the conservation of the past in the present, with Guadalupe as the spiritual capital of the pilgrimage system. At this changed post-Columbian level, though, the system has come to symbolize the widest, most generic bond between Mexicans—like the Earth shrines of the Tallensi—rather than to represent the segmental oppositions and power cleavages of a sociopolitical structure. The pilgrimage system is at once an instrument and an expression of normative communitas.

Sixth, for those many pilgrims who travel on foot and donkeyback, the traditional way of going to a major pilgrimage center is very important in itself. One gains more merit or grace by ignoring modern means of transportation. More important than this, as John Hobgood has written with reference to the Zapotec Indians of the Isthmus of Tehuantepec, who travel for over a month to visit the great Cristo of Chalma near Mexico City, "it is considered essential to visit sacred way-stations on the way to Chalma, and if it has been important to make the pilgrimage by following exactly the same route every year, since before the time of the Spanish conquest, then it may be possible to gain additional information on how both *ideas* and *trade goods* moved back and forth throughout Mesoamerica" (1970a:2). Hobgood himself traveled with a party of Otomí Indians from the town of Huizquilucán, near the shrine of Our Lady of the Remedies, just west of Mexico City, all the way to Chalma on foot and confirmed that there were indeed sacred way stations which appeared to be connected with pre-Columbian archeological sites (see Map 4). But here, once more, there has probably been convergence with the European pilgrimage pattern, for there grew up established routes to the great European shrines—and these also passed through a number of sacred way stations. As in Mexico, too, hostelries, hospitals, and markets grew and flourished beside these routes stimulated by the flow of pilgrims. In his book, *The Road to Santiago* (1965:6–7), Walter Starkie provides an excellent map of the network of routes leading to Compostella in northwestern Spain where the important pilgrimage shrine of St. James the Apostle was located. These routes, which brought pilgrims from Germany, England, and the Low Countries, as well as from Spain and France, were each punctuated with lesser pilgrimage centers and with abbeys, churches, and hospitals to cater for the spiritual and material needs of pilgrims. Yet here, too, as always in considering pilgrimages, we must beware of too narrow a view. The Indian and Muslim pilgrimages for which I have evidence exhibit the same picture of a multiplicity of routes converging on a great shrine, each lined with sacred way stations (see Map 2). It is as though such shrines exerted a magnetic effect on a whole communications system, charging up with sacredness many of its geographical features and attributes and fostering the construction of sacred and secular edifices to service the needs of the human stream passing along its arterial routes. Pilgrimage centers, in fact, generate a "field." I am tempted to speculate whether they have played at least as important a role in the growth of cities, markets, and roads as economic and political factors. Certainly, Otto von Simson has argued that the "religious impulse was so all-pervading an element of medieval life that even the entire economic structure depended upon it. Almost static otherwise, the economy received from religious customs and experiences the impulse it needed for its growth" (*The Gothic Cathedral*, 1962:170). He cites the growth of Chartres, Canterbury, Toledo, and Compostella, all major pilgrimage centers in the period of Gothic architecture, in support of this view. If the Protestant ethic was a precondition of capitalism, perhaps the pilgrimage ethic helped to create the communications net that later made capitalism a viable national and international system. Recently, Ralph della Cava (1970) has shown how the backland hamlet of Joaseiro in Brazil's impoverished northeast has increased in population from 2,500 to about 80,000 between 1889 and the present day. This sensational demographic growth has been almost entirely due to the development of the town as a pilgrimage center, as the result of an alleged miracle whose authenticity was sternly denied by the official representatives of the Catholic church, both in Brazil and Rome. In ancient Mexico, it is likely that several important Maya cities developed because they were pre-Christian pilgrimage centers. For example, J. Eric S. Thompson writes of several important Maya cities, such as Chichén Itzá, Cozumel, and Izamal, that they possessed sacred wells or *cenotes* which formed "the focal point of pilgrimages" (1967:133). "To these places," he writes, "came immense concourses of pilgrims, many of them from quite distant parts" (p. 135). The first bishop of Yucatán, the Franciscan, Landa, compares the pilgrimages to Chichén Itzá and Cozumel with the

Christian pilgrimages to Rome and Jerusalem. "Furthermore, Izamal, as the home of Kinichkakmo, a manifestation of the sun god, and of Itzamna, one of the greatest of Maya gods, was also a most important shrine" (p. 135). We shall have more to say about Izamal elsewhere; it was for centuries the most important Christian pilgrimage center in Yucatán, dedicated not to gods but to the Christian Mother of God. If we take this view that pilgrimages sometimes generate cities and consolidate regions, we need not abandon the view that they are sometimes also the ritualized vestiges of former sociopolitical systems. There may well be a process going on here by which, under certain conditions, communitas petrifies into politico-economic structure but may be regenerated as a communitas center when a new alternative politico-economic center develops or forcibly replaces the old. The new secular structure enters into a complementary relationship with the old structure, which then becomes sacralized and infused with liminal communitas. Former centrality has become peripherality, but peripherality may then become the setting for new centrality, as waves of pilgrims invade, and many settle near the peripheral shrines. But new pilgrimage shrines are constantly coming into existence as rumors of miracle workers and saints and their therapeutic deeds spread among the masses. These shrines may be situated in new locations. It remains a problem for intensive investigation to study the conditions under which such folk devotions survive until they become established pilgrimages legitimated by the authorities of the religious system in whose field of beliefs they have sprung up. This is where such historical studies as Ralph della Cava's are so valuable. Failure to survive is just as important an anthropological problem as survival. I am at present inclined to favor the view that a pilgrimage's best chance of survival is when it imparts to religious orthodoxy a renewed vitality, rather than when it asserts against an established system a set of heterodox opinions and unprecedented styles of religious and symbolic action. In this latter situation one finds sects, heresies, and millenarian movements, but not pilgrimage centers. The old has to be shown to be still alive if pilgrimages are to develop and to be still capable of producing miracles; but it must patently remain the traditional, even if the pilgrimage devotion renovates certain areas of tradition that have lapsed into latency or near oblivion for decades or even centuries. Religions persist as cultural systems partly because popular interest and energy are not equally distributed at all times over all their levels and sectors, but at each epoch get focused on one or a few. The rest are not abandoned or obliterated but remain unmanifest, or at a low pulse, until they are quickened again by popular devotions—which are only seeming novelties or challenges to the total system, but in the long run show themselves to be among its maintenance mechanisms. It may also be the case, as we have seen, that those pilgrimage centers which survive and thrive have been grafted onto even older centers, like scions on mentors. This would be true for Guadalupe, Chalma, Izamal, and Ocotlán, at least, in Mexico. Such a superimposition may involve a conscious rejection at the same time as an unconscious acceptance of the old religion. What is here rejected is the former structure, declared anathema; what is tacitly accepted is the perennial communitas, no longer normative (for the norms are consciously rejected) but seen as promising renewed true fellowship.

References

Aguilar, Carlos M. 1966. *Nuestra Señora de Ocotlán, Tlaxcala.* Tlaxcala.
Burton, Sir Richard. 1964. *Personal Narrative of a Pilgrimage to Al-Madinah and Meccah.* 2 vols. New York: Dover. First published 1893.
Cava, Ralph della. 1970. *Miracle at Joaseiro.* New York: Columbia University Press.
Cohen, Abner. 1969. *Custom and Politics in Urban Africa.* London: Routledge & Kegan Paul.

Deleury, G. A. 1960. *The Cult of Vithoba*. Poona: Sangam Press.

Dowse, Ivor. 1963. *The Pilgrim Shrines of England*. London: Faith Press.

——. 1964. *The Pilgrim Shrines of Scotland*. London: Faith Press.

Evans-Pritchard, E. E. 1948. *The Divine Kingship of the Shilluk of the Nilotic Sudan*. Cambridge: Cambridge University Press.

Excelsior. August 12, 1947. Mexico City (Daily newspaper.)

Fortes, Meyer. 1945. *The Dynamics of Clanship among the Tallensi*. London: Oxford University Press.

Garbett, G. Kingsley. 1963. "Religious Aspects of Political Succession among the Valley Korekore." In *The History of the Central African Peoples*, eds. E. Stokes and R. Brown. Lusaka: Government Press.

Gennep, Arnold van. 1960. *The Rites of Passage*. London: Routledge & Kegan Paul. First published 1908.

Gluckman, Max. 1965. *Politics, Law and Ritual in Tribal Society*. Oxford: Blackwell.

Hansa, Bhagwan Shri. 1934. *The Holy Mountain*. London: Faber and Faber.

Hobgood, John. 1970a. *A Pilgrimage to Chalma*. Huixquilucan Project, Working Papers No. 12. Madison: University of Wisconsin.

——. 1970b. *Chalma: A Study in Directed Cultural Change*. Huixquilucan Project, Working Papers No. 14. Madison: University of Wisconsin.

Ingham, John. 1971. "Time and Space in Ancient Mexico," *Man* 6 (December):615–629.

Jarett, Dom Bede. 1911. "Pilgrimage." In *The Catholic Encyclopedia*, ed. Charles G. Herbermann. New York: Appleton.

Jiménez, Luz. 1968. *De Porfirio Díaz a Zapata: Memoria Nahuatl de Milpa Alta*. Mexico City: Universidad Nacional Autónoma Mexicana, Instituto de Investigaciones Historicas.

Juan Diego. Published monthly in Mexico City.

Karve, Irawati. 1962. "On the Road: A Maharashtrian Pilgrimage," *Asian Studies* 22 (November):13–29.

Lewis, B. 1966. "Hadjdj." In *The Encyclopedia of Islam*. Leiden: Brill.

Maine, Henry. 1861. *Ancient Law*. London: Murray.

Malcolm X. 1966. *Autobiography of Malcolm X*. New York: Grove.

Milburn, R. L. P. 1963. Foreword to *The Pilgrim Shrines of England*, by I. Dowse. London: Faith Press.

Newett, M. Margaret. 1907. *Canon Pietro Casola's Pilgrimage to Jerusalem*. Manchester: University Press.

Nutini, Hugo G. 1968. *San Bernardino Contla*. Pittsburgh: University of Pittsburgh Press.

Oursel, Raymond. 1963. *Les Pèlerins du Moyen Age*. Paris: Fayard.

Peacock, James L., and A. Thomas Kirsch. 1970. *The Human Direction*. New York: Appleton-Century-Crofts.

Redfield, Robert. 1941. *The Folk Culture of Yucatan*. Chicago: University of Chicago Press.

Reina, Ruben. 1966. *The Law of the Saints*. Indianapolis and New York: Bobbs-Merrill.

Ricard, Robert. 1966. *The Spiritual Conquest of Mexico*. Los Angeles and Berkeley: University of California Press.

Romano, V., O. I. 1965. "Charismatic Medicine, Folk-Healing, and Folk-Sainthood," *American Anthropologist* 67 (October):1151–1173.

Shields, Rev. J. A. 1971. *Guide to Lourdes*. Dublin: Gill.

Simson, Otto von. 1962. *The Gothic Cathedral*. New York: Harper Torchbooks. First published 1956.

Singer, Isadore, ed. 1964. *Jewish Encyclopedia*. New York: Ktav.

Starkie, Walter. 1965. *The Road to Santiago*. Berkeley: University of California Press.

Tepeyac. Published monthly in Mexico City.

Thompson, J. Eric S. 1967. *The Rise and Fall of Maya Civilization*. Norman, Oklahoma: University of Oklahoma Press.

Turner, Victor. 1969. *The Ritual Process: Structure and Anti-structure*. Chicago: Aldine.

Voz Guadalupana, La. Published monthly in Mexico City.

Watts, Francis. 1917. *Canterbury Pilgrims and Their Ways*. London: Methuen.

Wensinck, A. J. 1966. "Hadjdj." In *The Encyclopedia of Islam*. Leiden: Brill.

Wheatley, Paul. 1971. *Pivot of the Four Quarters*. Chicago: Aldine.

Yang, C. K. 1961. *Religion in Chinese Society*. Berkeley: University of California Press.

CHAPTER 6

Passages, Margins, and Poverty: Religious Symbols of Communitas[1]

This chapter is concerned with the study of a modality of social interrelatedness which I have called "communitas" in my book *The Ritual Process*, and which I oppose to the concept of social structure. Communitas is a fact of everyone's experience, yet it has almost never been regarded as a reputable or coherent object of study by social scientists. It is, however, central to religion, literature, drama, and art, and its traces may be found deeply engraven in law, ethics, kinship, and even economics. It becomes visible in tribal rites of passage, in millenarian movements, in monasteries, in the counterculture, and on countless informal occasions. In this chapter I shall try to define more explicitly what I mean by "communitas" and by "structure." Something should be said about the kind of cultural phenomena that started me on this quest for communitas. Three aspects of culture seemed to me to be exceptionally well endowed with ritual symbols and beliefs of non-social-structural type. These may be described, respectively, as liminality, outsiderhood, and structural inferiority.

Liminality is a term borrowed from Arnold van Gennep's formulation of *rites de passage*, "transition rites"—which accompany every change of state or social position, or certain points in age. These are marked by three phases: separation, margin (or

[1] First read at a conference at Dartmouth College on Myth and Ritual, August 1967, and first published in a revised form in *Worship* 46 (Aug.-Sept. 1972):390–412; (Oct):432–494.

limen—the Latin for threshold, signifying the great importance of real or symbolic thresholds at this middle period of the rites, though *cunicular*, "being in a tunnel," would better describe the quality of this phase in many cases, its hidden nature, its sometimes mysterious darkness), and reaggregation.

The first phase, separation, comprises symbolic behavior signifying the detachment of the individual or the group from either an earlier fixed point in the social structure or from an established set of cultural conditions (a "state"). During the intervening liminal period, the state of the ritual subject (the "passenger," or "liminar,") becomes ambiguous, neither here nor there, betwixt and between all fixed points of classification; he passes through a symbolic domain that has few or none of the attributes of his past or coming state. In the third phase the passage is consummated and the ritual subject, the neophyte or initiand reenters the social structure, often, but not always at a higher status level. Ritual degradation occurs as well as elevation. Courts martial and excommunication ceremonies create and represent descents, not elevations. Excommunication rituals were performed in the narthex or porch of a church, not in the nave or main body, from which the excommunicated was being expelled symbolically. But in liminality, the symbolism almost everywhere indicates that the initiand (*initiare*, "to begin"), novice (*novus*, "new," "fresh"), or neophyte (νεος-φυτον, "newly grown") is structurally if not physically invisible in terms of his culture's standard definitions and classifications. He has been divested of the outward attributes of structural position, set aside from the main arenas of social life in a seclusion lodge or camp, and reduced to an equality with his fellow initiands regardless of their preritual status. I would argue that it is in liminality that communitas emerges, if not as a spontaneous expression of sociability, at least in a cultural and normative form—stressing equality and comradeship as norms rather than generating spontaneous and existential communitas, though of course spontaneous communitas may and does arise in most cases of protracted initiation ritual.

As well as the betwixt-and-between state of liminality there is the state of outsiderhood, referring to the condition of being either permanently and by ascription set outside the structural arrangements of a given social system, or being situationally or temporarily set apart, or voluntarily setting oneself apart from the behavior of status-occupying, role-playing members of that system. Such outsiders would include, in various cultures, shamans, diviners, mediums, priests, those in monastic seclusion, hippies, hoboes, and gypsies. They should be distinguished from "marginals," who are simultaneously members (by ascription, optation, self-definition, or achievement) of two or more groups whose social definitions and cultural norms are distinct from, and often even opposed to, one another (see Stonequist, Thomas, and Znaniecki). These would include migrant foreigners, second-generation Americans, persons of mixed ethnic origin, parvenus (upwardly mobile marginals), the déclassés (downwardly mobile marginals), migrants from country to city, and women in a changed, nontraditional role. What is interesting about such marginals is that they often look to their group of origin, the so-called inferior group, for communitas, and to the more prestigious group in which they mainly live and in which they aspire to higher status as their structural reference group. Sometimes they become radical critics of structure from the perspective of communitas, sometimes they tend to deny the affectually warmer and more egalitarian bond of communitas. Usually they are highly conscious and self-conscious people and may produce from their ranks a disproportionately high number of writers, artists, and philosophers. David Riesman's concept of "secret" marginality where there are people who subjectively fail to feel the identities expected of them seems to overinflate the concept (1954:154). Marginals like liminars are also betwixt and between, but unlike ritual liminars they have no cultural assurance of a final stable resolution of their ambiguity. Ritual liminars are often moving symbolically to a higher status, and their being stripped of status temporarily is a "ritual," an "as-if," or "make-believe" stripping dictated by cultural requirements.

The third major aspect of culture that is of concern to the

student of religion and symbolism is "structural inferiority." This again may be an absolute or a relative, a permanent or a transient matter. Especially in caste or class systems of social stratification we have the problem of the lowest status, of the outcast, the unskilled worker, the *harijan*, and the poor. A rich mythology has grown around the poor, as also has the "pastoral" genre of literature (according to W. Empson); and in religion and art, the peasant, the beggar, the *harijan*, Gandhi's "children of God," the despised and rejected in general, have often been assigned the symbolic function of representing humanity, without status qualifications or characteristics. Here the lowest represents the human total, the extreme case most fittingly portrays the whole. In many tribal or preliterate societies, with little in the way of stratification along class lines, structural inferiority often emerges as a value-bearer whenever structural strength is dichotomously opposed to structural weakness. For example, many African societies have been formed by militarily more powerful incomers conquering the indigenous people. The invaders control high political office, such as the kingship, provincial governorships, and headmanships. On the other hand, the indigenous people, through their leaders, frequently are held to have a mystical power over the fertility of the earth and of all upon it. These autochthonous people have religious power, the "power of the weak" as against the jural-political power of the strong, and represent the undivided land itself as against the political system with its internal segmentation and hierarchies of authority. Here the model of an undifferentiated whole whose units are total human beings is posited against that of a differentiated system, whose units are status and roles, and where the social persona is segmentalized into positions in a structure. One is oddly reminded of those Gnostic notions of an extraterrestrial "fall" in which an originally undivided "Human Form Divine" became divided into conflicting functions, each incompletely human and dominated by a single propensity, "intellect," "desire," "craftsmanship," and so on, no longer in orderly harmonious balance with the others.

A similar contrast may be found, in societies based primarily on kinship, between the "hard" legal *line* of descent, patrilineal or matrilineal, through which authority, property, and social placement pass, and the "soft," "affectional" side of the family through the parent of so-called "complementary filiation," mother's side in patrilineal systems, father's side in matrilineal systems. This *side*, as distinct from the legal *line*, is often attributed with mystical power over a person's total welfare. Thus in many patrilineal societies, the mother's brother has powers of cursing or blessing his sister's child, but no legal power. In others, the mother's kin may act as a sanctuary against paternal harshness. A man is, in any case, more clearly an individual in relation to his kin of complementary filiation, or of what Meyer Fortes calls the "submerged side of descent" (1949:32) than he is to his lineal kin, for whom he is importantly a bundle of jural rights and obligations.

In this chapter I will examine several aspects of the relationship between liminality, outsiderhood, and structural inferiority, and show in the course of it something of the dialectical relationship over time between communitas and structure. But if we are to say that a process such as ritualization tends to occur frequently in the interstices or on the edges of something, we have to be fairly clear about what that something is. What *is* social structure? The term "structure" is, of course, commonly employed in all analytical sciences, and even in geology, which is mainly taxonomic or descriptive. It evokes architectural images, of houses awaiting inhabitants, or bridges with struts and piles; or it may invoke the bureaucratic image of desks with pigeon holes—each hole being a status, and some being more important than others.

The social sciences, like biology, are partly analytical and partly descriptive; the result is that there is wide variation in the meaning of structure in the work of anthropologists and sociologists. Some regard structure as primarily a description of repeated patterns of action, that is, of an observable uniformity of action or operation, of something "out there," capable of being empirically observed and, hopefully, measured. This viewpoint, represented most prominently in anthropology by the work of Radcliffe-Brown and his British followers, has been severely criticized by Lévi-Strauss, who holds that social structures are "entities independent of men's consciousness of them (although they in fact govern men's existence)" (1963:121). All that can be directly observed in societies, he says, is "a series of expressions, each partial and incomplete, of the same underlying *structure*, which they reproduce in several copies without ever completely exhausting its realities." Lévi-Strauss asserts that

if the structure can be seen it will not be at the . . . empirical level, but at a deeper one, previously neglected; that of those unconscious categories that we may hope to reach, by bringing together domains which, at first sight, appear disconnected to the observer; on the one hand, the social system as it actually works, and on the other, the manner in which, through their myths, their rituals and their religious representations, men try to hide or to justify the discrepancies between their society and the ideal image of it which they harbor [1960:53].

He taxes Radcliffe-Brown for his "ignorance of hidden realities" and for believing that structure is of the order of empirical observation when in fact it is beyond it.

But it is not with Lévi-Strauss's concept of "social" structure, really cognitive structure, that I wish to begin this analysis. Nor shall I invoke here the concept of structure as "statistical categories," or regard "structural" as what Edmund Leach has called "the statistical outcome" of multiple individual choices. Sartre's view of structure as "a complex dialectic of freedom and inertia," where "the formation and maintenance of each group is contingent on the free engagement of each individual in its joint activities" (L. Rosen on Sartre in "Language, History, and the Logic of Inquiry in Lévi-Strauss and Sartre," 1971:281) is closer to my own theoretical position, though it is not what I mean by structure in this argument. What I intend to convey by social structure here—and what is implicitly regarded as the frame of social order in most societies—is not a system of unconscious categories, but quite simply, in Robert Mertonian terms, "the patterned arrangements of role-sets, status-sets, and status-sequences" *consciously* recognized and regularly operative in a given society. These are closely bound up with legal and political norms and sanctions. By "role-sets" Robert Merton designates "the actions and relationships that flow from a social status"; "status-sets" refers to the probable congruence of various positions occupied by an individual; and "status-sequences" means the probable succession of positions occupied by an individual through time. Thus, for me, *liminality* represents the midpoint of transition in a status-sequence between two positions, *outsiderhood* refers to actions and relationships which do not flow from a recognized social status but originate outside it, while *lowermost status* refers to the lowest rung in a system of social stratification in which unequal rewards are accorded to functionally differentiated positions. A "class system," for example, would be a system of this type.

Nevertheless, Lévi-Strauss's concept of "unconscious social structure" as a structure of relationships between the elements of myth and rituals must enter into our reckoning when we consider liminal ritual phenomena. Here I must pause to consider once more the difference between structure and communitas. Implicitly or explicitly, in societies at all levels of complexity, a contrast is posited between the notion of society as a differentiated, segmented system of structural positions (which may or may not be arranged in a hierarchy), and society as a homogeneous, undifferentiated *whole*. The first model approximates to the preliminary picture I have presented of "social structure." Here the units are statuses and roles, not concrete human individuals. The individual is segmentalized into roles which he plays. Here the unit is what Radcliffe-Brown has called the *persona*, the role-mask, not the unique individual. The second model, communitas, often appears culturally in the guise of an Edenic, paradisiacal, utopian, or millennial state of affairs, to the attainment of which religious or political action, personal or collective, should be directed. Society is pictured as a communitas of free and equal comrades—of total persons. "Societas," or "society," as we all experience it, is a process involving both social structure and communitas, separately and united in varying proportions.

Even where there is no mythical or pseudohistorical account of such a state of affairs, rituals may be performed in which egalitarian and cooperative behavior is characteristic, and in which secular distinctions of rank, office, and status are temporarily in abeyance or regarded as irrelevant. On these ritual occasions, anthropologists who have previously, from repeated observations of behavior and interviews with informants in nonritual situations, built up a model of the socioeconomic structure cannot fail to note how persons deeply divided from one another in the secular or nonreligious world nevertheless in certain ritual situations cooperate closely to ensure what is believed to be the maintenance of a cosmic order which transcends the contradictions and conflicts inherent in the mundane social system. Here we have an unstated model of communitas, an operational model. Practically all rituals of any length and complexity represent a passage from one position, constellation, or domain of structure to another. In this regard they may be said to possess "temporal structure" and to be dominated by the notion of time.

But in passing from structure to structure many rituals pass through communitas. Communitas is almost always thought of or portrayed by actors as a timeless condition, an eternal now, as "a moment in and out of time," or as a state to which the structural view of time is not applicable. Such is frequently the character of at least parts of the seclusion periods found in many protracted initiation rites. Such is the character, too, I have found, of pilgrimage journeys in several religions. In ritual seclusion, for example, one day replicates another for many weeks. The novices in tribal initiations waken and rest at fixed hours, often at sunrise and sunset, as in the monastic life in Christianity and Buddhism. They receive instruction in tribal lore, or in singing and dancing from the same elders or adepts at the same time. At other set times they may hunt or perform routine tasks under the eyes of the elders. Every day is, in a sense, the same day, writ large or repeated. Then again, seclusion and liminality may contain what Eliade calls "a time of marvels." Masked figures, representing gods, ancestors, or chthonic powers may appear to the novices or neophytes in grotesque, monstrous, or beautiful forms. Often, but not always, myths are recited explaining the origin, attributes, and behavior of these strange and sacred habitants of liminality. Again, sacred objects may be shown to the novices. These may be quite simple in form like the bone, top, ball, tambourine, apples, mirror, fan, and woolly fleece displayed in the lesser Eleusinian mysteries of Athens. Such *sacra*, individually or in various combinations, may be the foci of hermeneutics or religious interpretations, sometimes in the form of myths, sometimes of gnomic utterances hardly less enigmatic than the visible symbols they purport to explain. These symbols, visual and auditory, operate culturally as mnemonics, or as communications engineers would no doubt have it, as "storage bins" of information, not about pragmatic techniques, but about cosmologies, values, and cultural axioms, whereby a society's deep knowledge is transmitted from one generation to another. Such a device, in the setting of "a place that is not a place, and a time that is not a time" (as the Welsh folklorist and sociologist Alwyn Rees once described for me the context of Celtic bardic utterance), is all the more necessary in cultures without writing, where the whole cultural deposit has to be transmitted either through speech or by repeated observation of standardized behavioral patterns and artifacts. And I am beginning to wonder whether it is not the structuring of functionless elements in myth and ritual patterns which preserves such elements through centuries until they find a socioeconomic milieu in which they may become functional again—as the Cruzob replicated pre-Columbian Maya social organization in Quintana Roo during the War of the Castas in nineteenth-century Yucatán, described by Nelson Reed in his exciting book *The Caste War of Yucatan*. Major liminal situations are occasions on which a society *takes cognizance of itself*, or rather where, in an interval between their incumbency of specific fixed positions, members of that society may obtain an approximation, however limited, to a global view of man's place in the cosmos and his relations with other classes of visible and invisible entities. Also, importantly, in myth and ritual an individual undergoing passage may learn the total pattern of social relations involved in his transition and how it changes. He may, therefore, learn about social structure in communitas. This view need not depend heavily on explicit teaching, on verbal explanations. In many societies it seems to be enough that neophytes learn to become aware of the multiple relationships existing between the *sacra* and other aspects of their culture, or learn from the positioning of sacred symbols in a structure of relationships—which are above, which are below; which are on the left, which are on the right; which are inside, which are outside, or from their prominent attributes, such as sex, color, texture, density, temperature—how critical aspects of cosmos and society are interrelated and the hierarchy of such modes of interlinkage. The neophytes may learn what Lévi-Strauss calls the "sensory codes" underlying the details of myth and ritual and the homologues between events and objects described in different codes—visual, auditory, and tactile. The medium here is the message, and the medium is nonverbal, though often meticulously structured.

It can be seen from all this that there is a certain inadequacy in the contrast I have just made between the concepts "structure" and "communitas." For clearly the liminal situation of communitas is heavily invested with a structure of a kind. But this is not a social structure in the Radcliffe-Brownian sense but one of symbols and ideas, an instructional structure. It is not too difficult to detect here a Lévi-Straussian structure, a way of inscribing in the mentalities of neophytes generative rules, codes, and media whereby they can manipulate the symbols of speech and culture to confer some degree of intelligibility on an experience that perpetually outstrips the possibilities of linguistic (and other cultural) expression. Within this, one can find what Lévi-Strauss would call "a concrete logic," and behind this, again, a fundamental structure of human mentality or even of the human brain itself. In order to implant this instructional structure firmly in the minds of neophytes it seems necessary that they should be stripped of structural attributes in the social, legalistic, or political sense of the term. Simpler societies seem to feel that only a person temporarily without status, property, rank, or office is fit to receive the tribal gnosis or occult wisdom which is in effect knowledge of what the tribespeople regard as the deep structure of culture and indeed of the universe. The content of such knowledge, is, of course, dependent on the degree of scientific and technological development, but, so Lévi-Strauss argues, the "savage" mental structure which can be disengaged from the palpable integument of what often seem to us bizarre modes of symbolic representation is identical with our own mental structure. We share with primitive men, he holds, the same mental habits of thinking in terms of binary discriminations or oppositions; like them, too, we have rules, including deep structural rules, governing the combination, segregation, mediation, and transformation of ideas and relations.

Now men who are heavily involved in jural-political, overt, and conscious structure are not free to meditate and speculate on the combinations and oppositions of thought; they are themselves too crucially involved in the combinations and oppositions of social and political structure and stratification. They are in the heat of the battle, in the "arena," competing for office, participating in feuds, factions, and coalitions. This involvement entails such affects as anxiety, aggression, envy, fear, exultation, an emotional flooding which does not encourage either rational or wise reflection. But in ritual liminality they are placed, so to speak, outside the total system and its conflicts; transiently, they become men apart—and it is surprising how often the term "sacred" may be translated as "set apart" or "on one side" in various societies. If getting a living and struggling to get it, in and despite of a social structure, be called "bread" then man does not live "by bread alone."

Life as a series and structure of status incumbencies inhibits the full utilization of human capacities, or as Karl Marx would have said, in a singularly Augustinian fashion, "the powers that slumber within man." I am thinking of Augustine's *rationes seminales*, "seminal reasons," implanted in the created universe at the beginning and left to work themselves out over historical time. Both Augustine and Marx favored organic metaphors for social movement, seen in terms of development and growth. Thus, for Marx, a new social order "grows" in the "womb" of the old and is "delivered" by the "midwife", force.

Preliterate societies, out of the need for mere survival, provide little scope for leisure. Thus it is only by ritual fiat, acting through the legitimate authority vested in those who operate the ritual cycle, that opportunities can be created to put men and women outside their everyday structural positions in family, lineage, clan, and chieftainship. In such situations as the liminal periods of major *rites de passage* the "passengers" and "crew" are free, under ritual exigency, to contemplate for a while the mysteries that confront all men, the difficulties that peculiarly beset their own society, their personal problems, and the ways in which their own wisest predecessors have sought to order, explain, explain away, cloak, or mask ("cloak" and "mask" are different: "cloak" is to "conceal," "mask" is to impose the "features" of a standardized interpretation) these mysteries and difficulties. In liminality resides the germ not only of religious *askesis*, discipline, and mysticism, but also of philosophy and pure science. Indeed, such Greek philosophers as Plato and Pythagoras are known to have had links with the mystery cults.

I would like to make it clear at this point that I am here referring not to such spontaneous behavioral expressions of communitas as the kind of good fellowship one finds in many secular marginal and transitional social situations, such as an English pub, a "good" party as distinct from a "stiff" party, the "eight-seventeen A.M. club" on a suburban commuters' train, a group of passengers at play on an ocean voyage, or, to speak more seriously, at some religious meetings, a "sit-in," "love-in," "be-in," or more dramatically, the Woodstock or Isle of Wight "nations." My focus here is rather on cultural—and hence institutionalized—expressions of communitas, communitas as seen from the perspective of structure, or as incorporated into it as a potentially dangerous but nevertheless vitalizing moment, domain, or enclave.

Communitas is, existentially speaking and in its origins, purely spontaneous and self-generating.[2] The "wind" of existential communitas "bloweth where it listeth." It is essentially opposed to structure, as antimatter is hypothetically opposed to matter. Thus, even when communitas becomes normative its religious expressions become closely hedged about by rules and interdictions—which act like the lead container of a dangerous radioactive isotope. Yet exposure to or immersion in communitas seems to be an indispensable human social requirement. People have a real need, and "need" is not for me "a dirty word," to doff the masks, cloaks, apparel, and insignia of status from time to time even if only to don the liberating masks of liminal masquerade. But they do this freely. And here I would like to point out the bond that exists between communitas, liminality, and lowermost status. It is often believed that the lowest castes and classes in stratified societies exhibit the greatest immediacy and involuntariness of behavior. This may or may not be empirically true, but it is at any rate a persistent belief held perhaps most firmly by the occupants of positions in the middle rungs of structure on whom structural pressures to conformity are greatest, and who secretly envy even while they openly reprobate the behavior of those groups and classes less normatively inhibited, whether highest or lowest on the status ladder. Those who would maximize communitas often begin by minimizing or even eliminating the outward marks of rank as, for example, Tolstoy and Gandhi tried to do in their own persons. In other words, they approximate in dress and behavior the condition of the poor. These signs of indigence include the wearing of plain or cheap apparel or the assumption of the peasant's smock or worker's overalls. Some would go even further and try to ex-

[2] Here I would contrast "existential" with "normative" communitas.

press the "natural" as opposed to "cultural" character of communitas, even though "natural" is here, of course, a cultural definition, by allowing their hair and nails to grow and their skin to remain unwashed, as in the case of certain Christian saints and Hindu and Muslim holy men. But since man is inveterately a cultural animal, nature here itself becomes a cultural symbol for what is essentially a human social need—the need to be fully together with one's fellows and not segregated from them in structural cells. A "natural" or "simple" mode of dress, or even undress in some cases, signalizes that one wishes to approximate the basically or merely human, as against the structurally specific by way of status or class.

A random assortment of such aspirants to pure communitas would include: the mendicant friars of the Middle Ages, especially those of the Franciscan and Carmelite orders, for example, whose members by their constitutions were forbidden to possess property, not merely personally, but even in common so they had to subsist by begging and were hardly better clothed than beggars; some modern Catholic saints, like St. Benedict Labré, the palmer (d. 1783), who was reputed to be always covered with vermin as he traveled ceaselessly and silently around the pilgrimage shrines of Europe; similar qualities of poverty and mendicancy are sought by Hindu, Muslim, and Sikh holy men of India and the Middle East, some of whom even dispense with clothing altogether; in America today we have the counterculture people, who like holy men of the East wear long hair and beards and dress in a variety of ways ranging from the clothes of the urban poor to the attire of underprivileged rural and ethnic groups, such as Amerindians and Mexicans. So critical were some hippie men, not long ago, of the principles underlying the structure out of which they had opted that they even rejected in their dress the dominant American stress on virility and successful aggressiveness in a competitive business milieu by wearing beads, bangles, and earrings, just as "flower power," in the late 1960's, was opposed to military strength and business aggressiveness. In this they share common ground with the Vīraśaiva saints of medieval south India. My colleague A. K. Ramanujan has recently translated from the Kannada language some poems known as *vacanas* which in their protest against traditional structural dichotomies in orthodox Hinduism reject the differences between man and woman as superficial. One of these *bhakti* poems is quoted below, page 286.

There is no doubt that from the perspective of incumbents in positions of command or maintenance in structure, communitas— even when it becomes normative—represents a real danger and, indeed, that for all those, including even political leaders, who spend much of their lives in structural role playing it also represents a temptation. Who does not really want to shuck off that old armor plating? This situation was dramatically exemplified in the early history of the Franciscan order. So many rushed to join St. Francis' following that recruitment to the secular clergy fell off sharply, and the Italian bishops complained that they could not maintain ecclesiastical discipline when their dioceses were overrun by what they considered to be a mendicant rabble. In the last quarter of the thirteenth century Pope Nicholas III decreed that the order modify its rule with regard to the abandonment of all property. In this way a communitarian threat to the jural structure of the church was turned to her advantage, for the doctrine of poverty has left a permanent impress on Catholicism acting as a constant check on the growth of Roman legalism, with its heavy involvement in political and economic structures.

Liminality, then, often draws on poverty for its repertoire of symbols, particularly for its symbols of social relationship. Similarly, as we have seen, the voluntary outsiders of our own society, particularly today's voluntary rural communards, also draw upon the symbolic vocabulary of poverty and indigence. Both the mendicant orders and today's counterculture have affinities with another social phenomenon which has recently aroused great interest among anthropologists and historians. I refer to that range of religious movements, scattered throughout history and of wide geographical provenience, which have variously been described as "enthusiastic," "heretical," "millenarian," "revitalistic," "nativistic," "messianic," and "separatist"—to cite but a few of the terms by which they have been called by theologians, historians, and social scientists. I shall not enter into the problem of providing an adequate taxonomy of such movements, but will content myself with mentioning a few of their recurrent attributes which seem closely similar to those of (1) ritual liminality in tribal societies, (2) religious mendicancy, and (3) the counterculture. In the first place, it is common for members of these movements either to give up what property they have or to hold all their property in common. Instances have been recorded of the destruction of all property by the members of religious movements at the command of their prophetic leaders. The rationale here, I believe, is that in most societies differences in property correspond to major differences of status or else in simpler stateless societies relate to the segmentation of corporate groups. To "liquidate" property, or "pool" it (the fluid metaphors are perhaps significant and may sometimes be concretely expressed in water symbolism, such as baptism, perhaps an instance of Lévi-Strauss's "concrete logic"), is to erase the lines of structural cleavage that in ordinary life prevent men from entering into communitas.

Similarly, the institution of marriage, source of the family, a basic cell of social structure in many cultures, also comes under attack in many religious movements. Some seek to replace it by what Lewis Morgan would have called "primitive promiscuity" or by various forms of "group marriage." Sometimes this is held to demonstrate the triumph of love over jealousy. In other movements, on the contrary, celibacy becomes the rule and the relationship between the sexes becomes a massive extension of the sibling bond. Thus some religious movements are similar to religious orders in abstaining from sexual activity, while others resemble some groups of hippies in breaking down sexual exclusiveness. Both attitudes toward sexuality are aimed at homogenizing the group by "liquidating" its structural divisions. In tribal societies, too, there is abundant ethnographic evidence to testify that an interdiction is laid on sexual relations during the liminal period in major *rites de passage*. Sometimes, too, episodes of sexual license may follow periods of sexual abstinence in such ceremonies, in other words, both antithetical modes of representing the destruction of monogamous marriage are utilized.[3]

To digress briefly, it seems to make more sense of the facts if we regard sexuality not so much as the primordial source of sociality and sociality as neutralized libido but as the expression, in its various modalities, either of communitas or structure. Sexuality, as a biological drive, is culturally and hence symbolically manipulated to express one or the other of these major dimensions of sociality. It thus becomes a means to social ends, quite as much as an end to which social means are contrived. Whereas structure emphasizes, and even exaggerates, the biological differences between the sexes, in matters of dress, decoration, and behavior, communitas tends to diminish these differences. Thus in many tribal initiations where both sexes appear as neophytes, men and women, boys and girls, are often dressed alike and behave similarly in the liminal situation. Afterward, custom segregates them and stresses sexual differences as they are restored to the structural order. In religious movements, at some of the critical rites of incorporaton, such as baptism by immersion, male and female neophytes or catechumens may wear the same type of robe—a robe which often deliberately conceals sexual differences, as among one of the offshoots from the Bwiti cult of Gabon as described by James Fernandez. It is still today a commonplace of conversation in situations dominated by structural (or middle-class) values to hear such comments on hippies as, "How can one tell whether it's a boy or a girl—they all have long hair and dress alike?"

Nevertheless, similarity in appearance between males and females does not necessarily mean the disappearance of sexual at-

[3] Clearly the organizational outcomes of celibacy versus orgy must be very different as must the attitude of the guardians of orthodox structure to movements of these rival types.

traction between them. There is no evidence to suggest that members of the alternate culture are less sexually active than their "straight" fellows. But sexuality, sometimes perhaps in the "polymorphously perverse" forms recommended by Norman Brown and extolled by Allen Ginsberg, seems to be here regarded by them rather as a way of enhancing the inclusiveness of communitas, as a means to wide-range mutual understanding. Such a means is positively opposed to asserting the exclusive character of certain structural bonds, such as marriage or unilineality.

The many traits that such "enthusiastic" and chiliastic religious movements share with the liminal situation in traditional ritual systems suggest that these movements too have a liminal quality. But their liminality is not institutionalized and preordained. Rather should it be viewed as spontaneously generated in a situation of radical structural change, what Parsons, following Weber, calls the "prophetic break," when seemingly fundamental social principles lose their former efficacy, their capacity to operate as axioms for social behavior, and new modes of social organization emerge, at first to transect and, later, to replace traditional ones. Religion and ritual, it is well known, often sustain the legitimacy of social and political systems or provide the symbols on which that legitimacy is most vitally expressed, so that when the legitimacy of cardinal social relations is impugned, the ritual symbolic system too which has come to reinforce such relations ceases to convince. It is in this limbo of structure that religious movements, led by charismatic prophets, powerfully reassert the values of communitas, often in extreme and antinomian forms.

This primal impetus, however, soon attains its apogee and loses its impetus; as Weber says, "*charisma* becomes routinized," and the spontaneous forms of communitas are converted into institutionalized structure, or become routinized, often as ritual. What the prophet and his followers actually did becomes a behavioral model to be represented in stereotyped and selected liturgical form. This ritual structure has two important aspects: on the one hand, the historical deeds of the prophet and his closest companions become a sacred history, impregnated with the mythical elements so typical of liminality, that becomes increasingly resistant to criticism and revision and consolidates into a structure in the Lévi-Straussian sense as binary oppositions are set up and stressed between crucial events, individuals, groups, types of conduct, periods of time, and so on; on the other hand, both the deeds of the founder and his visions and messages achieve crystallization in the symbolic objects and activities of cyclical and repetitive rituals. Indeed, it may well be that even in tribal religions, where there is no written religious history, the cyclical rites that seem so closely in their stability and repetitiveness to resemble natural phenomena, such as the seasonal round and the life cycles of birds and animals, may well have originated in times of social crisis, whether man-made or due to natural catastrophes, in the novel and idiosyncratic visions and deeds of inspired shamans or prophets.

Freud's notion of "repetition compulsion," whatever may be its causes, fairly well describes the process whereby the inspirational forms generated in some experiences of communitas get repeated in symbolic mimesis and become the routinized forms of structure. The outcomes of "vision" become the models or patterns of repetitive social behavior. The word or act that appeared to heal or amend personal or social disorder comes to be accorded intrinsic power in isolation from its original context and is formally repeated in ritual and incantatory utterance. A creative deed becomes an ethical or ritual paradigm.

Let me give a simple illustration from my own field experience. Among the Ndembu of Zambia, I have been able to allocate approximate dates to the introduction of certain rites to the hunting and curative cult systems which, although they now share many of the properties of the more traditional rites, nevertheless betray their origins in some disturbed phase of Ndembu history. Here external threat seemed to intensify the sentiment of Ndembu unity. For example, the Wuyang's gun hunters' cult and the Chihamba curative cult, in their prayers and symbolism, refer unmistakably to the traumatic impact of the nineteenth-century slave trade on the harassed and fleeing Ndembu; the quite recently introduced Tukuka cult, marked by hysterical trembling and a concept of possession by alien, notably European spirits, stands in marked contrast to the almost Apollonian dignity and restraint of many of the traditional ritual performances. These rituals, however, despite their differences, present the Ndembu as a communitas of interdependent sufferers.

It is not only among the Ndembu but also in the history of most of the great religions that we see crisis disclosing communitas and the manifest form of such communitas subsequently reinforcing an old structure or replacing it by a new one. Various reform movements within the Catholic church, the Protestant Reformation itself, not to mention the innumerable evangelical and revivalistic movements within the whole Christian world, attest to this. In Islam, Sufism and Sanusi reform movements among the Bedouin and Berbers exemplify but two among many. The many attempts in Indian Hinduism to liquidate the caste structure, from Buddhism, through Jainism and Lingayatism and the Vīraśaiva saints to Gandhism—not to mention such syncretic Hindu-Islamic religions as Sikhism—are further examples.

I mention this correlation between crisis, communitas, and the genesis of religions mainly because it is too often held by sociologists and anthropologists that "the social" is at all times identical with the "social-structural," that man is nothing but a structural animal and consequently a *homo hierarchicus.* Thus the breakdown of a social system can only result in *anomie, angst,* and the fragmentation of society into a mass of anxious and disoriented individuals, prone, as Durkheim would have said, to pathologically high rates of suicide. For if such a society is unstructured it is nothing. It is less often seen that the dissolution of structural relationships may sometimes give communitas a positive opportunity.

One recent historical example of this is the "miracle of Dunkirk," when from the destruction of the formal organization of the Allied armies in 1940 an informal organization arose, deriving from the liberated spirit of communitas. The rescue of small groups of soldiers by the crews of small boats gave rise to a spirit of resistance generally known as "the spirit of Dunkirk." The general careers of guerrilla bands as against formally regulated and hierarchical armies in the recent history of China, Bolivia, Cuba, and Vietnam may be further examples. I am not suggesting that there is no *anomie*, no *angst*, no alienation (to mention three currently popular "A"s) in such situations of drastic structural change—one must not be surprised or indignant that in any social field contrary social processes may be simultaneously at work—but I am suggesting that there are socially positive forces at work here too. Structure's breakdown may be communitas' gain.

Durkheim, whose work has been so influential both in England and France, is often difficult to understand precisely because, at different times, he uses the term "society" to represent, on the one hand, a set of jural and religious maxims and norms, coercing and constraining the individual and, on the other, "an actual living and animating force" closely approximate to what we are here calling "communitas." Yet it is not a complete approximation, for Durkheim conceives of this force as "anonymous and impersonal" and as passing through the generations, whereas we see communitas rather as a relationship between persons, an I-Thou relationship in Buber's terms or a We, the very essence of which is its immediacy and spontaneity. It is structure that is transmitted, by rote and repetition; though under favorable circumstances some structural form, generated long ago from a moment of communitas, may be almost miraculously liquified into a living form of communitas again. This is what revitalistic or revivalistic religious movements, as against radical or transformist ones, aim to do—to restore the social bond of their communicants to the pristine vigor of that religion in its days of generative crisis and ecstasy. For example, as Ramanujan writes, "Like European Protestants, the Vīraśaivas returned to what they felt was the original inspiration of the ancient traditions no different from

true and present experience" (1973:33). Perhaps this, too, under-
lies the notion of permanent revolution. It was certainly present
in the Événements de Mai-Juin 1968 in Paris when the students
adopted symbols of unity and communitas from earlier French
revolutions. Just as during the Paris Commune of 1871, the communards identified themselves with the revolutionaries of 1789,
even to the point of adopting the revolutionary calendar for the
commune's magazines, so the 1968 events identified themselves as
a kind of re-enactment of the Paris Commune. Even the barricades
erected there had little instrumental value, but were a symbol of
continuity with the grandeur of the 1871 uprising.

When a social system acquires a certain stability as in most of
the societies until recently studied by anthropologists, there tends
to develop in the temporal relationship between structure and
communitas a process to which it is hard to deny the epithet "dialectical." The life cycles of individuals and groups exhibit al-
ternating exposure to these major modes of human intercourse.
Individuals proceed from lower to higher statuses through interim periods of liminality, where they are stripped of all secular
status, though they may possess a religious status. But this status
is the antithesis of status in the structural domain. Here the high
are obliged to accept the stigmata of the lowly and even to endure patiently the taunts of those who will become their inferiors,
as in the installation rites of many African chiefs and headmen.

Since liminality represents what Erving Goffman would call
"a leveling and stripping" of structural status, an important
component of the liminal situation is, as we saw earlier, an enhanced stress on nature at the expense of culture. Not only does it
represent a situation of instruction—with a degree of objectivity
hardly found in structural situations where status differences have
to be explained away or, rather, merely accepted—but it is also
replete with symbols quite explicitly relating to biological processes, human and nonhuman, and to other aspects of the natural
order. In a sense, when man ceases to be the master and becomes
the equal or fellow of man, he also ceases to be the master and

becomes the equal or fellow of nonhuman beings. It is culture that fabricates structural distinctions; it is culture too that eradicates these distinctions in liminality, but in so doing culture is forced to use the idiom of nature, to replace its fictions by natural facts—even if these facts themselves only possess what reality they have in a framework of cultural concepts. Thus it is in liminality and also in those phases of ritual that abut on liminality that one finds profuse symbolic reference to beasts, birds, and vegetation. Animal masks, bird plumage, grass fibers, garments of leaves swathe and enshroud the human neophytes and priests. Thus, symbolically, their structural life is snuffed out by animality and nature, even as it is being regenerated by these very same forces. One dies *into* nature to be reborn *from* it. Structural custom, once broken, reveals two human traits. One is liberated intellect, whose liminal product is myth and protophilosophical speculation; the other is bodily energy, represented by animal disguises and gestures. The two may then be recombined in various ways.

One classical prototype of this revealed duality is the centaur Cheiron, half wise old man, half stallion, who in his mountain cavern—epitomizing outsiderhood and liminality—instructed, even initiated, the adolescent sons of Achaean kings and princes, who would later occupy leading positions in the social and political structure of Hellas. Human wisdom and animal force meet in this liminal figure, who is both horse and man. As is well known, theranthropic figures combining animal with human characteristics abound in liminal situations; similarly, human beings imitate the behavior of different species of animals. Even angels in the Iranian, Judaeo-Christian, and Islamic traditions may perhaps be regarded in this way—as ornithanthropic figures, birdhumans, messengers betwixt and between absolute and relative reality.

Yet it would be unwise, and in fact incorrect, to segregate structure too radically from communitas. I stress this most vigorously for both modes are human. For each level and domain of structure there is a mode of communitas, and there are cultural links established between them in most stable, ongoing, sociocultural systems. Usually, in the seclusion or liminal phases of *rites de passage*, at least some of the symbols, even of the *sacra* displayed, have reference to principles of social structure. For example, among the Nyakyusa of Tanzania, who are patrilineal, an important symbolic medicine in all *rites de passage* is a reddish fluid, rather endearingly called *ikipiki*, which represents the principle of patrilineal descent. And, as Terence Turner of Chicago showed in his paper on the Kayapo Indians of Brazil, sacred myths, which, if not always actually told in the secrecy or seclusion of liminal situations, often refer to crucial points of passage or transition in the lives of individuals or groups. When they are regarded globally, these myths often "relate to the social situation to which they refer [in a relation which] is one of analogy rather than of dialectical contrast or opposition" (T. Turner, 1967: Abstract, p. 2). Here Terence Turner is referring to the dialectics of Lévi-Strauss. Turner distinguishes between two aspects of the structure of the myth: "the internal structure of logical relations of opposition and mediation between the discrete symbolic elements of the myth (the aspect of structure upon which Lévi-Strauss prefers to concentrate), and the relation between the myth as a whole and the social situation to which it refers" (T. Turner, 1967; Abstract, p. 2). This continuous thread of structure through ritualized communitas in liminality is, to my mind, highly characteristic of long-established and stable cultural systems, in which, as it were, communitas has been thoroughly domesticated, even corralled—as among the Elks and Kiwanis in the United States. Raw or wild communitas is, more typically, a phenomenon of major social change, or, it may be, sometimes, a mode of reaction against too rigid a structuring of human life in status and role-playing activities—as some of the counterculture people claim their revolt to be—against what they call "American middle-class values," or against the "organization men," or against the tacit regimentation imposed on many levels and domains of society by the dominance of a military-industrial complex with its complicated repertoire of covert social controls.

To my mind it is the analysis of culture into factors and their free recombination in any and every possible pattern, however weird, that is most characteristic of liminality, rather than the establishment of implicit syntax-like rules or the development of an internal structure of logical relations of opposition and mediation. The limitation of possible combinations of factors by convention would indicate to me the growing intrusion of structure into this potentially free and experimental region of culture.

Here, a remark of Sartre (1969:57–59) seems apposite: "I [agree] that social facts have their own structure and laws that dominate individuals, but I see in this the reply of *worked matter* to the *agents* who work it. *Structures are created by activity which has no structure*, but suffers its *results as structure*." I see liminality as a phase in social life in which this confrontation between "activity which has no structure" and its "structured results" produces in men their highest pitch of self-consciousness. Syntax and logic are *problematic* and not *axiomatic* features of liminality. We have to see if they are there—empirically. And if we find them we have to consider well their relation to activities that have as yet no structure, no logic, only potentialities for them. In long-established cultural systems I would expect to find the growth of a symbolic and iconographic syntax and logic; in changing or newly established systems I would expect to find in liminal situations daring and innovation both in the modes of relating symbolic and mythic elements and in the choice of elements to be related. There might also be the introduction of new elements and their various combination with old ones, as in religious syncretisms.

The same formulation would apply to such other expressions of liminality as Western literature and art. Sometimes art expresses or replicates institutionalized structure to legitimate or criticize; but often it combines the factors of culture—as in cubism and abstract art—in novel and unprecedented ways. The unusual, the paradoxical, the illogical, even the perverse, stimulate thought and pose problems, "cleanse the Doors of Perception," as Blake put it. This is especially likely to be the case when art is presented in preliterate societies in an instructional situation like initiation. Thus the portrayal of monsters and of unnatural situations in terms of cultural definitions, like the incestuous ties connecting the gods in the myths of some religions, may have a pedagogical function in forcing those who have taken their culture for granted to rethink what they have hitherto taken to be its axioms and "givens." For each society requires of its mature members not only adherence to rules and patterns, but at least a certain level of skepticism and initiative. Initiation is to rouse initiative at least as much as to produce conformity to custom. Accepted schemata and paradigms must be broken if initiates are to cope with novelty and danger. They have to learn how to generate viable schemata under environmental challenge. Something similar may be found in European literature, for example, in the writings of Rabelais and Gênet. Such mastery over phenomena taken for granted by the uninstructed may well be thought to give enhanced power during the later incumbency of a new and higher status.

But the frequency with which such unnatural—or rather anti-cultural or anti-structural—events as incest, cannibalism, murder of close kin, mating with animals are portrayed in myth and liminal ritual surely has more than a pedagogical function. It is more too than a mere cognitive means of coding relationships between ritual elements, of assigning to them pluses or minuses or indicating transformations as Lévi-Strauss would assert. Here, I think, we must return to our earlier point about certain aspects of nature asserting themselves in liminal situations. For human nature as well as culture has its unconscious regularities, though these regularities may be precisely such as have to be denied expression if human beings are to go about their business of getting a living and maintaining social control as they do so. Much that the depth psychologists insist has been repressed into the unconscious tends to appear, either in veiled form, or, sometimes, perfectly explicitly, in liminal ritual and its connected myths. In many mythologies, the gods slay or unman their fathers, mate with their mother and sisters, copulate with mortals in the form of animals and birds—while in rites that act these out, their human representatives or imitators imitate, in symbol, or sometimes even literally, these immortal amoralities. In rituals, especially in the seclusion rites of initiations into manhood, womanhood, or into tribal associations and secret societies, there may be episodes of real or symbolic cannibalism—in which men eat the flesh of the recent dead or of captives, or else eat the symbolic flesh of deities spoken of as their "fathers," "brothers," or "mothers." Here there are regularities and repetitions indeed, yet they are not those of law and custom but of unconscious cravings which stand opposed to the norms on which social bonding secularly depends—to the rules of exogamy and the prohibition of incest, to those enjoining respect for the bodily person of others, to veneration of elders, and to definitions that class men differently from animals. Here again I would revert to my characterization in several articles of certain key symbols and central symbolic actions as "semantically bipolar," as "culturally intended" to arouse a gross quantity of affect—even of illicit affect—only to attach this quantum of affect divested of moral quality, in a later phase of a great ritual, to licit and legitimate goals and values, with consequent restoration of moral quality, but this time positive instead of negative. Perhaps Freud and Jung, in their different ways, have much to contribute to the understanding of these nonlogical, nonrational (but not irrational) aspects of liminal situations.

What seems to emerge from this brief glance at some of the cultural apparatus of liminal rituals, symbols, and myths is that all these phenomena exhibit great depth and complexity. They emphatically do not lend themselves to being reduced to the terms of practitioners of a single discipline or subdiscipline, such as the various and opposed schools of psychology, emotionalist

and intellectualist, the various schools of sociologistic reduc-
tionism from the followers of Radcliffe-Brown to those of Lévi-
Strauss, or philosophers and theologians who may tend to neglect
the contextual involvement of these phenomena with the social
structure, history, economy, and ecology of the specific groups
in which they occur. What we do not want is a Manichean
separation of what is purely intellectual or spiritual in such
pivotal religious phenomena from what is material and specific.
Nor should we separate—in considering the liminal symbol—
something which offers itself to experience from *someone* who
actually does experience it. Here I would say that if the cultural
form of communitas—as found in liminality—can correspond
with an actual experience of communitas, the symbols there presented may be experienced more deeply than in any other context, if the ritual subject has what theologians would call the
"proper dispositions." Here what Matthias Vereno [4] has called
"the essentially *relational* or predicative *esse*" of the symbol is
most fully exemplified—a relation which he calls a "gnostic" one.
Men "know" less or more as a function of the quality of their
relationship with other men. Gnosis, "deep knowledge," is highly
characteristic of liminality, certainly in many parts of Africa, as
Germaine Dieterlen has shown for the Dogon and Audrey
Richards for the Bemba, where it is believed that the esoteric
knowledge communicated in symbols in the girls' puberty rites
changes the inmost being of the neophytes. It is not merely that
new knowledge is imparted, but new power is absorbed, power
obtained through the weakness of liminality which will become
active in postliminal life when the neophytes' social status has
been redefined in the aggregation rites. Among the Bemba a
woman has been grown from a girl through the importation of
gnosis in a communitas of women.

To recapitulate the argument so far: in a situation which is
temporally liminal and spatially marginal the neophytes or "pas-

[4] Matthias Vereno of the University of Salzburg made this comment at
the Conference at Dartmouth College (August 1967) on Myth and Ritual.

sengers" in a protracted *rite de passage* are stripped of status and authority— in other words removed from a social structure which is ultimately maintained and sanctioned by power and force— and further leveled to a homogeneous social state through discipline and ordeal. Their secular powerlessness may, however, be compensated by a sacred power, the power of the weak derived on the one hand from resurgent nature and on the other from the reception of sacred knowledge. Much of what has been bound by social structure is liberated, notably the sense of comradeship and communion, in brief, of communitas; on the other hand, much of what has been dispersed over many domains of culture and social structure is now bound or cathected in the complex semantic systems of pivotal, multivocal symbols and myths which achieve great conjunctive power and possess what Erik Erikson, following Rudolf Otto, would call "numinosity." It is as if social relations have been emptied of their legal-political structural character, which character, though not, of course, its *specific* structure, has been imparted to the relations between symbols, ideas, and values rather than between social *personae* and statuses. In this no-place and no-time that resists classification, the major classifications and categories of the culture emerge within the integuments of myth, symbol, and ritual.

In everyday life people in tribal societies have little time to devote to protophilosophical or theological speculation. But in protracted liminal periods, through which everyone must pass, they become a privileged class, largely supported by the labor of others—though often exposed by way of compensation to annealing hardships—with abundant opportunity to learn and speculate about what the tribe considers its "ultimate things." Here we have a fruitful alienation of the total individual from the partial *persona* which must result in the development at least in principle or potentiality if not always in practice of a total rather than a partial perspective on the life of society. After his immersion in the depths of liminality—very frequently symbolized in ritual and myth as a grave that is also a womb—after this profound experience of humiliation and humility, a man who at the end of the ritual becomes the incumbent of a senior political status or even merely of a higher position in some particularistic segment of the social structure can surely never again be quite so parochial, so particularistic, in his social loyalties. This can be seen in many tribal societies which practice protracted circumcision rites: the initiands are drawn from diverse tribal segments; when the rites are completed they form an association with mutual rights and obligations which may last until death and which cuts across cleavages on the basis of ascribed and achieved status.

It would seem that where there is little or no structural provision for liminality, the social need for escape from or abandonment of structural commitments seeks cultural expression in ways that are not explicitly religious, though they may become heavily ritualized. Quite often this retreat from social structure may appear to take an individualistic form—as in the case of many post-Renaissance artists, writers, and philosophers. But if one looks closely at their productions, one often sees in them at least a plea for communitas. The artist is not really alone, nor does he write, paint, or compose for posterity, but for living communitas. Of course, like the initiand in tribal society, the novelistic hero has to be reinducted into the structural domain, but for the "twice-born" (or converted) the *sting* of that domain—its ambitions, envies, and power struggles—has been removed. He is like Kierkegaard's "knight of faith" who having confronted the structured and quantitative crowd as "the qualitative individual" moves from antithesis to synthesis and though remaining outwardly indistinguishable from others in this order of social structure is henceforth inwardly free from its despotic authority, is an autonomous source of creative behavior. This acceptance or forgiveness, to use William Blake's term, of structure in a movement of return from a liminal situation is a process that recurs again and again in Western literature, and, indeed, in the actual lives of many writers, artists, and political folk heroes from Dante and Lenin to

Nehru and the African political exiles who became leaders. It represents a secularization of what seems to have been originally a religious process.

Recently there was a tendency among many people, especially those under thirty, to try to create a communitas and a style of life that is permanently contained within liminality. Their motto was Timothy Leary's "Tune in, turn on, and drop out." Instead of the liminal being a passage, it seemed to be coming to be regarded as a state, although some seemed to think of communes as initiation lodges rather than permanent homes. Of course, this conversion of liminality, in modified form, into a way of life, has also been true of the monastic and mendicant orders in, for example, Christianity and Buddhism, but the religious state has been there clearly defined as an exceptional condition reserved for those who aspire after perfection, except, of course, in Thailand where all young men spend a year as monks. The religious life is not for everyone, but only for those "elected by grace." Even so we have seen how dangerous primitive Franciscan communitas was held to be by the structured church.

But the Western urbanized hippies shared with many historical enthusiastic sects a desire to generalize and perpetuate their liminal and outsider condition. One of my graduate students in a seminar at Cornell gave me some Haight-Ashbury [5] literature, produced during the brief heydey of the "Hashbury" culture, and I would like to quote some passages from a journal called the *Oracle* which used to be published "approximately bi-monthly" in San Francisco, where it was described as the hippies' "house journal." I quote from Volume I, number, 6 which appeared in February 1967, and has subsequently been spoken of as "a vintage number." Most of the features which we have ascribed to the liminal phases of *rites de passage* and to the early stages of religous movements reappear in this literature with startling clarity.

[5] This district in San Francisco was the main center of "hippiedom" in 1966 and 1967. Its name gave rise to such posters and grafitti as: "Haight is love."

We have seen that in liminality social structure disappears or is simplified and generalized while the cultural apparatus often becomes structurally complex. Well, then, we find on the very first printed page of this copy of the *Oracle* a series of statements about "rock" (described as "the first 'head' music we've had since the end of the baroque"). Rock is clearly a cultural expression and instrumentality of that style of communitas which has arisen as the antithesis of the "square," "organization man" type of bureaucratic social structure of mid-twentieth-century America. I will now quote freely (but exactly) from this page, on which it seems that the term "rock" sometimes represents a form of music and sometimes a modality of communitas. The author of "Notes for the New Geology" (geology—the study of rock!) is enunciating "some principles." These include:

That rock principles are not limited to music, and that much of the shape of the future can be seen in its aspirations today (these being namely total freedom, total experience, total love, peace and mutual affection) [note: the emphasis on totality or "totalism" rather than partial perspectives and on the *"prophetic"* character of this liminal manifestation];

That rock is a way of life, international and verging in this decade on universal; and can't be stopped, retarded, put down, muted, modified or successfully controlled by typeheads, whose arguments don't apply and whose machinations don't mesh because they can't perceive (dig) what rock really is and does [note: the stress on the pan-human yet immediate quality of this "new" social relationship and its cultural product—both called "rock"];

That rock is a *tribal* phenomenon [*sic*.], immune to definition and other typographical operations, and constitutes what might be called a Twentieth Century magic [note: "typeheads"—as against acid heads —"define" and "stereo*type*"—but of course truly "tribal" phenomena are really highly involved with classifications as Levi-Strauss and the "thought structuralists" have shown];

That rock is a vital agent in breaking down absolute and arbitrary distinctions [note: the expression of communitas' power of dissolving structural divisions];

That group participation, total experience and complete involvement are rock's minimal desiderata and those as well of a world that
has too many people [note: the stress on the need for face-to-face relationships—in which communities best flourishes];

That rock is creating the social rituals of the future [note: the
stress on the creative role of certain social situations in which new
definitions and models for behavior are constructed];

That rock presents an aesthetic of discovery [note: the experimental
quality of liminality is here recognized];

That rock is evolving Sturgeonesque *homo gestalt* configurations.

So much for the social characteristics of this "*rock* communitas." "Typographic" for this author designates that kind of
analytical thinking that presupposes a corpse, as against "vital agen-
cies" of discovery; "typeheads" are sterile and authoritarian "la-
belers"; and "Sturgeonesque" refers not to the Russian fish, but
to an American author of science fiction who wrote a novel,
popular some years ago among the hippies, about a group of
people who constituted a human *gestalt*—"the next stage in human evolution"—when the individual is replaced by the cluster
as the crucial human unit. These people "bleshed" together, just
as Robert Heinlein's cult group in *Stranger in a Strange Land*
"grocked" together. Incidentally, students of symbolism and
myth should take note of science fiction, for this genre provides
many examples of just such a juggling of the factors of culture
in new and often bizarre combinations and settings as was postu-
lated earlier as a feature of liminality in initiations and mystery
religions. Here we are dealing with "an esthetic of discovery," a
mythology of the future, an "omega" mythology, as appropriate
for a society undergoing rapid and unceasing change as a mythology of the past, or an "alpha" mythology, is appropriate for a
stable and relatively repetitive and cyclical social order.

The structure-dissolving quality of liminality is clearly present,
for "rock . . . breaks down absolute and arbitrary distinctions."
I have written elsewhere (1969) that communitas is, in principle,
universal and boundless, as against structure which is specific and

bounded. Here we find rock described as "international and . . . universal." But now let us look at what the *Oracle*'s "geologist" says about rock as a cultural manifestation rather than a mode of social relationship:

Rock is a legitimate *avant-garde* art form with deep roots in the music of the past (especially the baroque and before), great vitality and vast potential for growth and development, adaptation, experiment, etc.;

Rock shares most of its formal/structural principles with baroque music . . . and it and baroque can be judged by the same broad standards (the governing principles being those of mosaic structure of tonal and textural contrast: tactility, collage).

Here again we see the contrast between the unstructured communitas (or in the words of the author, "the groups themselves far more intimately interrelated and integrated than any comparable ensemble in the past") and its highly elaborate cultural product and medium, which, like the myths analyzed by Lévi-Strauss and Leach, has a logical framework of "formal/structural principles."

The pedigree of "rock" communitas is, of course, much longer than our author supposed. There was no doubt a paleolithic "rock"! And anthropologists the world over have participated in tribal "scenes" not dissimilar to the rock "scene"—in the seclusion lodges of initiation or in the rhythmical dances, with improvised singing—of many kinds of ritual in many kinds of societies. Our author speaks, too, of "synaesthesia," the union of visual, auditory, tactile, spatial, visceral, and other modes of perception under the influence of various stimuli such as music, dancing, and drugs. This "involvement of the whole sensorium" is found in tribal ritual and in the services of many modern religious movements. Arthur Rimbaud, one of the folk heroes of the counterculture, would have approved of this as "*un dereglement ordonné de tous les sens*," "a systematic derangement of all the senses." Just as Rimbaud wrote about the vowel sounds having distinctive colors, so our author talks about "sensory counter-

point—the senses registering contradictory stimuli and the brain
having fun trying to integrate them . . . imagine *tasting* G-minor
. . . the incredible synaesthesiae!"

One could point out the detailed resemblances between liminal
phenomena of all kinds. But I will conclude the chapter by calling
attention to the way that certain cultural attributes of ascribed
inferior status acquire a communitas significance as attributes of
liminal situations or liminal *personae*. This stress on the symbolism
of weakness and poverty is not confined to the counterculture.
Here, of course, I am not talking about the actual social behavior
of persons of structurally inferior caste, class, or rank. Such behavior may be as much or as little dependent upon social-structural considerations as the behavior of their status superiors. What
I have in mind is the symbolic value of the poor man or *harijan*
of religion, literature, and political philosophy. In religion, the
holy man who makes himself to all appearances poorer than the
meanest beggar may, and in fact often does, come from a wealthy
or aristocratic, or at least highly educated stratum of the social
structure. St. Francis, for example, was the son of a rich merchant; Gautama was a prince. In literature, we find the values of
communitas represented by such types as Tolstoy's peasants and
by such characters as Dostoevsky's prostitute Sonia, Chekhov's
poor Jewish fiddler Rothschild (the irony of that name!), Mark
Twain's Negro slave Jim and youthful vagrant Huckleberry Finn
of whom Lionel Trilling has said that they form "a primitive
community of saints . . . because they do not have an ounce of
pride between them" (*The Liberal Imagination*, 1953: 110ff.),
and the Fool in Shakespeare's *King Lear*. In political philosophy
we have the images of Rousseau's Noble Savage, Marx's prole-
tariat, and Gandhi's Untouchables, whom he called *harijans* or
"the children of God." Each of these thinkers, however, had
different structural recipes and different formulae for relating
communitas to structure. Liminal poverty must not be confused
with real poverty, although the liminally poor may become
actually poor. But liminal poverty, whether it is a process or a

state, is both an expression and instrumentality of communitas. Communitas is what people really seek by voluntary poverty. And because communitas is such a basic, even primordial mode of human interlinkage, depending as it does neither on conventions nor sanctions, it is often religiously equated with love—both the love of man and the love of God. The principle is simple: cease to have and you are; if you "are" in the relationship of communitas to others who "are," then you love one another. In the honesty of being, people "naturally" relate to or "dig" one another. The difficulty experienced by these Edenic prescriptions in a post-Edenic world is that men have to organize structurally in order to exist materially at all, and the more complex the technology of living becomes, the more finely cut and finely intermeshed does its social division of labor become, and the more time-consuming and absorbing become society's occupational and organizational statuses and roles. One great temptation in this milieu is to subordinate communitas totally to structure so that the principle of order will never be subverted. The opposite temptation is to opt out of structure altogether. The basic and perennial human social problem is to discover what is the right relation between these modalities at a specific time and place. Since communitas has a strong affectual component, it appeals more directly to men; but since structure is the arena in which they pursue their material interests, communitas perhaps even more importantly than sex tends to get repressed into the unconscious, there to become either a source of individual pathological symptoms [6] or to be released in violent cultural forms in periods of social crisis. People can go crazy because of communitas-repression; sometimes people become obsessively structural as a defense mechanism against their urgent need of communitas.

The major religions have always taken account of this bipolarity and have tried to maintain these social dimensions in balanced relationship. But the countless sects and schismatic movements in the history of religions have almost always asserted the

[6] "The need to relate" to others.

values of communitas against those of structure and claimed that the major religions from which they have seceded have become totally structured and secularized, mere empty forms. Significantly, such separatist movements have almost invariably adopted a cultural style dominated by the cultural idiom of indigence. In their first impetus, such movements often strip their members of the outward show of wealth or status, adopt a simple form of speech, and to a considerable extent strip their religious practices of ritualism and visual symbolism. Organizationally, they often abolish priestly hierarchies and substitute for them either prophetic charismatic leadership or democratic methods of representation. If such movements attract great numbers and persist for many years, they often find it necessary to compromise with structure once again, both in their relations with the wider society and in their own internal concerns both liturgical and organizational.

The great historical religions have, in the course of time, learned how to incorporate enclaves of communitas within their institutionalized structures—just as tribal religions do with their *rites de passage*—and to oxygenate, so to speak, the "mystical body" by making provision for those ardent souls who wish to live in communitas and poverty all their lives. Just as in a ritual of any complexity there are phases of separation from and reaggregation to the domain of social structure—phases which themselves contain many structural features, including symbols which reflect or express structural principles—and a liminal phase representing an interim of communitas with its own rich and elaborate symbolism, so does a great religion or church contain many organizational and liturgical sectors which overlap with and interpenetrate the secular social structure but maintain in a central position a sanctuary of unqualified communitas, of that poverty which is said to be "the poetry of religion" and of which St. Francis, Angelus Silesius, the Sufist poets, Rumi and Al-Ghazali, and the Vīraśaiva poet Basavanna were melodious troubadours and jongleurs.

The link between inferior structural status and communitas can also be found in tribal societies; it is not merely a mark of structural complexity. Now I would like to bring my argument round full circle and state that from the standpoint of structural man, he who is in communitas is an exile or a stranger, someone who, by his very existence, calls into question the whole normative order. That is why when we consider cultural institutions we have to look in the interstices, niches, intervals, and on the peripheries of the social structure to find even a grudging cultural recognition of this primordial human modality of relationship. On the other hand, in times of drastic and sustained social change, it is communitas which often appears to be central and structure which constitutes the "square" or "straight" periphery. If one may dare to venture a personal evaluation of such matters, one might say that much of the misery of the world has been due to the principled activities of fanatics of both persuasions. On the one hand, one finds a structural and ultimately bureaucratic *übermensch* who would like to array the whole world of lesser men in terms of hierarchy and regimentation in a "New Order," and on the other the puritanical levelers who would abolish all idiosyncratic differences between man and man (even necessary organizational differences for the sake of the food quest), and set up an ethical tyranny that would allow scant scope for compassion and forgiveness. "One Law for the Lion and the Ox is Oppression," said Blake with reference to such ethical tyranny. Yet since both social modalities are indispensable for human social continuity, neither can exist for long without the other. Indeed, if structure is maximized to full rigidity, it invites the nemesis of either violent revolution or uncreative apathy, while if communitas is maximized, it becomes in a short while its own dark shadow, totalitarianism, from the need to suppress and repress in its members all tendencies to develop structural independences and interdependences.

Moreover, communitas, which is in principle boundless and universal, has been in historical practice limited to particular geographical regions and specific aspects of social life. Thus the varied expressions of communitas such as monasteries, convents, socialist bastions, semireligious communities and brotherhoods, nudist colonies, communes in the modern countercultures, initiation camps, have often found it necessary to surround themselves with real as well as symbolic walls— a species of what structural sociologists would call "boundary maintaining mechanisms." When large-scale communites are involved, these tend to take the form of military and police organizations, open and secret. Thus to keep out structure, structure has to be constantly maintained and reinforced. When the great principles regard one another as antagonists, each "becomes what it beholds." What seems to be needed, to quote William Blake again, is to "destroy the negation" and thus "redeem the contraries," that is, to discover what is the right relationship between structure and communitas at a given time and place in history and geography, to give to each its due.

To sum up, a major stumbling block in the development of sociological and anthropological theory has been the almost total identification of the social with the social structural. Even informal relations are considered structural. Many of them are, of course, but not all; these include the most relevant ones, and it is possible to distinguish the deep from the shallow here. This has created enormous difficulties with regard to many problems, such as social change, the sociology of religion, and role theory, to name but a few. It has also led to the view that all that is not social structural is "psychological"—whatever this may mean. It has also led to the positing of a false dichotomy between the individual as subject, and society as object. What seems to be the case is that the social has a free or unbound as well as a bonded or bound dimension, the dimension of communitas in which men confront one another not as role players but as "human totals," integral beings who recognizantly share the same humanity.

Once this has been recognized, it will be possible for the social sciences to examine more fruitfully than hitherto such cultural phenomena as art, religion, literature, philosophy, and even many aspects of law, politics, and economic behavior which have hitherto eluded the structuralist conceptual net. Such domains are rich with reference to communitas. The vain task of trying to find out in what precise way certain symbols found in the ritual, poetry, or iconography of a given society "reflect" or "express" its social or political structure can then be abandoned. Symbols may well reflect not structure, but anti-structure, and not only reflect it but contribute to creating it. Instead, we can regard the same phenomena in terms of the relationship between structure and communitas to be found in such relational situations as passages between structural states, the interstices of structural relations, and in the powers of the weak.

References

Durkheim, Emile. 1961. *The Elementary Forms of the Religious Life.* Tr. J. S. Swain. New York: Collier. First published 1912.

Fortes, Meyer. 1949. *The Web of Kinship among the Tallensi.* London: Oxford University Press.

Gennep, Arnold van. 1960. *The Rites of Passage.* London: Routledge & Kegan Paul. First published 1908.

Lévi-Strauss, Claude. 1960. "On Manipulated Sociological Models," *Bijdragen tot de Taal, Land en Volkenkunde* 116(1):45–54.

——. 1963. *Structural Anthropology.* Tr. Claire Jacobson. New York: Basic Books. First published 1958.

The Oracle (San Francisco). 1967. Vol. 1, no. 6 (February).

Ramanujan, A. K. 1973. *Speaking of Śiva.* Baltimore: Penguin Books.

Reed, Nelson. 1964. *The Caste War in Yucatan.* Stanford: Stanford University Press.

Riesman, David. 1954. *Individualism Reconsidered and Other Essays.* Glencoe, Illinois: The Free Press.

Rosen, Lawrence. 1971. "Language, History, and the Logic of Inquiry in Lévi-Strauss and Sartre," *History and Theory* 10(3):269–294.

Sartre, Jean-Paul. 1963. *Search for a Method.* New York: Knopf.

——. 1969. "Itinerary of a Thought," *New Left Review* 58:57–59.

Stonequist, E. V. 1937. *The Marginal Man.* New York: Scribner.

Trilling, Lionel. 1953. *The Liberal Imagination.* New York: Anchor Books.

Turner, Terence. 1967. "The Fire of the Jaguar: Myth and Social Organization among the Northern Kayapo of Central Brazil." Paper given at the Conference on Myth and Ritual at Dartmouth College, August 1967 (including Abstract).

Turner, Victor. 1969. *The Ritual Process*. Chicago: Aldine.

Znaniecki, F., and W. I. Thomas. 1918. *The Polish Peasant in Europe and America*. Boston: Badger.

CHAPTER 7

Metaphors of
Anti-structure in
Religious Culture[1]

In my book *The Ritual Process*, I posited a difference between
society as "structure" and society as "anti-structure." Perhaps I
was wrong, as some reviewers have suggested, to make the over-
worked term "structure" work again like a good and patient
cart-horse in yet another capacity, but I consider that its traditional connotations make it an effective operator in the argument.
By structure I meant, roughly, social structure as most British
and many American anthropologists and sociologists have defined
the term, that is, as a more or less distinctive arrangement of
mutually dependent institutions and the institutional organization
of social positions and/or actors which they imply. Class structures are only one species of structures so defined, and a measure
of alienation adheres to all, including so-called tribal structures,
insofar as all tend to produce distance and inequality, often leading to exploitation between man and man, man and woman, and
old and young. Even the egalitarian reciprocities involved in
exchanges of consumer goods such as uncooked food assert some
degree of distance, as against sharing the same meal, the anthropologists' "commensality"—which, caught into the exemplary and
paradigmatic medium of ritual becomes "communion."

I have used the term "anti-structure," but I would like to make
clear that the "anti" is here only used strategically and does not

[1] First published in *Changing Perspectives in the Scientific Study of Religion*, ed. Allan W. Eister (New York: John Wiley, 1974).

imply a radical negativity. Structure has been the theoretical point of departure for so many social anthropological studies that it has acquired a positive connotation—even though I would prefer to regard structure rather as the "outward bound or circumference," as Blake might have said, than as the center or substance of a system of social relations or ideas. When I speak of anti-structure, therefore, I really mean something positive, a generative center. I do not seek the eradication of matter by form as some of my French-inspired colleagues have tried to do in recent years, but suppose a matter from which forms may be "unpacked," as men seek to know and communicate.

Roughly, the concepts of liminality and communitas define what I mean by anti-structure. Liminality—a term borrowed from van Gennep's formulation of the processual structure of ritual in *Les Rites de passage*—occurs in the middle phase of the rites of passage which mark changes in an individual's or a group's social status and/or cultural or psychological state in many societies past and present. Such rites characteristically begin with ritual metaphors of killing or death marking the separation of the subject from ordinary secular relationships (in which status-role behavior tends to prevail even in informal situations) and conclude with a symbolic rebirth or reincorporation into society as shaped by the law and moral code. The biological order of birth and death is reversed in rites of passage—there one dies to "become a little child." The intervening liminal phase is thus betwixt and between the categories of ordinary social life. Symbols and metaphors found in abundance in liminality represent various dangerous ambiguities of this ritual stage, since the classifications on which order normally depends are annulled or obscured—other symbols designate temporary antinomic liberation from behavioral norms and cognitive rules. This aspect of danger requiring control is reflected in the paradox that in liminality extreme authority of elders over juniors often coexists with scenes and episodes indicative of the utmost behavioral freedom and speculative license. Liminality is usually a sacred condition protected against secularity by taboos and in turn prevented by them from disrupting secular order, since liminality is a movement between fixed points and is essentially ambiguous, unsettled, and unsettling.

In liminality, communitas tends to characterize relationships between those jointly undergoing ritual transition. The bonds of communitas are anti-structural in the sense that they are undifferentiated, equalitarian, direct, extant, nonrational, existential, I-Thou (in Feuerbach's and Buber's sense) relationships. Communitas is spontaneous, immediate, concrete—it is not shaped by norms, it is not institutionalized, it is not abstract. Communitas differs from the camaraderie found often in everyday life, which, though informal and egalitarian, still falls within the general domain of structure, which may include interaction rituals. Communitas, to borrow a phrase of Durkheim's, is *"de la vie serieuse"* (Durkheim, *The Elementary Forms of the Religious Life*, 1961:427; first published 1912), part of the "serious life." It tends to ignore, reverse, cut across, or occur outside of structural relationships. In human history, I see a continuous tension between structure and communitas, at all levels of scale and complexity. Structure, or all that which holds people apart, defines their differences, and constrains their actions, is one pole in a charged field, for which the opposite pole is communitas, or anti-structure, the egalitarian "sentiment for humanity" of which David Hume speaks, representing the desire for a total, unmediated relationship between person and person, a relationship which nevertheless does not submerge one in the other but safeguards their uniqueness in the very act of realizing their commonness. Communitas does not merge identities; it liberates them from conformity to general norms, though this is necessarily a transient condition if society is to continue to operate in an orderly fashion.

I have discussed elsewhere (1969:99–106) how, among the Ndembu people of Zambia, in the liminal phase of their rites of passage, communitas is both metaphorically represented and actually engendered by ritual leveling and humiliation. Other

societies exhibit similar features. In more pronouncedly hierarchical societies with what Benjamin Nelson (1971:19), interpreting Weber, might call "sacro-magical structures of consciousness" communitas is frequently affirmed by periodic rituals
in which the lowly and the mighty reverse social roles. In such
societies, too, and here I have drawn examples from European
and Indian history, the religious ideology of the structurally
powerful tends to idealize humility, orders of religious specialists
undertake ascetic lives, while, on the contrary, cult groups among
those of low status ritually play with symbols of power. These
contrary processes go on in the *same* religious field, modifying,
opposing, and being transformed into one another as time goes
on. I would like here to give some examples of how such
processes operate in the religious field of India, drawing on the
work of two Indian colleagues and friends.

The first example is taken from a paper by J. Singh Uberoi, of
Delhi University, formerly my colleague at the University of
Manchester. It is entitled "Sikhism and Indian Society" (1967).
Uberoi opens with the proposition that the Hindu system of
caste relations (using the term "caste" to include both *varna*, the
all-India classification, and *jati*, the localized subcaste classification) is, in fact, only half of Hinduism. Here, of course, he parts
company with Max Weber, who regarded caste (and particularly
the position of Brahmins) as "the fundamental institution of
Hinduism." The whole Hindu *dharma*, literally "law," "justice,"
sometimes "religion," which might perhaps be paraphrased in
this context as "religio-moral field," is often described by the
term *varnashramdharma*. Thus, there are, *in addition to caste*
(*varna*), the institution of the four stages or statuses (*ashramas*),
student, householder, forest dweller, and homeless mendicant
through which high-caste Hindus were traditionally supposed to
pass. If social anthropologists tended to focus on the institution
of caste to the exclusion of the *ashram* system, it is probably because they preferred to work with stable, localized systems of
social relations and positions bound up in easily isolable customary

regularities rather than with processual models. But, as Uberoi points out, the social system of caste seems always to have been surrounded by a "penumbral region" of noncaste, or even anticaste, where there throve the renunciatory religious orders whose principles repudiated the ascribed statuses resting on caste and birth. And, indeed, the fourth *ashram* or stage, that known as *sannyas*, the state of being a holy man or ascetic, who has dedicated himself completely to the quest for *moksha* or "salvation," was always a metaphorical door through which the individual was recommended by sages and teachers to pass from the world of caste to that of its negation—from structure to anti-structure, one might say, for there is a moment when the *sannyasi* divests himself of all structural ties and is even recommended to erase from his memory all kinship connections. As Uberoi argues, "the mutual relation of the two worlds, caste and anti-caste, seems to be of the greatest significance to a broad understanding of either." For there is a social and corporate aspect of the *ashrama* system. *Sannyas* is not only a stage in an individual life cycle but may represent a religious order of renunciation. Uberoi considers that the total structure of medieval India could be split into three main segments, even if this involves for historians an exercise in gross oversimplification. There was a division between (1) the rulers (the world of *rajya*), (2) the caste system (*varna*, with an emphasis here also on the ashram of the householder, *grihasta*), and (3) the orders of renunciation (*sannyas*). The interrelations of these features would seem to define a sociocultural field in the medieval period, each part of which achieves its full significance only in terms of its relationship to all the others.

In this field, Uberoi continues, there were many orders which rejected caste initially or broke pollution rules, regarding nothing as common or unclean—he instances the Sanyogis of the Punjab. In the course of time, many of these came back from mendicancy to householding again. Uberoi suggests that this apparent contradiction may be resolved by regarding both these conditions as forming the different stages or phases of a single developmental cycle. From this standpoint, any specific order or suborder that once renounced caste with all its social rights and duties and its notions of sacred space and time, and "walked out through the open front door of *sannyas* into the ascetic wilderness, could later become disheartened or lose the point of its protest, and even end by seeking to re-enter the house of caste by the backdoor." In so doing, it would reverse the individual's institutionalized life path from householder to world-renouncer, but, then, groups do not move irreversibly deathward as individuals do. They tend to find that after a few generations they still confront the same old problems under approximately the same old conditions, and that what seemed a grand climactic gesture of world-renunciation was, in fact, no climax at all, possibly an evasion, and certainly not a solution. What seems to have happened in medieval India was that as a particular order or section fell back, so to speak, from the frontier of asceticism, and abandoned its nonprocreative, propertyless, occupationless, liminal existence, its function within the total field of *varnashrandharma* would be fulfilled by some other order or section. The ascetic, we may venture to say, "protestant," impulse itself remained a constant feature. If we were making an extended-case study of the genesis of a new order we might say that the *sannyas* principle was a perduring "latent-field-characteristic" of that field of *varnashrandharma*. Parallels with the modern American and West European alternative or counterculture may be inaccurate and superficial here, but it does appear as though the frontier of protest against "straight" or establishment Western culture has been occupied by different types of groups every two or three years or so. For example, some specific groups have transformed themselves from ghetto family to city commune to manufactory or farm commune in a way that suggests broad parallels with the return from *sannyas* to *grihasta*. Western *askesis* (though this may have Near Eastern roots) parallels *sannyas* here—and the other major counterstructural modality, sexual community, had an affinity with certain Tantric notions—often the Eastern and Western notions converge in syncretic metaphors. Paperbacks and travel have brought Eastern religion into many Western milieus. But in the West the tempo is much more rapid under conditions of large-scale industrialism and urbanism and multiple communications media, and the tempos of change in East and West might be compared with the differential effects of sun and incubator. But the processual form is similar, though the transformations are speedier and more blurred.

Reverting to medieval India, Uberoi suggests that "during an order's ascetic period it may occupy one or the other of two positions, or pass through both successively. . . . It may either adopt a theory and practice completely opposed to that of caste and be for that reason regarded as heterodox and esoteric; or it might remain within the fold and link itself to the caste system through the normal sectarian affiliations of caste people." It could be said that a heterodox or antinomian sect is one opposed to caste as its living shadow, while an orthodox sect is complementary to the caste system, being its other half within Hinduism. Uberoi was interested in the special position of the Sikhs, being one himself and having problems about it. In his view, the Sikhs barred the door to asceticism, but did not return to the orthodox citadel of caste. What they tried to do, he thought, was to "annihilate the categorical partitions, intellectual and social, of the Indian medieval world," to liquidate its formal structure, one might say. Sikhism rejected the orthodox opposition between the states of common citizen or householder and renouncer, and of the ruler vis-à-vis both of these, refusing to acknowledge them as separate and distinct modes of existence, let alone stages in a developmental cycle. The Sikhs did acknowledge the powers or qualities inhering in the domains of *rajya*, *sannyas*, and *grihasta*, but sought to invest their virtues conjointly in a single body of faith and conduct, like some Protestant sects during the European Reformation, who took the virtues of monasticism into the world, as Weber has shown so cogently. Nevertheless,

Sikhism did not make for the internalization of conscience in the individual; corporate values were highly stressed even to the point of militancy. The Sikhs, in fact, renounced renunciation, and Uberoi goes on to show how this renunciation of renunciation is expressed in detail in the cultural symbolism of the five "K's," the *kes* ("long hair," or acceptance of "nature"), *kangha* ("comb," to control the "natural" hair), *kara* ("steel arm band," to control the sword arm), *kripan* ("sword," directed aggression), and *katsh* ("short drawers that end above the knee," to control the genitalia). I will not go into his analysis here except to say that he argues that all these symbols imply both a recognition of natural processes and forces and simultaneously their religiocultural control, a nice synthesis of asceticism and acceptance of natural urges. Sikh anti-structure became in time counter-structure, as the gurus succeeded one another from Nanak (1469–1539) to Govind Singh (1675–1708), but remained outside Hindu structure (Macauliffe, 1909).

My second case to illustrate how processes of structure, anti-structure, counter-structure, and restructuring can coexist and modify one another continuously over time in the same ritual field, and how field properties influence the metaphors in which religious experiences within it are expressed, is taken from a valuable paper by my colleague at the University of Chicago, A. K. Ramanujan ("Structure and Anti-Structure: the Vīraśaiva Example," 1971, later published in his translation of poems, *Speaking of Śiva*, 1973), on the religious literature of Vīraśaiva saints of the tenth to twelfth centuries in South India. The Vīraśaivas, though not ascetics, followed a different path to *moksha*, or salvation, from that taken by orthodox Hindus. They stressed devotion, love, and faith rather than the scrupulous performance of caste duties and rituals. Yet their "way" has become one of the three recognized ways of attaining salvation in Hinduism, alongside (1) complex and exacting performance of ritual, and (2) knowledge through meditation or Yoga. Nevertheless the Vīraśaiva movement was, in its inception in the Kannada-speaking regions, "a social upheaval by and for the poor, the lowcaste and the outcaste against the rich and the privileged; it was a rising of the unlettered against the literate pundit, flesh and blood against stone" (Ramanujan, 1973:21). Ramanujan suggests that, like other *bhakti* religions, Vīraśaivism is an Indian analogue to European Protestant movements. The Indian and European movements have in common such characteristics as:

protest against mediators like priest, ritual, temples social hierarchy, in the name of direct, individual, original experience; a religious movement of and for the underdog, including saints of all castes and trades (like Bunyan, the tinker) speaking the sub-standard dialect of the region, producing often the first authentic regional expressions and translations of inaccessible Sanskritic texts (like the translations of the Bible in Europe); a religion of arbitrary grace, with a doctrine of the mystically chosen elect, replacing a social hierarchy-by-birth with a mystical hierarchy-by-experience; doctrines of work as worship leading to a puritan ethic; monotheism and evangelism, a mixture of intolerance and humanism harsh and tender [pp. 53–54].

Dr. Ramanujan had written his paper for a seminar on Aspects of Religion in South Asia at the School of Oriental and African Languages, University of London, March 30–April 2, 1971, before he read my book *The Ritual Process: Structure and Anti-Structure.* He was so much struck by the resemblance between the opposition indicated in its subtitle and that which he had noticed in the Indian data that he made it the title of his paper, "Structure and Anti-structure: The Vīraśaiva Example." This was because the strategic thrust of his paper centered on an attempt "to unpack the meaning of a single 'binary opposition' in Vīraśaivism, i. e. *Sthāvara* [*stasis*] and *Jangama* [*dynamis*] . . . and show how it organizes attitudes towards religion, society, language, metrical form, imagery, etc. . . . as seen in the *vacanas* [the body of religious lyric poetry produced by the early saints of the movement)" (p. 1). Since I am dealing with metaphors of anti-structure,

I can hardly do better than present in some detail Ramanujan's exegesis of a poem written by Basavaṇṇa, the Vīraśaiva leader, which exemplifies the opposition sthāvara and jaṅgama, an opposition which, stripped of its Indian integument, I hold to be cross-cultural and universal. The metaphorical opposition, too, draws much of its significance, from its function within the South Indian religiomoral field of *varnashramdharma*. Here is Basavaṇṇa's poem:

> The rich
> will make temples for Śiva.
> What shall I,
> a poor man,
> do?

> My legs are pillars,
> the body the shrine,
> the head a cupola
> of gold.

> Listen, O lord of the meeting rivers,
> things standing shall fall,
> but the moving ever shall stay. [Ramanujan, 1973:19]

According to Ramanujan this poem "dramatizes several of the themes and oppositions characteristic of Vīraśaiva protest" (p. 19). Thus, Indian temples are "built traditionally in the image of the human body" (just as European Gothic cathedrals represent in many cases the crucified Christ, even to the extent that the hanging head is symbolized by a slight curvature of the building beyond the altar at the east end).

The ritual for building a temple begins with digging in the earth and planting a pot of seed. The temple is said to rise from the implanted seed, like a human. The different parts of a temple are named after body parts. The two sides are called the hands or wings, the *hasta*. The top of the temple is the head, the *śikhara*. The shrine, the innermost and the darkest sanctum of the temple is a *garbhagṛha*, the womb-house. The temple thus carries out in brick and stone the primordial blueprint of the human body.

But in history the human metaphor fades. The model, the meaning, is submerged. The temple becomes a static standing thing that has forgotten its moving originals. Basavaṇṇa's poem calls for a return to the original of all temples, preferring the body to the embodiment.

The poems . . . suggest a cycle of transformation—temple into body into temple, or a circle of identities—a temple is a body is a temple [pp. 19–20].

I am tempted here to see this also as a metaphor for the process whereby communitas becomes structure and then communitas again and for the ultimate identification of both modalities as human sociality.

Ramanujan points out that the poem draws a distinction between *making* and *being*.

The rich can only *make* temples. They may not *be* or become temples by what they do. Further what is made is a mortal artifact, but what one *is* is immortal—things standing shall fall, but the moving ever shall stay.

This opposition, the standing *vs.* the moving, *sthāvara vs. jaṅgama*, is at the heart of Vīraśaivism. The Sanskrit work *sthāvara* is cognate with the Indo-European words in English like *stand, state* (estate), *stature, static, status, stay,* and carries connotations of these related words. *Jaṅgama* contains a cognate of English *go. Sthāvara* is that which stands, a piece of property, a thing inanimate. *Jaṅgama* is moving, moveable, anything given to going and coming. Especially in Vīraśaiva religion a *Jaṅgama* is a religious man who has renounced world and home, moving from village to village, representing god to the devoted, a god incarnate. *Sthāvara* could mean any static symbol or idol of god, a temple, or a *liṅga* worshipped in a temple. Thus the two words carry a constrast between two opposed conceptions of god of worship. Basavaṇṇa . . . prefers the original to the symbol, the body that remembers to the temple that forgets, the poor, though living, moving *jaṅgama* to the rich petrified temple, the *sthāvara*, standing out there [pp. 20–21].

As Ramanujan indicates, "the polarities are lined up and judged:

the rich	: the poor
temple	: body
make	: be
the standing (*sthāvara*)	: the moving (*jaṅgama*)" [p. 22]

There is an evaluation asymmetry here: *jaṅgama* is better than *sthāvara*. Here, too, evangelism begins. Metaphors in other religious cultures make similar oppositions, but do not take sides. For example, the *Analects of Confucius* distinguish between the concepts *li* and *jen* but regard them both as necessary to a virtuous human social life. According to D. Howard Smith (*Chinese Religions from 1000 B.C. to the Present Day*, 1971:40), the character *li* originally was closely associated with the sacrificial cult by which the *manes* of the ancestors and the gods and spirits were worshiped and honored. In Confucius' day it had come to represent the "unwritten customary usages which regulated all the various relationships of society and family." It has been variously translated as "propriety, rites, ceremonies, ritual." The character *jen* has been variously translated as "love, goodness, benevolence, humaneness, man-to-man-ness" (p. 42). A few quotations from the *Analects* will indicate its operational meaning.

Fan Ch'ih asked the meaning of *jen*. The master said, "love men" [12:21].
There may be a noble man who failed in *jen*, but never was there a mean man who possessed *jen* [14:7].
A man who possesses *jen* will not seek to preserve his life at the expense of *jen*. There are those who through death bring their *jen* to perfection [15:8].

Jen is reconciled with *li* in the following:

Jen is self denial and a return to *li* (propriety, ritual). For by self-denial and return to *li* the whole world would return to *jen* [12:1. Quoted from Smith, 1971:42–43].

Here Confucius sees the extremes as touching. I think that it would be possible to translate *jen* as "the sentiment of human-kindness or for humanity," and its social expression as communitas, while *li* is not so far from what I have called structure. Confucius seems to be saying that if men operated within and according to the norms of the structure without seeking to subvert those norms to their own self-interest or factional goals, then the result in terms of peaceful, just, social coexistence would be similar to those produced by spontaneous, existential communitas. This is the position which his critics down the ages have called "conservative." This position implies, on the one hand, a bonding of individuals by ritual or propriety, and, on the other, a safeguarding of each individual's independence within the general interdependence. Here distancing is not constraint, but the safeguarding of each person's dignity. To be perfectly fair, the Vīraśaivas, too, sometimes saw that *sthāvara* and *jaṅgama* were ultimately one. Ramanujan writes:

The Vīraśaiva trinity consists of *guru, liṅga,* and *jaṅgama*—the spiritual teacher, the symbolic stone emblem of Śiva, i.e., the structural signs of the cult, its incipient *sthāvara,* and his wandering mendicant representative. They are three yet one. Basavaṇṇa insists, in another poem, "*sthāvara* and *jaṅgama* are one" to the truly worshipful spirit. Yet if a devotee prefer external worship of the stone *liṅga* (*sthāvara*) to serving a human *jaṅgama,* he would be worthy of scorn [p. 22].

This identification of the moving and the standing, the speaking and the spoken, man-to-man-ness and ritual, together with the process of their mutual recognition, forms a metaphorical triple classification found not infrequently in religious culture. The social correlates of these may be termed, in my view, anti-structure, structure, and societas, the process whereby anti-structure is periodically transformed into structure and structure into anti-structure.

I have here not stressed opposition between communitas and structure, but between anti-structure or astructure and structure.

This is because the Vīraśaivas have elected to stress liminality, and the Confucians communitas, as the essential contrary to structure. For while *li* has a marked affinity to *sthāvara*, both being translatable without forcing as "structure," *jangama*, "the moving," is closer to liminality, and *jen*, "humaneness," to communitas, than either is to the other. One archmetaphor for that which is outside structure, between structures, a dissolvent of structures, is "movement," "nomadism," "transience"—it is this aspect that concerns me in my current research on comparative pilgrimage processes past and present. *Jangama*, "anything given to going and coming," fits well with this notion. In passing, we would seem to be in a period of history when *jangama* values occupy a considerable place in public attention—exemplified, for instance, despite their manipulation for box-office purposes, by such films as *Five Easy Pieces, Easy Rider*, and other "road" movies and literature of moving people who, unable to belong to any institutionalized group, any *sthāvara* status, must travel from place to place, bed to bed, class to class, but may never stay anywhere long: in brief, the "hang-loose ethic" people. In *The Ritual Process*, I suggested that history itself seems to have its discernable liminal periods, which share certain distinctive features, between relatively stablized configurations of social relations and cultural values. Ours may well be one of them. One difference between East and West here, though, may lie in the sadness of Stoicism of the Western wanderers and the gladness and faith of the Eastern. The former are positively negative, the latter negatively positive. Thereby hangs a tale it would take volumes even to begin to tell.

Liminality often provides favorable conditions for communitas, but it may have the reverse effect, either a Hobbesian war of all against all, or an existentialist anarchy of individuals, each "doing his or her own thing." This is clearly not what Confucius had in mind when he dichotomized *li* and *jen*. Love of one's fellows could go very well, he thought, with propriety, or the maintenance of those structures which depend upon the proper fulfill-

ment of customary obligations (*li*). Thus for him there was no
essential opposition between *li* and *jen*—*jen* was *li*'s inner dynamic.

Yet traces of communitas adhere to *jangama* in Vīraśaiva
thought. In his protest against traditional structural dichotomies,
the poet Dāsimayya, translated by Ramanujan, for example, rejects the differences between man and woman as superficial, stressing their fundamental unity, thereby anticipating certain modern
Western trends by nine centuries (p. 26):

> If they see
> breasts and long hair coming
> they call it woman,
> if beard and whiskers
> they call it man:
> but, look, the self that hovers
> in between
> is neither man
> nor woman
> O Rāmanātha. [Ramanujan, 1973:27]

Note here the *jangama* metaphors, "coming," "hovers," "in
between," "neither-nor," coupled with the communitas metaphor,
the single "self" underlying cultural differences.

In connection with the earlier Sikh illustration, I mentioned
the sequence, structure/anti-structure/counter-structure/restruc-
turing, as characterizing in India the fate of protest movements.
Ramanujan gives further illustration of this. For him, the division
made by Redfield between "great" and "little" traditions in Indian
civilization, or between such similar antitheses as popular/learned,
folk/classical, folk/elite, low/high, parochial/universal, peasant/
aristocratic, lay/hieratic, is of little importance to the founders of
protest religious movements such as Vīraśaiva. Great and Little
traditions were rejected alike as the "establishment," as structure,
and what was stressed was religious experience, *kṛpa* or "grace."

The religious poems distinguish between *anubhava*, "experience," and
anubhāva, "*The* Experience." The latter is a search for the unmediated

vision, the unconditioned act, the unpredictable experience. Living in history, time and cliche, one lives in a world of the pre-established, through the received (*śruti*) and the remembered (*smṛti*). But the Experience when it comes, comes like a storm to all such husks and labels. . . . The grace of the Lord is nothing a devotee can invoke or wheedle by prayer, rule, ritual, mystical word, or sacrificial offering. A mystical opportunist can only wait for It, be prepared to catch It as it passes [pp. 31–32].

One is irresistibly reminded here of William Blake's

> He who binds to himself a joy
> Does the winged life destroy
> But he who kisses the joy as it flies
> Lives in eternity's sunrise. ["Eternity," Everyman's edition]

For Ramanujan, "structure" includes cognitive, linguistic, and ideological, as well as physical and social structures—it is, in brief, that which confers order and regularity on phenomena or assumes that these will be found in the relations among phenomena. It does so even as it breaks the continuity of the world into "sign" and "signified," "code" and "codified," in order to make that external reality intelligible and communicate knowledge of it. Here we have the perennial problem of resolving the contradiction between distinction, or discontinuity (briefly, structure), and connection, or continuity; of experiencing unity while knowing it by means of contrasts. The Experience—what is often in Hinduism called *samādhi*, a state in which all distinction between subject and object is lost—appears to obliterate all structure, cognitive or communicational. In it, not only is the distinction between subject and object felt to be lost, but all is experienced either as One Self or as formless void. This is sometimes represented in Hindu mythology and ritual metaphor by the apparently amoral, capricious, yet creative acts of the major deities, who transcend the laws and limitations of men. In *anubhāva*, the Vīraśaiva devotee "needs nothing, he is Nothing," writes Ramanujan, "for to be someone, or something, is to be differentiated and separate from God. When he is one with Him, he is the Nothing without names" (pp. 32–33).

Structure depends upon binary oppositions in the last analysis —or so some of our French colleagues would have it. But anti-structure abolishes all divisiveness, all discriminations, binary, serial, or graduated. This creative moment of rejection of structures, social, philosophical, and theological, what Ramanujan calls "this fierce rebellion against petrification" (p. 33), in the name of the "moving" of "grace" tended, however, in practice and in Indian social history to be merely a rebellion against what Hindus were currently doing. It was not only an assertion of the value of interior experience against outward forms—it was simultaneously an attempt to legitimate such experience by having recourse to what were felt to be pure ancient traditions that were no different from true and present experience. The originally enunciated Truth, the "deposit of faith," was just such as the devotee had personally experienced. Since these traditions had become part of structure, the structure of both Great and Little traditions, the paradox existed that rejection of structure was legitimated by recourse to structure, as in Europe the Protestants appealed to the simple, communitarian church of the founding fathers as their paradigm for rejection of the Catholic pharisaical formalism intervening between the pristine and contemporary states of Christianity. But once this has been done we cannot speak any more of "anti" structure, but only of "counter" structure. Ancient Hindu scriptures were cited by the Vīraśaivas to support a return to immediate experience. "Alienation from the immediate environment can mean continuity with an older ideal. Protest can take place in the very name of one's opponents' ideals" (p. 33). The danger in doing this is, of course, that one thereby already puts one's foot on the first rung of the structural escalator. Liminality is terminating; the return to the structural fold has begun. Ramanujan, since he is at once a professor of linguistics and a literary critic, saw the Vīraśaiva return to structure via counter-structure in terms of the rhetorical structure of their literary output. I will not enter its technical dimension here, except to echo his conclusion that "spontaneity has its own rhetorical structure; no free verse is truly free," and that "without a repertoire of structures to rely on, there can be no spontaneity" (p. 38). The common Hindu stock of similes, analogies, and metaphors is drawn upon in the Vīraśaiva poetry although used in new and startling ways—while the apparently inspirational poems can be shown to have a consistent metrical structure, characterized by what Roman Jakobson has called "grammatical parallelism," as well as other major symmetries and patterns. In the American tradition the poetry of Walt Whitman might provide an apt analogy.

To summarize drastically: Vīraśaiva protest mysticism initially collapses and rejects both all-India and regional structures and traditions and stresses mystical experience as the basic source of human meaning and social bondedness. In its developing group expression it becomes counterstructural socially and culturally and ransacks past traditions to validate immediate experience. For analyzing the next stage Redfield's distinction between Great and Little traditions becomes useful again. Ramanujan has shown, for example, how in the course of time the Vīraśaiva heretics are canonized; temples are erected to them, Sanskrit hagiographies are composed about them. Not only local legend and ritual, but an elaborate theology assimilating various Great tradition elements may grow around them. They become, in retrospect, founders of a new caste, and are defied in turn by new egalitarian movements—as the Jains, originally a Hindu heresy, were defied by the first Vīraśaivas. Anthropologists should take note from all this that a scientific study of any component of Indian religion, from *jati*-system to Jain ideology, at a given point in history, should really take into account and represent by appropriate constructs the total field of Indian religion as context.

It is now time to look more closely at the structure of metaphor in these religious contexts. We have already seen how "the body" is stated as being in relation to what Vīraśaiva poets call *jaṅgama,* "the moving," and "the temple" to *sthāvara* "the stand-ing." Although each of these terms is what I would call a multi-vocal symbol, there is sufficient similarity and analogy between the various referents of each symbol for it to represent fairly well the ensemble of referents. One approach to the study of meta-phor, which draws somewhat on Lévi-Strauss, Jakobson, and Noam Chomsky, is Elli Köngäs Maranda's discussion in her recent article "The Logic of Riddles" (1971:193–194). She relates meta-phors to the concepts "analogy" and "metonymy," accepting Aristotle's definition of the first: "There is an analogy whenever there are four terms such that the relation between the second and the first is similar to that between the fourth and the third," for example, $A/B = C/D$. Analogy is a "technique of reasoning, resting on two kinds of connectives between phenomena: similar-ity and contiguity, in other words metaphor and metonymy. In the analogy formula [therefore] two members in the same structural position (A and C) constitute a sign, a metaphor in which one of them (A) is the signans, or the 'signifier,' and the other (C) is the signatum, or the 'signified.' . . . The members on one side of the equation mark are in a metonymic relation to each other (A and B)." Thus, in the analogy, she arranges metaphor and metonymy as in the following diagram:

ANALOGY

METAPHOR

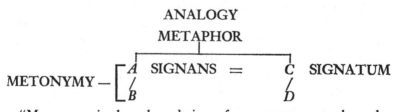

"Metonymy is thus the relation of two terms; metaphor, the equation of two terms." In the Vīraśaiva poem translated by Ramanujan an analogy is constructed in the following terms: temple/*sthāvara* (standing) = body/*jaṅgama* (moving). The re-lation between *sthāvara* to temple is similar to that between *jaṅgama* and body. This analogy is then subjected to evaluation. In the abstract it may be true that the relation between stasis and temple is similar to the relation between dynamis and body, but the context of the poem introduces the paradox that "things standing shall *fall* but the moving shall ever *stay*" (my italics). While the temple begins as a metaphor of the body, the poem suggests that in reality, even in eternity, there is no temple, only body (shades of the Christian doctrine of the resurrection of the body), but that the body has in it the holiness which is only metaphorically ascribed to the temple: "the body the shrine," as Basavaṇṇa puts it. I would posit another metaphorical relationship here: *sthāvara:jaṅgama* :: structure:anti-structure (that is, communitas + liminality). *Sthāvara* is to *jaṅgama* as structure is to communitas. For *sthāvara*, as Ramanujan writes, has such social structural connotations as "status, estate, a piece of property." And *jaṅgama*, like the transitional period in rites of passage represents "moving, anything given to going and coming." The *jaṅgama* in Vīraśaiva religion represents a permanently liminal man, a "religious man who has renounced world and home, moving from village to village" (p. 21). Even those who did not wander physically did not feel themselves bound by the strict rules of caste or kinship. Ramanujan, in his exposition, stresses that the "Vīraśaiva movement was a social upheaval by and for the poor, the lowcaste and the outcaste against the rich and the privileged" (p. 21), a communitas based on the dissolution of caste ties in favor of immediate experience—for the Vīraśaivas, "the Lord of the meeting rivers" which regularly appears as the refrain of their poems, does not exactly refer to the personal Śiva of the Hindu pantheon, but rather to the experience of *samādhi* in which such distinctions as I-Thou, God-human, subject-object, become unimportant and all seems to be one or nothing, in the sense that language has nothing positive to say about such an experience. This position, common to both Eastern and Western mysticism, is perhaps most clearly formulated by the great scholar of Zen religion D. T. Suzuki (*On Indian Mahayana Buddhism*), when he writes:

Our language is the product of a world of numbers and individuals of todays and yesterdays and tomorrows, and is most usefully applicable to this world (known as *loka* in Indian *Mahayana*). But our experiences have it that our world extends beyond that *loka*, that there is another called by Buddhists *loka-uttara*, a "transcendental world", and that when language is forced to be used for things of this world, it becomes warped and assumes all kinds of crookedness: oxymora ["figures of speech with pointed conjunction of seeming contradictories, e.g., 'faith unfaithful kept him falsely true,' " *Oxford English Dictionary*], paradoxes, contradictions, contortions, absurdities, oddities, ambiguities, and irrationalities. Language itself is not to be blamed for it. It is we ourselves who, ignorant of its proper functions, try to apply it to that for which it was never intended [1968:243].

In my view it is no accident that this *jaṅgama* or mystical **rhetoric, charged** with oxymora and metaphors, is very often characteristic of movements of egalitarian, popular protest during liminal periods of history when social, economic, and intellectual structures showing great stability and consistency over long periods of time begin to show signs of breaking up and become objects of questioning both in structural and anti-structural terms. We have been accustomed to thinking of mystical utterance as characterizing solitary individuals meditating or contemplating in mountain, desert, or monastic cell, and to see in it almost anything but a social fact. But the continuous operational conjunction of such language with movements of a communitas type, the Friends of God with the Rhineland mystics, for example, leads me to think that at least something of what is being uttered refers metaphorically to extant social relationships. "Withdrawal" there is, "detachment," "disinterest," there is, to mention terms common to the mystical lexicon of many cultures, but this withdrawal is not from humanity, but from structure when it has become too long petrified in a specific shape. Here it is not merely a question of one component of the social structure, a class or caste or ethnic group, seeking to better its circumstances within a total structural system, nor to make a new structural system free from the exploitative tendencies inherent in the structure of its predecessor. What is being sought is emancipation of men from all structural limitations, to make a mystical desert outside structure itself in which all can be one, *ein bloss niht,* "a pure nothingness," as the Western mystic Eckhart once wrote— though this "nothingness" has to be seen as standing in meta- phorical opposition to the "somethingness" of a historically de- rived structure. It has as yet content but no manifest structure, only explosively stated anti-structure. History will of course un- pack its latent structure, especially as experience encounters tradi- tional structures of culture and thought. Those who have had *the Experience* now have to confront the establishments both of Great and Little traditions as they try to realize their vision in social relational terms. Now vision becomes sect, then church, then in some cases dominant political system or a prop for one— until communitas resurges once more against it from the liminal spaces and instants every structure is forced by its nature to provide—since structure depends on distance and discontinuity between its units, and these interstitial spaces provide homes for anti-structural visions, thoughts, and ultimately behaviors. Com- plex societies, too, provide a multiplicity of structural subsystems, manifest or latent, forming a field propitious for the growth of counterstructures, as individuals pass between subsystems. So- ciety is a process which embraces the visions and reflections, the words and work, of religious and political mendicants, exiles, and isolated prophets, as much as the activities of crowds and masses, the ceremonies of the forum and marketplace, and the deeds of legislators, judges, and priests. If we can see it as having such seemingly solitary or withdrawn purifiers, and minuses and zeros as well as pluses, in its central developments, anti-structure as well as structure, and that there is a constant interplay between these on various levels and in various sectors of sociocultural fields, then we will begin to avoid some of the difficulties in- herent in systems of thought which recognize only structurally positive values, rules, and components; and these are only positive because they are the rules recognized as legitimate by the political and intellectual elites at a given time. Such systems throw out at least one half of human sociality, the creative (and also destructive) half which insists on active, extant, vital unity, and upon novelty and extemporization in styles of human interrelations. But it should also be observed that fanaticism and intolerance tend to characterize movements that stress communitas as the counterstructural negation of structure. Iconoclasts, evangelists, Roundheads, as well as mystics, poets, and saints, abound in their ranks. The Vīraśaivas were fierce evangelists; the symbol of the Sikhs, the *khanda*, two curved swords, a double-edged dagger, and a discus, symbolizes martial virtue as well as spiritual power. "Liberty, fraternity and equality" were shouts that drove Bonaparte on to seize an imperial crown.

Societies which stress structure—and establish mystiques of hierarchy and status, setting unalterable divisions and distances between categories and groups of human beings—become equally fanatical in the eradication of communitas values and the liquidation of groups which outstandingly exemplify them. Often we find communitarians unforgivingly arrayed against structuralists, and vice versa. The basic cleavage in social man finds frequent historical expression. Those religions or humanistic systems which preach love as a major ethical principle—and all so-called "universal" religions profess this value as central—beam out some version of the Confucian reconciliation between *li* and *jen*, "ceremony" and "man-to-man-ness," this reconciliation being broadly what is meant by love. The great religious systems harmonize rather than oppose structure and communitas and call the resultant total field the "body" of the faithful, the *umma* ("comity") of Islam, or some similar term which reconciles love with law, communitas with structure. In fact, neither law nor love can be such when they are implacably opposed; both are then hate; all the more so, when masked as moral excellence.

Both structure and anti-structure are represented in the concrete imageries and acts of the ritual process in tribal and peasant societies. Such societies are no less Man than we are, and their nonverbal symbols may even afford swifter access to the human matter than sophistries and apologetics. There structure and anti-structure have not become as yet generalized into opposed ideological positions, well adapted to political manipulation, but the metaphors of iconoclasm exist *within* the texture of ceremonies heavily endowed with icons. The construction and destruction of images are moments of a single ritual process. Most descriptions, since they have been made by alien observers, fail to describe adequately the communitas aspect of anti-structural metaphorical actions and their symbolic components in tribal ritual, but this will be increasingly remedied as literate members of these cultures describe what it has meant to them to participate collectively in ritual of an anti-structural tenor. Here novels, plays, and poetry currently being published in the new nations form an important body of data—personal documents that give us what Znaniecki calls the "humanistic coefficient" of a social analysis. An analogous instance may be helpful here. In my current study of pilgrimage processes in historical religions such as Christianity, Islam, Judaism, Hinduism, and Buddhism, I am beginning to accumulate evidence from pilgrims' narratives that experiences of a communitas type are often the subjective correlates of constellations of symbols and metaphors objectively indicative of anti-structure. Nevertheless, despite this grave lacuna about the presence of communitas in tribal limina, I will give one example out of many that may be cited from studies of tribal ritual of the deliberate effacement or destruction of complex structures of symbols, each of which is a semantic system of great complexity.

These instances of orthodox and permitted iconoclasm always take place in the liminal or marginal phase of major rites of passage, in the portion of institutionalized time assigned to the portrayal of anti-structure. Sometimes they are associated with an act of sacrifice, but often they occur independently of such an act though they have a sacrificial character. One of the best examples of the metaphorical destruction of structure that I know is given in Audrey Richards' account of the Bemba girl's initiation ceremony at puberty, *Chisungu* (1956). Among the Bemba of northeastern Zambia the *chisungu* is a long, elaborate sequence of ritual acts—which include miming, singing, dancing, and the handling of sacred objects—preceding the marriage of a young girl, and is an "integral part of the series of ceremonies by which a bridegroom [is] united to the family group of his bride, in a tribe in which descent is reckoned through the woman and not the man, and in which a man comes to live with his wife's relatives at marriage rather than a woman with her husband's" (p. 17). One of the distinctive features of this ceremony is the elaborate modeling of figurines in clay—Richards counted forty-two in one performance she studied—over several days of the protracted ritual, which lasted twenty-three days and in the past may have been longer, with many symbolic actions taking place each day. Further pottery figurines or "emblems," made in a hut (all are known as *mbusa;* the mistress of ceremonies is known as *nachimbusa*, or "mother" of the emblems) are suddenly pulled to pieces two hours after the ensemble of emblems is completed. The emblems are used to teach the girl-novice the duties, norms, values, and typical cultural settings of her coming structural position as wife and mother. Each has a specific ritual name, a cryptic song attached to it, and is interpreted to the girl for her social benefit by the senior ladies present, especially by the senior "mother of the emblems." Dr. Richards and Fr. E. Labreque, of the Missionary White Fathers, have collected much material on these didactic exegeses. Richards' appendix to *Chisungu*, giving informants' interpretations of *mbusa*, is particularly valuable. In brief, they add up to a fairly full account of a mature woman's structural fate in a matrilineal society, such as that of the Bemba, with many of its structural problems and tensions also represented—as I have indicated in chapter 4, "Betwixt and Between," of my book *The Forest of Symbols* (1967:193–194). Richards shows how the emblems refer, *inter alia*, to domestic duties, agricultural duties, the obligations of husband and wife, obligations to other relatives, the duties and circumstances of legitimate motherhood, the authority of chiefs, and to the general ethics incumbent upon mature Bemba. In Richards' words:

In terms of time spent, the ritual handling and presentation of the sacred emblems probably occupied more hours than any other part of the rite. The handling, preparation and presentation of the pottery emblems and the collection of the woodland and domestic *mbusa* cost the organizers much time and energy. . . . The long day's work on the pottery emblems in the [novice's] hut has been described and it will be remembered that this long day's work was destroyed at the end of the very same day. . . . Apart from the making and finding of *mbusa*, their presentation by the different women in order of rank seemed, to me at least, the most interminable part of the *chisungu* rite since it involved the singing of every doggerel rhyme (interpreting the meaning of each *mbusa*) some twenty times or more [1956:138].

The swift destruction of images and emblems laboriously constructed is not precisely comparable to the demolition of religious statues, paintings, and icons by Byzantine iconoclasts, Moguls in Banaras, Henry VIII's commissioners, Cromwell's Roundheads, or Scottish Covenanters. But behind it lies perhaps the same human impulse to assert the contrary value to structure that distances and distinguishes man from man and man from absolute reality, describing the continuous in discontinuous terms. The important thing for those who use metaphorical means is to build up as elaborately as they may a structure of ideas, embodied in symbols, and a structure of social positions, symbolically expressed, which will keep chaos at bay and create a mapped area of security. Elaboration may, as in Chinese cosmological schemes, become obsessional in character. Then a metaphorical statement is made of what lies at once between the categories of structure ("inner space") and outside the total system ("outer space"). Here words prove useless, exegesis fails, and there is nothing left to do but to express a positive experience by a negative metaphorical act —to destroy the elaborate structure one has made and admit transcendence, that is, over all that one's culture has been able to say about the experience of those who bear or have borne it to its present point in time. Actually, what is conceptually transcendent may well be experimentally immanent—communitas itself. Only those who know how to build know how to collapse what has been built. Mere literal destruction is not the metaphorical destruction illustrated in ritual. Here the metaphor of destruction is a nonverbal way of expressing a positive, continuous aspect of social reality which tends to escape the discontinuous character of most codes of communication, including linguistic codes. Perhaps this is because man may still be an *evolving* species; his future is in his present, but as yet unarticulated, for articulation is the presence of the past. This state Western thinkers share with the aborigines, and both of us reveal the dilemma in our nonverbal symbols, in our metaphors. *Chisungu*, we might say in conclusion, presents ritual and antiritual, in a relation of complementarity rather than contradiction. Structure and anti-structure are not Cain and Abel, to use a metaphor familiar to ourselves; they are rather Blake's Contraries that must be "redeemed by destroying the Negation." Otherwise we must all perish, for behind specific historical and cultural developments, East versus West, hierarchical versus egalitarian systems, individualism versus communism, lies the simple fact that man is both a structural and an anti-structural entity, who *grows* through anti-structure and *conserves* through structure.

References

Durkheim, Emile. 1961. *The Elementary Forms of Religious Life*. Tr. J. S. Swain. New York: Collier. First published 1912.

Gennep, Arnold van. 1960. *The Rites of Passage*. London: Routledge & Kegan Paul.

Macauliffe, M. J. 1909. *The Sikh Religion*. Oxford: The Clarendon Press.

Maranda, Elli Köngäs. 1971. "The Logic of Riddles." In *Structural Analysis of Oral Tradition*, eds. P. and E. K. Maranda. Philadelphia: University of Pennsylvania Press.

Nelson, Benjamin. 1971. "Civilizational Complexes and Intercivilizational Encounters." Paper read at the American Sociological Association Conference, August 30.

Ramanujan, A. K. 1971. "Structure and Anti-structure: The Vīraśaiva Example." Paper given at the Seminar on Aspects of Religion in South Asia at the School of Oriental and African Languages, University of London.

———. 1973. *Speaking of Śiva.* Baltimore: Penguin Books.

Richards, Audrey. 1956. *Chisungu.* London: Faber and Faber.

Smith, Howard D. 1971. *Chinese Religions from 1000 B.C. to the Present Day.* New York: Holt Paperbacks. First published 1968.

Suzuki, D. T. 1968. *On Indian Mahayana Buddhism.* New York: Harper Torchbooks.

Turner, Victor. 1969. *The Ritual Process: Structure and Anti-structure.* Chicago: Aldine.

———. 1970. *The Forest of Symbols.* Ithaca: Cornell Paperbacks. First published 1967.

Uberoi, J. Singh. 1967. "Sikhism and Indian Society," *Transactions of the Indian Institute of Advanced Study,* vol. 4. Simla.

Index

Action, symbolic and ritual, 55, 56
Actors in political field, 127
African cultures, and symbol systems, 163-164
Agnes, St., martyr, 86
Aldáma, Juan, 102, 107, 112
Alexander III, pope, 61, 73, 77-78, 88, 93
Alhóndiga granary, 102, 125; battle of, 102, 112; as symbol, 112
Allende, Ignacio, 102, 103, 107, 113, 115, 117-118, 124-125; leader of criollos, in disagreement with Hidalgo, 109, 110, 111, 112-113, 119, 121
Anamnesis, 208
Anouilh, Jean, 86
Anthropologists' handling of history, 132
Anti-structure, 45, 46, 50, 202, 272-298 passim; see also Structure and anti-structure, pairs of opposed terms
Archetype, conceptual, 26-27, 28
Arena, 98, 102, 103, 129, 135-136; definitions discussed, 17, 132-135; in Hidalgo Insurrection, 102, 128, 139-140
Ashram, system of (stages in life), 275-277
Atemporal structure, 35-37
Augustine, St., 151, 161, 242
Azcárate, Juan Francisco de, 143, 144

Bailey, Frederick, 38, 129, 140
Barbarossa, see Frederick I
Barth, Frederick, 129, 140
Becket, St. Thomas, 23-58 passim; sources, 61-63, 69; controversy

about, 62-63; his pride and humility, 66, 88-89; as chancellor, 70, 82; as martyr, 72, 74, 85-86, 89; chronology, 73; refuses to sign Constitutions of Clarendon, 77; origins, 77, 86, 95; and bishops, 80-83, 88, 90, 92-94; forced to pay fines and debts, 81-83; his low point, 84; says St. Stephen's Mass, 84-87; and barons, 84, 94-95; appeals to pope, 93; refuses sentence and leaves council, 95
Berington, Joseph, 62
Bernstein, Basil, 158
Betrayal, a myth of culture, 122-124
Bierstedt, Robert, 32
Black, Max, 25, 27-28, 29-30
Blake, William, 50, 68, 114, 151, 159, 256, 260, 268, 269, 287, 298
Body symbols: among the Dogon, 161-162; in India, 281-282
Boehme, Jakob, 159
Bonaparte, Napoleon, 103, 137, 142
Breach, in social drama, 38
Brown, Jerald, 18
Brown, Paul Alonzo, 63
Brown Virgin of Guadalupe, see Virgin of Guadalupe
Buber, Martin, 47, 251, 274
Bunge, Mario, 51-52
Burton, Sir Richard, 167

Cabildos, local municipal councils, 143, 145
Caesaropapalism, 77, 151
Calame-Griaule, Madame G., 156-164
Calleja, General Felix, 116, 118, 120
Canon law, 75, 76-77, 94
Casola, Canon Pietro, 167